GW01458525

Unbecoming Catholic

Reimagining Ireland

Volume 139

Edited by Dr Eamon Maher,
Technological University Dublin – Tallaght Campus

PETER LANG

Unbecoming Catholic

Being Religious in Contemporary Ireland

Tom Inglis

PETER LANG

Oxford - Berlin - Bruxelles - Chennai - Lausanne - New York

Library of Congress Cataloging-in-Publication Data

Names: Inglis, Tom, author.
Title: Unbecoming Catholic : being religious in contemporary Ireland / Tom Inglis.
Description: Oxford ; New York : Peter Lang, [2025] | Series: Reimagining Ireland,
    1662-9094 ; volume 139 | Includes bibliographical references.
Identifiers: LCCN 2024055717 (print) | LCCN 2024055718 (ebook) |
    ISBN 9781803748177 (paperback) | ISBN 9781803748184 (ebook) |
    ISBN 9781803748191 (epub)
Subjects: LCSH: Inglis, Tom--Religion. | Catholics--Ireland--Biography. |
    Ireland--Religious life and customs.
Classification: LCC BX4705.I535 I54 2025 (print) | LCC BX4705.I535 (ebook) |
    DDC 282/.415--dc23/eng/20250206
LC record available at https://lccn.loc.gov/2024055717
LC ebook record available at https://lccn.loc.gov/2024055718

A catalogue record for this book is available from the British Library.

Bibliographic Information published by the Deutsche Nationalbibliothek
The Deutsche Nationalbibliothek lists this publication in the Deutsche Nationalbibliografie;
detailed bibliographic data is available in the internet at <http://dnb.d-nb.de>.

Cover image: © Arron Inglis
Cover design by Peter Lang Group AG

ISSN 1662-9094
ISBN 978-1-80374-817-7 (Print)
E-ISBN 978-1-80374-818-4 (E-PDF)
E-ISBN 978-1-80374-819-1 (E-PUB)
DOI 10.3726/b22436

© 2025 Peter Lang Group AG, Lausanne, Switzerland

Published by Peter Lang Ltd, Oxford, United Kingdom
info@peterlang.com

Tom Inglis has asserted his right under the Copyright, Designs and Patents Act, 1988,
to be identified as Author of this Work.

All rights reserved.

All parts of this publication are protected by copyright. Any utilisation outside the strict
limits of the copyright law, without the permission of the publisher, is forbidden and liable
to prosecution. This applies in particular to reproductions, translations, microfilming, and
storage and processing in electronic retrieval systems.

This publication has been peer reviewed.

www.peterlang.com

Table of Contents

Acknowledgements   ix

CHAPTER 1

Introduction   1

    Religion begins with experience   4

    Dimensions of being religious   11

CHAPTER 2

Catholic Colonisation   19

    Being Catholic   19

    Catholic enchantment   24

    Catholic doctrine   39

    Self-denial, sexual repression and fear   50

    Catholic enforcement   60

    Breaking free   83

    Religious reformation   96

CHAPTER 3

A New Era of Being Religious   101

    Attunement   101

    Collective effervescence   103

    Sport as a new religion?   106

    Belonging   108

    Being enchanted   117

CHAPTER 4

God and Nature 125

    The question of God 125

    Being spiritual 133

    Being in nature 137

    Mammon and being religious 149

CHAPTER 5

Conclusion 155

Notes 161

Select Bibliography 177

Index 179

Acknowledgements

I have been a little obsessed with trying to understand how I have come to be the way I am. I have explored many avenues, mostly sociological. When it came to the latest attempt, I did not want to write an academic treatise. Nor did I want to write another memoir. It was something in-between. My experience of the world is profoundly personal. What I have experienced in becoming and unbecoming Catholic is unique to me, but it is also similar to what many other people have experienced in Ireland. I have met and talked with people who have inspired me, friends, colleagues and loved ones. I am grateful to you all. I am particularly grateful to Eamon Maher and Tony Mason who believed in this project when others did not. I would also like to thank the two anonymous reviewers of the text and the many other scholars who have contributed to my learning.

There are others who have been especially inspiring and insightful, Michael Cussen, Manus Charleton, David Blake Knox, Marta Abromowicz, Donal McAnaney, Michael Murphy, Charles Crockatt, Hugo Hamilton, Paddy Masterson and the late Gerard McCarthy. And there is family, particularly my son Arron, who did the cover image, and daughter Olwen who became the rock on which this self was realised.

Finally, there is Carol. She is kind, loving and patient. She has been my editor for many years now and, once again, has steered me in the right direction with quiet determination and great patience.

CHAPTER I

Introduction

I stand at the window in my bedroom. I look over the garden that runs down to a small lake. On the far side there is an abundance of reeds that reach out from the shore into the lake. Beyond them there are hedgerows and patchy green fields where cattle come in summer. The fields rise up to a white house on a hill.

As I look out the window, I pick a spot in the distance and begin to focus on it. It is never the same spot. I concentrate on it. I like this moment. It is as if my whole being is reaching out into the infinite. I am a body and mind in time and space. There is just me and this one arbitrary leaf, branch, flower petal, blade of grass that I have come to focus on. I try to be still and to empty my mind.

I start my breathing. Slowly in through my nose for five, six, seven seconds. As I do, I say to myself that this is what it means to be alive. That there is just this moment in time. That this is everything. And then I hold my breath. Maybe for ten seconds. Then I slowly let it out. And I focus on the idea that I am nothing. That in the scheme of things, I have never been anything, that I will never be anything and that any other thought is a delusion.

And then slowly I lift my right leg and, when my foot reaches above my left knee, I place it against my thigh. The balance is maintained by controlling the pressure of the foot into the thigh. The more I practice, the easier it gets.

But there are wobbles. These can occur through loosing concentration through some thought or some change in the environment. It could be a change in the light, the arrival of a bird into view or the sound of a tractor roaring down the road that runs along the lakeside. The distraction can also come from within. Thoughts of things to do, places to go, people to meet, books to be read and sentences to be written.

I am supposed to stand erect like a tree, with my arms down by my side, raised up from the elbows like branches. More often, instead of being still, my arms are flaying up, down and around, as I desperately try to find my balance. In these moments, I feel like a drunken conductor in front of an orchestra. My attempts to remain still and balanced depend on how much wine I drank the night before.

As I stand there, half-naked, with my little pot belly hanging out over my shorts, I try to close my eyes. This must be done very slowly, still focusing on the exact spot and concentrating on my breathing, I begin to close my eyes until they are barely open. I have tried on occasions imagining that I am walking on a tightrope between two enormous skyscrapers, looking down at the ant-like people below. I think it might help me concentrate. It doesn't. I have never managed to close my eyes completely. As soon as the light fades, I lose the pose, and my leg goes to ground.

My daily posing is a form of ritual practice. It is a version of a well-known pose in yoga. I think if I did it often enough, I might become a Buddhist. Most religions have an element of ritual. Repeating the same actions, the same words, helps eliminate the thoughts and concerns of the day, and enables the person enter into another realm of being. My tree pose helps me distance myself from the world of coming and going, doing, getting and spending. I am, so to speak, not just in the world but, for this brief period of time, at one with it.

Is this some form of soul searching? Some new-age spirituality? A way of being religious that has nothing to do with churches and doctrines. Or is it just a means towards an end: it has nothing to do with being closer to God, the supernatural or nature, and everything to do with wanting to be healthy and live longer? Or is it more about self-realisation, about being able to work, read and write and produce texts, about being recognised, respected and listened to? Is it about being successful?

There are physical and mental benefits to people standing on one leg.[1] It increases the sense of balance which improves the connections between the brain and the body, and this reduces the risk of falling. You are less likely to be able to stand on one leg if you have medical conditions such as Parkinson's or Alzheimer's disease. An inability to balance on one leg for 20 seconds or longer is linked to an increased risk of small blood vessel damage in the brain.

There are other times when I sit in a chair or lie still on my bed and concentrate on my breathing. You could call it a form of meditation. I am not sure if it is mindfulness or mindlessness. I think it is a form of just being in the world without the distractions of day-to-day concerns. Whatever it is, it helps me remember that I am an insignificant grain in time and that it is good to try and put the cosmos at the centre of my being rather than me thinking that I am the centre of the cosmos. It helps me realise that I am an infinitesimal, fleeting part of some whole consciousness, some meaning which is real and palpable but always mysterious.

Most mornings I walk down a nearby lane. It takes about a half hour. It is calming, beautiful and inspiring. There is a sense of being immersed in nature, of being caught in time between the earth and the sky and all the attendant species in the fields, trees and hedgerows. Again, I try not to think. Just to be. Again, am I being religious? Would it become religious if I said the rosary or some other prayers or recited a poem while I'm walking?

Where does being religious begin and end? What makes my trying to pose as a tree different from a Catholic going to Mass? Is there a way of being religious beyond traditional religion? Is there a way of thinking about God that has nothing to do with being Christian, Jewish or Muslim? This, in turn, raises questions about secularisation. Are we living in a new age that is leaving aside the institutional world of religion, of churches, theologians and priests, and finding new ways of being religious?

For many people, being religious means believing in a God or gods. That there is something beyond this material world, some supernatural realm. But belief in God is always vague, ambiguous and uncertain. This is what makes it personal. It is more emotional than rational.

Does God think? Does God have a mind? How can I know God? I have difficulty knowing what is going on in the minds of those I love. I have difficulty knowing what they are feeling. So even if there is a God, how could I know him, her or it? When someone says, 'I believe in God', I am not sure what they mean.

Being religious is traditionally associated with shared beliefs. These beliefs give rise to shared values and practices. Together beliefs, values and practices are central to creating and maintaining shared meanings and identities which are woven into tight webs that sustain people in their everyday lives.[2] We can trace a line from shared beliefs to values and morals which become the basis of laws.

If you probe people about what it is they believe about God and life after death, unless they revert to some official Church doctrine, they are likely to be vague and uncertain. This leads me to argue that when it comes to being religious, it is not so much what people believe, but more about what they do. It is not about doctrine. It is more about engaging in practices and rituals. It is about generating feelings of bonding and belonging, about creating times and places that are sacred. It is about experiences of mystery and enchantment. It is about an intuitive rather than scientific knowledge of life.[3]

For me, being religious revolves around feelings and experiences and a great sense of mystery and uncertainty. I have no explanation for the meaning of life, but I feel that I am part of some extraordinary whole, something majestic and beautiful. It is similar to the feeling of love. I cannot explain it, but I know it exists and that it is a powerful force in my life.

Albert Einstein said he was an atheist. He did not believe in a personal God, but he believed that there was something mysterious, beautiful and enchanting about life.

> To know what is impenetrable to us really exists, manifesting itself as the highest wisdom and the most radiant beauty which our dull faculties can comprehend only in their most primitive forms—this knowledge, this feeling, is at the center of true religiousness. In this sense, and in this sense only, I belong in the ranks of devoutly religious men.[4]

Religion begins with experience

Taking a different perspective

For most people, religion revolves around the notion of God. They believe that God transcends time and space and intervenes in this world. I take a broader view. I think religion revolves around a sense of wonderment, about humans trying to make sense of the world in which they live, of nature, the cosmos, and life here on earth. I think that from the beginning, human groups learnt to develop a shared sense of meaning. This meaning, evolved into a notion of spirits and gods and was maintained through symbols and rituals. These became sacred to the group. They enabled members to communicate and collaborate with each other and to live in harmony.[5]

I think it is time to take off the conceptual glasses with which we have looked at traditional conceptions of religion and being religious.[6]

Our inherited ways of thinking about religion have blinkered us from understanding and appreciating the impulses that have been at the heart of being religious in the past and from the feelings, emotions and experiences that are central to being religious today. We associate religion with people belonging to churches, denominations, sects and other groups. We think of religious specialists or leaders such as priests, bishops, rabbis, imams, brahmins or gurus. We think of sacred texts such as the Bible, the Koran and the Veda that have been read and analysed and turned into teachings, doctrine and dogma.[7]

All of these dimensions to being religious began to emerge two and a half thousand years ago with the birth of the Axial age.[8] Given that human society has been developing for more than two hundred thousand years, these forms of being religious are relatively new. For most of human history, being religious revolved around feelings, around rituals and beliefs that emerged from language, art and symbolic life. These were fundamental to humans living in groups. As evolution progressed, humans began to name and classify the world around them. There were forces that they could not explain. They began to distinguish them as different spirits and gods.[9]

The emergence of churches, leaders and texts can be seen as a rationalisation of the religious field particularly in Judaism, Christianity and Islam. The big turn in these Abrahamic religions was the move away from spirits and gods to the notion of there being one God. Religious experts began to puzzle over the nature of God, his relationship with humans, the notion of salvation and how it could be attained. This led to theologies, doctrines and dogmas.[10] This institutionalisation can be seen as the second era of religion.

But although religion became more rationalised, organised and institutionalised, the fundamental dimension of being religious remained the same. There will never be definitive answers to the meaning of life. Religion has always been founded on mystery, on not knowing. It is based on feelings of awe, beauty, fear, of people coming together to share these feelings and, in doing so, developing a love, care and concern for each other.[11] What is happening in the West today is that religion has become less institutional. It has become more private and personal. It is a matter of individual choice. People come together in families and groups but there is no doctrine or dogma.

I think humans have always been, and will always be, religious. I think that people today, in the so-called secular West, are as religious as people have ever been. It is just that they are being religious in a different way. Religious behaviour is rooted in a feeling that we are part of a wider whole. It is a mystical feeling we get from being a member of a family, a group or community, that becomes enmeshed in experiences of nature, love and beauty.[12] It is rooted in rituals that remind us that reason and science cannot explain these crucial dimensions of life. That there is something beyond material existence, that can be accessed and utilised and that has social and personal benefits.

Being religious revolves around humans trying to make sense of life and the world in which they live, of developing a sense of bonding and belonging and engaging in rituals that create a feeling of unity. We share memories. We gather in places at certain times, and we talk and perhaps eat and drink and maybe even sing. And it is not so much the words that are said; it is the way they are said. And these times and places become sacred. Family gatherings are set apart from the mundane world of working, going to school, getting and spending, cleaning, cooking and looking after children. Members come together to celebrate special times and events and to commiserate and grieve in times of death and tragedy. This raises a fundamental issue at the heart of the study of religion. Should we have a substantial definition of religion that makes reference to the notion of a supernatural realm, of God, and then of churches and priests, or should we have a loose definition that looks at feelings and experience, the rituals that bind people together and create a sense of insight, renewal, emergence and transcendence?[13]

Rituals around mourning are part of every human society.[14] Many of the oldest traces of human society relate to burial practices. But there is little evidence to relate these to a formally organised system of religion. Similarly, throughout history and around the world today, families, loved ones and friends gather together to celebrate birthdays, anniversaries, successes, departures and returns. In Ireland, families gather at Christmas and Easter, for Christenings, First Holy Communions and Confirmations. They are sacred occasions but, for many, have little to do with doctrine and belief. There are many doctrinal rituals in Catholic Ireland, such as going to Mass and saying the rosary, that are formal and repetitious. But there are other more informal, spontaneous, unscripted rituals which revolve around creating new dispositions, new insights, new ways of seeing and understanding the world.[15] People have epiphanies, experiences that change the way they live their lives. These can come through pilgrimage, penitential practice, sex, drugs, art, music and dance. They can come through being with and opening to another, a stranger, who sees and understands the world differently, or to immersing oneself in a different culture.

There is then, when it comes to everyday life, an artificial divide between the religious and the secular. As they have always done, humans will always come together to create and sustain meaning. This coming together is part and parcel of what it is to live ethically. What has happened over the last two thousand years in particular, is that these religious feelings, rituals and beliefs became institutionalised into churches, leaders and dogmas. Churches have developed a monopoly position in the religious field in the same way that the state has come to dominate the political field.[16] If the state created a monopoly over taxation and violence, institutional religions developed a monopoly over the meaning of life and what it is to flourish.

The strength of this monopoly is that many people believe that if they are not a member of some religious group, sect or Church, they are not religious. Would they say this about other aspects of their lives? Take, for example, sport. What is it to be sportive? I am not a member of any sports club, but I spend a lot of time playing, watching, following and talking about sport. Many people say that they are not into sport and yet they walk, hike, swim and cycle. I am not in any book club, but I enjoy reading and see myself as literary. I am not in any musical society. I don't play any instrument, but I enjoy listening to music. I like to sing songs, mostly to myself but to others when the occasion arises, usually after some wine. I listen and sing, therefore, I would argue, I am musical.

So why then, when it comes to religion, do many people feel the need to say with such vehemence that they are not religious? I think this relates not so much to the search for meaning and the desire to be a good person, which are universal impulses, and more to do with power. In Ireland, the Catholic Church colonised the notion of what it is to be religious. Through this, it gained significant power in other social fields, particularly the political, but also education, health, social welfare, the media, business and sport.[17] I think it is the legacy of this power that has created an antipathy to religion and the notion of being religious. It has, so to speak, given religion a bad name.

It has created a false binary opposition. Either one is religious, or one is not. Either one believes in God or a realm of the supernatural, or one does not.

But it doesn't have to be either/or. It can be and/both. Being religious does not have to be consistent. It is not about fully accepting teachings and doctrines. It can be riddled with doubt, ambiguity and inconsistency. People can believe in God one day and reject him the next. I am Catholic by culture but, generally, I am an agnostic searching for truth, love and beauty. When it comes to the meaning of life, I don't know. And yet I believe I am part of something that is more than a random collision of atoms. I am religiously fluid.

For me being religious is about not knowing. It is about accepting that we do not have an answer or explanation for everything. We don't know what happens when we die. We don't know if there is a God or gods and, if there is, what she, he, it or they are like. However, what makes me fearful is that so many people, particularly bishops, priests and theologians, can say with such conviction that they know that there is one God, that they know God, that He is a loving, caring, all-knowing but also judgemental father figure and that he can and does intervene in life on earth. It is not so much the idea that frightens me, it is the absolute conviction with which the belief is held. It is this conviction, this religious fundamentalism, that has been the cause of so much anger, conflict and violence.

This relates to another problem with many religions. They are instrumental in humans developing the notion that they are God's chosen people. They have persuaded themselves that they have a God-given right to master and control other species. It will take a religious revolution for humans to see themselves as just one species among millions, that they have no more right to be on this planet than any other species.[18]

Another endemic problem is that most world religions are patriarchal and hierarchical. They symbolically reproduce male dominance. Institutional religion started to emerge with the move from hunting and gathering societies, to settled pastoral farming. The animistic world of multiple spirits and gods who were in the world became rationalised into the notion of there being one transcendent, all-knowing, all-powerful God. The world of shamans, necromancers and druids, were replaced by a new cadre of priests, rabbis and mullahs. Beliefs and rituals became formalised. Theologians developed dogmas and doctrines. However, it could be argued that the emergence of liberal individualism has led to a decline in institutional religion and has ushered in new, third era of being religious. People are developing new understandings of God and nature. New ways of celebrating what is sacred. New ways of being spiritual. They are reengaging with ancient beliefs and rituals. This third era of being religious is informal, fluid and dynamic. It is still unknown if there will be new religious leaders in this era, from where they will emerge, whether they will be predominantly women and what their message might be.

Three eras of religion

I think it is important to realise that ways of being religious are embedded in a wider culture that is continually evolving. I mentioned earlier that the initial rationalisation within religion involved a move away from numerous gods and spirits to the notion of there being one God. But this rationalisation was part of a much bigger, long-term process of change. We now live in a world in which there is so much order. We operate in bureaucracies that demand predictable behaviour, in which everything is in its proper time and place.[19] The world is less magical, less unpredictable.

We now rely on science and technology to explain and control the world. People might bless themselves before boarding a plane and pray for a safe flight, but they rely more on the pilot knowing 'his' job and the plane operating properly. And yet it was only around five hundred years ago that science began to be seen as fully distinct from religion, with different theories and methods, and its own explanations of life.[20] There are still many people who believe that the world was created by God around five or six thousand years ago.

Scientific knowledge led to new techniques for mastering and controlling the environment. People no longer relied on magic and miracles. Rationalisation, and the drive to find the best way of living and organising life, extended into states and markets, and into families, schools, hospitals and welfare homes.

This rationalisation extended to religion. The Protestant Reformation was part of a process within which the world became less magical. The whole enterprise of indulgences, miracles and praying for favours was eroded. Individuals were free from the restrictions of the Church. They oversaw their own salvation. The bible was still seen as the word of God, but it was up to each individual to make their own choices about what was right and wrong. It ushered in an era of individual moral responsibility. People could go beyond the bible and church teaching. They were free to live their lives as they felt best.

In the current third era, the freedom for people to live their own lives has become a human right.[21] They can worship whatever God they like, be a member of whatever church, sect or group, and follow the advice of any sage or guru. And they are free to make up their own religious menus. As well as the *á la carte* Catholic who choses which Church teachings to follow, there is now the *smorgasbord* Catholic who mixes Catholic rituals, beliefs and values with advice from dietary gurus and self-help guides.[22]

Institutional religion may be on the decline in Ireland as elsewhere in the West, but there is still an interest in living morally and being a good person. Like many others, I have come to the conclusion that being a good person revolves around not just how I relate to other human beings, but includes how I relate to other animals, to other species and to nature in general. My understanding of sin has changed. When I was young, I was taught that every time I had sex with myself, I was hurting God. I was driving another nail into Jesus as he was dying on the cross. Now I have a different notion of morality. I have come to recognise that every time I climb aboard a plane, get into a car, or eat a steak, I am complicit in destroying nature, the very thing that I admire, love and depend upon.

Increasingly I think that the meaning of life is in nature, that if there is a God the only way we can know and understand 'her', is through nature. I think there are some religions, particularly Buddhism, that help develop a better relationship with nature, but the question is whether there are other ways of being religious that will help humans live a better life, a life more closely in harmony with nature. I don't know. But I do think that we need to think again about what it means to be religious. I think we need to go beyond the conception of being religious as revolving around God, churches, concerns about life after death and laying down laws about what is right and wrong. We need to go back to basics.

Dimensions of being religious

Although religion is always evolving, we can identify three key ingredients or dimensions to being religious. Most analysts argue that belief is the main ingredient that, for example within Christianity, it is the belief that Jesus is the son of God and that he rose from the dead. It is argued that it is this shared belief that leads people to engage in ritual practices. Religious beliefs and practices, it is claimed, create values about how to live a moral life. Finally, it is these beliefs, values and practices that give rise to religious experiences.[23]

While all these dimensions are clearly interconnected, I think that religion begins with feelings and experiences.[24] For me, it is religious experience that creates and maintains beliefs, practices and values. Doctrines, theologies, priests, prophets and gurus may come and go, but unless there is a feeling of belonging to some beautiful, mysterious order, that is universal though only ever experienced personally, there is no religion. However, while I think experience is primary, I recognise that the dimensions are all interconnected and each creates and maintains the others.

For me, the first dimension to being religious is the sense of awe, wonderment, beauty, mystery and excitement that comes from being in the world. This feeling of being in the presence of something awesome, call it God, is different from, and primary to, belief. I think it is reflected in the innocent but fundamental question of the child who asks, 'where did I come from? or the philosopher who wonders why there is something rather than nothing. I think this was the same question that our ancestors asked tens of thousands of years ago when they became self-conscious.

Participating in doctrinal practices, such as going to Mass or saying the rosary, is founded on a desire to bond together and to pay attention to the mysteries of life. Nature has become increasingly amenable to rational, scientific explanation but it is still a magical place full of intense experiences that are serendipitous and inexplicable. Strangers meet and fall in love. We are enchanted by the beauty and mysterious ways of nature. We engage in magical thinking. We encourage it. We see it as part and parcel of being human. We do not live in a scientific laboratory in which everything is predictable, regulated and controlled. We are conscious of a force of life. We cannot control it. Reason and science provide an explanation of death, but it is primarily an emotional experience. No explanation can ease the emotional pain. I think we can say that the impulse to be aware and appreciate the inexplicable beauty, unfairness and fragility of life is religious.[25]

The second dimension is attunement. This revolves around connectedness, of people being like-minded, sharing the same sense of purpose, the same values and beliefs. This sense of connectedness, being attuned to the dispositions, cares and concerns of others, is attained by engaging in rituals, creating times and places that are sacred to the group.[26] We associate this sense of connectedness with families but also with groups, organisations and nations. But throughout history and around the world today, this sense of connectedness, of identity and belonging, comes from engaging in rituals and practices that maintain a sense of sharing beliefs and values about the meaning of life and what it is to live ethically.

It seems to me that what has happened in Ireland, and the West generally, is that the supposed shared belief of what or who God is has become increasingly irrelevant when it comes to experiences of attunement. What people believe about God, has become personal and private. Individuals have developed their own sense of God, of what it means to be in the presence of God, and how they relate and communicate this eternal being.

The question then is when, where, how and among whom do individuals create a sense of attunement. Is it possible for a sense of bonding and belonging to reach beyond members of a particular family, group or community to wider society and perhaps even all human beings? Is it possible to become attuned to other species? Is striving to connect with nature a way of being religious? Is walking down a country lane and being inspired by the beauty of the landscape and trying to connect with the myriad of species who have lived there for thousands of years, just a different way of being religious, and is no different than going to Mass?[27] Can we say this desire to reach out and connect with nature is religious even though it may not have any supernatural reference, particularly in terms of a God? I think the answer is yes.

The third dimension relates to being spiritual and mystical, to trying to go beyond existing taken-for-granted ways of knowing the world, of being in it. What makes humans different is not just their self-consciousness and ability to critically reflect, imagine and re-present their world, but to change it. We have an ability to transcend the social, cultural and material conditions of our existence. The symbolisation of the world, the notion of there being gods and spirits, was the beginning of this transcendence, of humans becoming self-conscious. This developed into reflective self-consciousness which, in turn, gave rise to self-transcendence, of going beyond the inherited ways of seeing, thinking and being. In Catholic Ireland, being spiritual and seeking transcendence often revolved around fasting and abstinence from certain foods, particularly during Lent, doing the Stations of the Cross, saying the rosary and engaging in penitential practices such as pilgrimages to Lough Derg and Croagh Patrick.

Searching for new ways of being religious is not new. There have always been mystics, gurus and prophets. However, what is different is that over the last six hundred years, being religious, particularly in the West, became conflated with institutional religion and doctrine, rules and regulations. Self-transcendence and new forms of being spiritual were systematically repressed.

Self-transcendence has been closely allied with sex, drugs, dance, music, art and literature. But it can also include new religious rituals and trying to find new ways of being with others. Transcendence involves embracing the other, going beyond cherished beliefs that can become fundamental, intransigent dogmas. I suggest that the continual search for truth, the continual challenge of the taken-for-granted, of trying to go beyond the confines of the present, can be more than just spiritual; it can be the basis of creating new ideals, of creating social and cultural change.[28]

Spiritual feelings and experiences became labelled, classified and interpreted by religious specialists who weave them into institutionalised doctrines. A renewed emphasis on feelings and experiences is part of the deinstitutionalisation of religion and the intensification of religious individualisation. But although spiritual feelings are intensely private and personal, they can become part of a shared, communal sense of awe, mystery and uncertainty, that can be shared and celebrated in language, symbols and rituals.[29]

But because the primary impulse in being religious revolves around feelings, emotions and experiences, institutionalised religions seek to corral, label and control these forces. There is a fear of mysticism. But, like sexual feelings, the repression of mystical and spiritual feelings can never succeed. New conditions of existence, changes in the environment, lead to new understandings of what it is to be human, that are linked to new rituals, new forms of creating a sense of bonding and belonging.

Doctrinal Solidity Melts into Air

When it comes to being religious, the emphasis I place on feelings, experiences and rituals might suggest that I do not see belief as important. It is important but, as I suggested earlier, belief is variable. It varies throughout history and across cultures. And it varies across the life of an individual. What someone believes in, can vary in different circumstances, particularly in times of ill-health, tragedy and death. People can pray to a God that they are not sure really exists.

Moreover, religious beliefs are not consistent. They are often vague, ambiguous, uncertain and even contradictory. People may believe in heaven but have no clear conception of what it is. What a Catholic believes may be quite different from Church doctrine. Many Catholics, for example, reject belief in Hell and the Devil. Even if they do believe, they often have their own version. And yet, these beliefs are, ostensibly, central to the belief that salvation is attained in and through the Church.[30] But increasingly salvation is less about getting into the next life and more about how to live a good, long and healthy life and this might mean rearing children as Catholic, going to Mass as well as doing yoga and meditation and embracing Buddhist teachings and practices.

Variability and inconsistency mean that it is often difficult to determine what people 'really' believe and the depth and level of commitment to their beliefs. They may say that they believe in a personal God who intervenes in their lives, who listens to their prayers, who creates miracles. But to what extent is this belief put into practice in their daily lives?[31] How often do they talk to God? How often do they pray? And if they believe that the teachings of the Catholic Church are the path to salvation, to what extent do they fulfil these teachings? How often do they receive the sacraments? If someone said they believed in family, it would be difficult to believe them if they rarely thought of their parents, sisters and brothers, if they did not communicate with them and if they rarely attended family gatherings.

At a social level, beliefs operate as a form of social identity. People identify themselves as Christian as a means of distinguishing themselves from Jews and Muslims. It is a bit like ethnicity and nationality. It is not so much what people believe, but rather that they belong to a certain cultural tradition. Religious divisions still permeate society even when people no longer believe or practice the religion in which they were brought up. But again, things change. Irish Catholics may be increasingly willing to marry Protestants, but perhaps less willing to marry Jews or Muslims. And context is important. The willingness of Catholics to marry Protestants is, for example, different in Northern Ireland compared to the South.

Sometimes I think of humans as highly sophisticated ants that have developed incredibly complex forms of life. They live in huge colonies, in villages, towns and cities, some with nearly 40 million inhabitants. People live in relative harmony. They can communicate and cooperate. They are mostly rational, but they are also highly emotional creatures. They have antenna that enable them to pick up and respond to non-verbal forms of communication. Although they go out and about during everyday life, to work, to school, to the market and places of leisure and entertainment, most retire at night to live with family and friends in homes. There is then a sense of identity, of belonging with millions of others, of seeing them as the same, but this is nothing like the sentimental attachment there is to loved ones.

David Attenborough, the renowned natural scientist, when asked once if he believed in God, responded that he was an agnostic.[32] He went on, however, to say that if he were to take off the top of a termite hill and look down into it, he would see an incredibly complex form of life, with termites going hither and thither, building walls, looking after the queen and caring for the young. However, if the termites do not have the necessary senses, if they cannot see or hear, they might not be aware of his presence. Attenborough said that it might be the same for humans, that there is something out there, beyond us, that is looking down on us, but that we don't have the necessary sense organs to know and understand it.

I think there is another dimension to that image. It is not much different from the sight you get from the top of a skyscraper in a city. Thousands of people going along the streets, weaving in and out of each other, slowing down and speeding up, making sure not to bump into each other. They are highly sensitive to behaviour that is out of order. They are continually looking out for unusual behaviour, assessing the ever-changing territory, all the time looking but never staring, giving each other signals that everything is in its proper time and place. And, at the same, they may be lost in their thoughts, perhaps talking animatedly to someone either in person or on the phone, seemingly unaware of what is going on around them.

The question is to what extent religion plays a role in all this order.[33] There is obviously a close connection between being religious and being moral, in sharing the same outlook on life, the same beliefs and values. But I wonder to what extent people, as they go about their everyday lives, think about the meaning of life. How often do people reflect on the nature of the cosmos and the wonderous way social order comes about? Do they believe that God knows and is in charge of everything that happens, everything they do? Does the idea of this God provide the meaning that is necessary for them to move through life, to operate successfully, to communicate and collaborate? I think that most of the time, most of us go about our lives without worrying about any overall meaning. Religion steps in when our everyday meanings are threatened, undermined or attacked.

To recap. I think that being religious is part and parcel of being human. Religion provides an overall meaning to life and what it is to live ethically and to flourish. Being religious revolves around a sense of bonding and belonging, a feeling of attachment, of being attuned to others and caring for them. It also involves a sense of mystery, of being in a world that is full of order and beauty, that has a meaning that is beyond reason and science. And, finally, being religious involves being spiritual and mystical, of continually looking for new ways of being and understanding, of transcending the beliefs and practices that have become institutionalised. And throughout history, those times and places in which people become enchanted and attuned, in which they attain a sense of transcendence, become sacred.

I think for most people the ways of being religious are inherited, taken for granted and unquestioned. They revolve around engaging in time-old rituals, the reiteration of beliefs, that create a sense of bonding and belonging. These rituals and beliefs were central to group identity and because they were sacred, were often defended vehemently. The differences in religious identity, belief and practice have been, and still are, central to the deepest, long-lasting conflicts and wars. If we are to overcome these fundamental differences, we have to be able to debate and discuss, to defend and challenge each other's beliefs and, at the same time, be open and able to learn from each other. This means that we also have to be willing to let go what we were told was the truth, what we have grown to cherish and see as sacred.

My main objective in writing this book is to try to get people to think differently about what it is to be religious. I want to break down the barrier between being secular and being religious. I think there is a myriad of ways of being religious, that the notion of what is sacred changes, that people find different ways of being attuned with each other, of recognising the mysterious beauty of the world, and of seeking ways of seeing and being.

It has taken me a lifetime to try to transcend the Roman Catholic way of being into which I was socialised. It has taken the last twenty years for me to realise that I am as religious as any priest, nun or bishop. It is just that I am religious in my own way. I believe that if there is a God, he, she or it, can only be known through nature. I don't believe in heaven or hell. I have my own rituals. I don't go to Mass. Most days I walk a county lane near where I live. I feel immersed in nature and maybe God. I say my own prayers. I sing my own hymns.

Catholic Colonisation

Being Catholic

The climate breakdown is accelerating the debate about the meaning of life and what it is to live ethically. I think this involves questioning, challenging and resisting the taken-for-granted understanding of what it is to be religious. It means breaking the monopoly that institutional religions have developed in the religious field. To transcend their teachings and practices, we need to understand how they became embedded in people's ideas of themselves and the meaning of their lives. We think of institutionalised religions as forms of cultural imperialism, as forms of empires that colonised people's ways of thinking and being.

In Ireland, many scholars have investigated how the way we see and understand the world has emerged from how we were colonised and symbolically dominated by the English. But the Irish were also colonised by the Catholic Church. It was a different form of colonisation, mainly because for so long, so many people voluntarily and often eagerly acquiesced to being dominated.[34] The Catholic Church, and the ways of being and thinking that it promoted, became a form of dependency.

For almost two hundred years, generations of Irish people have been brought up in a Catholic ethos. The strength of this socialisation has waned, there may be less practice and more doubt, but most parents are happy to go with the Catholic flow, to engage in Catholic rituals, to send their children to Catholic schools and, generally, to follow a Catholic path. It may not be out of any strong conviction. It may be that it is part of a cultural legacy that is inherited and taken for granted and, generally, seen as good enough.

It is not easy to transcend one's socialisation. For most people, one's sense of self is embedded in family which is embedded in community. For most people throughout history and around the world today, this sense of identity is created and maintained through religious rituals. Learning to be religious is like wearing a vest every day that is never taken off. Over time, it begins to seep into the body and become part and parcel of who one is.[35] This is what happened over generations in Ireland. It is only in the last two generations that there has been a willingness and ability for people to take off their Catholic vests.

The recent growth in memoir writing provides insights into how socialisation takes place. This is especially important when it comes to religion. Because religion is based on feelings, emotions and experiences, we can develop a better understanding of how the Catholic Church developed a monopoly over what it is to be religious, by focusing on personal experiences. I cannot say anything about what it is, or was like, to grow up as a Jew in New York, a Presbyterian in Belfast, or a Muslim in Baghdad. I can only speak of what it was like to grow up Catholic in Ireland. I think, however, there are many similarities in growing up in any authoritarian orthodox religious culture. It is a colonisation of the soul, of religious experience and of the meaning of life and what it is to live ethically. It is a form of symbolic and emotional domination.

There is a tendency to think of emotions as something individual and belonging to the field of psychology. We are used to individuals trying to reveal their emotional history in therapy. How they emotionally came to be the way they are and how it impacts on their personal relations with others. But the ways in which people are emotional are central to understanding social life. There are times and places to be emotional. There are ways of expressing emotions. In our everyday interactions, we are constantly reading each other's actions for signs of emotional well-being. What we say and do and the ways in which they are said and done, become part not just of our being and sense and self, but of a cultural repertoire. There are ways of expressing happiness, sadness, anger, despair, sympathy and love. They are picked up and read before anything is said.

For generations in Ireland, being Catholic was central to a feeling of belonging, of everyone singing from the same hymn sheet. Understanding how this happened and how it is changing is key to understanding Irish culture and society. In some respects, then, what I am trying to do is develop an emotional understanding of how, as a member of Irish Catholic society, I came to be religious and how this has impacted on my understanding of religion generally and my own ways of being religious.[36]

For many years during my childhood, I had a feeling that I was lucky to be living on an island of pious, humble, devout Catholics who adored the Church, its icons and rituals, its bishops, priests, nuns and brothers. We saw ourselves as an island of saints and scholars. We were, as Scally labelled us, the best Catholics in the world.[37] It was all-enveloping. It produced a kind of religious high, an effervescence that reproduced beliefs and values.[38]

Trying to capture this religious high, is like trying to capture what it is like to fall in love. In most of my writings on Catholic Ireland, I have tried to be objective and detached. Now I want to add an emotional dimension, to try to describe the high that came from being Catholic, of how feelings of enrapture, enchantment and belonging were mixed with feelings of fear and shame and then, how these became overtaken by feelings of anger, frustration and alienation. And then, how in recent years I have discovered a new sensibility of what it is to be religious.

Like many other Irish people, I grew up in an intensely Catholic home, community and society. During my early childhood, I was a passionate Catholic. As I entered into my teenage years, this passion began to wane. The rituals and teachings of the church seemed archaic and irrelevant. I became more inspired by the messages that came through the media. The land I dreamed of was not of rural Ireland and comely maidens, it was of the vibrant, shinning cities of England, Europe and America. They became my new gods.

In the Catholic Ireland in which I grew up, there was no room for debate and discussion. It was difficult if not impossible to question the authority of the Church. It became a power that, if one wanted to be accepted, if one wanted to be successful and, most of all, if one wanted to be saved, it had to be obeyed. It became an institution of teachings, rules and regulations. There were still moments of enchantment and attunement, but for me the feelings had gone. It was all about doctrine and dogma that was dictated by Rome. The dominant emotion became fear. Slowly I began to realise that there was nothing to be afraid of. The Church was not a compulsory organisation like the state. I did not have to obey its laws. I could walk away from it. I was not alone. I was part of new generation that began to see and understand the power of the Church. All the certainty, pomp and arrogance began to shrivel and collapse like a leaky balloon. This was happening way before the clerical child sex abuse scandals. The attempt by the Church to deny and cover up the atrocities just accelerated the process.

But the feelings of attachment and belonging into which I had been socialised did not disappear. On the contrary, they linger deep within me. It is like still having an affection for someone you have broken up with. The emotional history of having been so deeply involved in the Church, so deeply imbued with a Catholic way of being, still lingers within me.

In 2022, when I was asked in the Irish Census of Population if I belonged to any religion, I ticked the first box 'No Religion'. I could, like I think many others, have ticked the next box 'Roman Catholic'. I don't think there was any chance of me ticking any of the other boxes provided. When it comes to being religious, whatever else I am, I am not Protestant, Muslim or Jewish.[39]

Being religious, is about identity. It is about belonging to a tradition. I grew up Catholic and while I may no longer see myself as Catholic – I don't practice, and I don't believe in most Church teachings – being Catholic has become part and parcel of who I am. It may not be as strong as being an Inglis, being male, white and Irish, or being a sociologist but, even though I can be repulsed by many things the institutional Church has done, I feel an affinity with other Catholics.[40] When I lived in the USA, I often felt more at ease with Catholics. There was a similar sense of self. A sense of being part of the same ethos, formed by the same rituals. I know that there are angry, alienated and disenchanted Catholics who feel nothing when they go into a Catholic Church. I still get a tingling sensation. I think it is this sentimental attachment to ritual and tradition that is at the heart of being a cultural Catholic.[41]

However, since I don't practice and don't believe in many of the fundamental teachings of the Church, it made no sense to tick the Roman Catholic box. But I had a major problem ticking the 'No Religion' box. It suggested that I am not religious. And this is something that goes to the heart of what I am writing about. I may no longer sing from the same hymn sheet as Catholics. I may no longer believe in God as in the Catholic interpretation. I may no longer pray or engage in Church rituals but, in recent years, I have come to the conclusion that I am as religious as any good Catholic. I may not be a saint or prophet, but I am as religious as any pope, bishop or priest. This may sound arrogant, but if I am to break free from the definitions of the meanings of life that have been ingrained in me and which I have embodied, and if I am to transcend inherited dispositions and assumptions about myself, I need to be confident that I am not a heretic when I say that there is no right or wrong when it comes to being religious, that we are all religious in our own way.

For a long time, I thought that if I did not believe in God, if I did not go to Mass, I was, almost automatically, an atheist or agnostic. That it was all or nothing. I was a classic case of washing the religious baby out with the Catholic bathwater. I am constantly bewildered, mesmerised and enchanted by the world in which I live. I engage in hundreds of rituals, some of which have become sacred. I get a feeling of effervescence when I am with family and friends, a sense of belonging, happiness and well-being. It makes me feel part of a social whole. I regularly get a similar feeling when I walk in the lanes and woods around me. A feeling of belonging to some mysterious, beautiful whole. That there is something spiritual about all this. Something beyond reason and science. I am regularly enchanted by love, by beauty and by the miraculous way that evolution has brought about this delicate, intricate, interdependent way of life among the millions of species that inhabit the earth. All of these feelings form the basis of my core values, of my attempt to live a good life. I also experience many times or moments, some stronger than others, that provide an insight into what life is about, a kind of epiphany, that changes how I see and understand myself and the world in which I live.

In saying all of this, I do not have a theology. I am very confused, ambiguous and, often, contradictory in my thoughts and actions when it comes to being religious. I am certainly not dogmatic. Indeed, it is the dogmatism of the Church which turns me off. I cannot understand how it knows *the* truth. That it claims to have a direct line to God. It was this dogmatism that enabled its personnel to dominate empires and states and do despicable things, all in the name of God. The Church is like all other forms of power. When its power became absolute, as it did in Ireland, it became so sacred that it was almost impossible to question or challenge it.

Catholic enchantment

One of the great achievements of the Catholic Church, which was central to the development of its symbolic domination and power, was to create a sense of awe, splendour and enchantment. During the nineteenth century, after Catholic emancipation and the end of the English state's attempt to turn the Irish into Protestants, there was a spectacular growth of church building throughout the country. People who lived in hovels willingly gave their pennies to help build the thousands of churches we see in every Irish village and town. These churches were beautiful, enchanting places. People flocked to them for all sorts of rituals. There was a heady mixture of praying, chanting and singing.[42] One can imagine after centuries of colonial oppression, of having to pass by and gaze at the splendour of Protestant churches, the sense of excitement, elation and enchantment at being able to go into one's own sacred space and celebrate.

When I was young, I was fed Catholic prayers, hymns and rituals. I was mesmerised by Catholic stories and mysteries, captivated by all the icons, sounds and aromas. The Church created a sense of majesty, awe and wonderment. It was heaven on earth. There was also a feeling of monarchy, of pomp and power that created a sense of deference, fear and trepidation.

I still get these feelings when I go into a Catholic church. I might try to expunge them, but part of me longs to go back to those beautiful, innocent days. They are part of who I am. It would be like trying not to be white, male and Irish. I can try and be rational about this feeling. I can write, read and talk about it. I can write chapters, articles and books. I can jump and shout and scream about the power of the Church. I am shocked and angered by the way it has abused, hurt and deeply damaged so many young and innocent boys and girls. I recoil when I think of the regimes of terror that took place in schools, homes and laundries. But such was the exquisite vice-like grip the Church developed over my emotions that the feelings of belonging and enchantment will not go away.

Like many others, it was my mother who instilled in me a love of God and all things Catholic. She taught me how to be pious, humble and holy. I was fervent in my desire to please her and God. I wanted her to be proud of me. I wanted to show the world what a good Catholic boy I was. In the world of Catholic thinking, she was a saint, and I was her little angel.

She taught me how to be pious. When she was getting me ready for bed, we would kneel down and she would show me how to put my two hands together, to bow my head, and to say my prayers, a Hail Mary, Our Father and Glory Be. They were repeated in the morning. At the end of the night prayers, I would ask Our Lady to look after absent family members and to help family and friends who were sick or in trouble. Being mindful of others was a way of keeping attuned.

Every evening during Lent and at other times during the year, she would call the family, my father, sister and brother, to say the rosary. We would kneel in the sitting room and face into a chair and the humming of the prayers would begin. It had its own cadence. Taking turns to sing out the first part of the Hail Mary and the others chanting out the second half. Round and round, fingering out the ten Hail Marys on the beads.

It was not just me; everyone said my mother was a saint. Every day, in all weathers, she walked the half mile up and back to the local church for ten o'clock mass. The preparations would begin after nine o'clock when the rest of the family had gone to school or work. She would sit at her dressing-table in the bedroom, in front of the mirror, puffing on a cigarette in between putting on her face. When she was dressed and ready to go, there was the ritual of opening and taking her missal and black mantilla from the drawer in the hall. She would then head down the small avenue on which we lived, walk up and across Lower Churchtown road, onto Upper Churchtown road and then cross over Beaumont Avenue and onto Nutgrove avenue. The same pilgrimage every day. I longed to go with her.

I grew up in the 1950s in the southern suburbs of Dublin. For me, for many years, the local church – 'The Good Shepard' – was a magical place, full of grandeur, even though there was no big stained-glass window at the end of the church to shine heavenly light down on the altar. The parish was too poor. The church was like hundreds of others that mushroomed around the new suburbs of Dublin in the 1950s and 60s. They were enormous. They towered over the suburban housing estates. They could accommodate hundreds, sometimes thousands. And pious, humble, obedient people like my family flocked to them for Mass each Sunday. The sense of reverence and obedience was inspiring.

I was an innocent boy in those days. I was in love with my mother, God and the world. I was extraordinarily happy as we walked into the church, she holding me with one hand and her handbag and missal in the other, me holding my little white prayer book. In summer, she wore a bright coloured dress, but still covered her head in a black mantilla. On Sundays in winter, she wore her fur coat. It was a class act as we paraded through the new council houses that had been built for the working classes that had escaped the tenements of the inner city.

And then, when we got to the church, more rituals ensued. The dipping of hands into the holy water font at the door, the putting of coins in the collection box. And then in through the big doors, into the space of God. It was mesmerising. The slow move up the right-hand side of the church under the 'stations of the cross', past Fr Hanlon's confession box (my mother did not like him) and on up to Fr Hyland's (she liked him). The genuflection before entering the pew. She always sat in the same place in the same pew.

She would kneel in prayer while I sat and stared and read my prayer book and waited for the bell to ring and the dramatic entrance of the priest from the small sacristy door at the side of the altar, striding in his richly coloured vestments to the bottom steps of the altar, followed by two boys in their black tunics and white surplices. And, like good Catholic soldiers, my mother and I would stand to attention.

The church had two side altars with large statues of Our Lady and St Joseph above them. During missions and retreats, these side altars would be busy with priests coming and going to say Mass. There could be three masses going on at the same time. It was a colourful hive of Catholic chaos, priests coming and going, prayers being chanted, bells being rung, hosts and chalices being raised. Except for Holy Week, there were always flowers on the altar. But the displays at Easter and Christmas were spectacular.

There was also a good display during the May Devotions. The smell and colour of the flowers, the soft evening light, the pungency of the incense burning in the thurible and the wisps of white smoke rising, the sonorous annunciation of the prayers, created a sense of ecstasy that gave a glimpse of what heaven might be like.

But most of all it was the singing of the hymns. It was one of the few occasions in which we were encouraged to sing. There were dozens of them, and everyone had their favourite. I still shiver when it comes to 'I'll Sing a

Hymn to Mary' and, most of all, 'Hail Queen of Heaven, the Ocean Star'. I was so enamoured by all this, that I created my own altar on top of the set of drawers in my bedroom. I put a statue of Our Lady in the middle and surrounded it with empty jam jars which I filled with bluebells, primroses, clover, lilac, daisies and buttercups. Every evening, I would go out into the garden, which itself was a magical place, and I would gather new flowers and redecorate my altar. And when it was all refreshed, I would kneel down, say my prayers and sing my hymns. Looking back, I think I was more enchanted with the world than I have ever been.

The feeling of enchantment was mixed with a sense of the inexplicable, the sense of awe and mystery. The idea that somewhere within this sacred place, there was an even more sacred place, a place that only priests could go. The tabernacle was in the middle of the altar, it was where the sacred hosts were kept, the hosts that had become the body and blood of Christ during the consecration. Every time I passed in front of the tabernacle, like everyone else, I bowed my head and genuflected. It was pure reverence. A reverence and sense of ecstasy that was overwhelming.

There was a sense of being inducted into a wonderful world in which everything made sense. Everyone had their role to play, the priests, the altar boys, the congregation. Everyone was blessed. On the way home, my mother would stop to talk with friends and neighbours. As a good boy, I would remain silent and pious. They would pat my head and tell my mother that I was a little angel.

Before I made my first Holy Communion, I was envious when she went up to receive the host. I longed to go. I imagined what it must be like to be filled with the body and blood of Christ, to feel God inside me. When people walked back to their pews, they seemed to be full of holiness. Like everyone else, my mother would kneel silently, letting the experience of God sink into her.

In those minutes, when she was experiencing God, I would take up her missal and go through the hundreds of pages, unable to make sense of the arcane language. There were no pictures. Just page after page of text. But her missal was laden with loose holy pictures and black memorial cards with photos of the people who had died and prayers to be said for their souls. They were in purgatory and needed prayers to help them get into heaven.

I wanted to play a bigger part. To be one of the altar boys. To ring the bell and bring up the cruets with the water and the wine to the priest during Mass. Most of all I longed to be the one who held out the incense to be put in the thurible that the priest then swung around. I was so obsessed with all this sacredness that, as young boys, my friend Jim Nunan and I would play priests and altar boys in the study at home. We would take turns in playing the lead role. We muttered the Latin prayers, stood, knelt and genuflected before the small box on the small table that had become the tabernacle. The big moment for me was, when as priest, I would take out a piece of bread from a bowl and hold it up and Jim would kneel down in front of me and, with eyes closed, would raise his head up, open his mouth and put out his tongue to receive.[43]

I loved it when the Church was full, and everyone prayed aloud and sang their hearts out. The intensity of that feeling, of everyone singing the hymns, was awesome. We were in unison with God. It was pure fervour and passion. What happened in those days in the Good Shepard church, was like many institutional rituals that have happened in churches, synagogues and mosques over the last two and a half thousand years, and before that, in myriads of sacred places developed in hunting and gathering societies. The creation of sacred spaces which have no material function, which create a sense of awe and enchantment which, in turn, create a sense of bonding, are central to being religious.[44]

We lived in Catholic time and space. Every morning when Radio Éireann, the national broadcaster, came on air, the announcer would first tell us the date and then which Catholic feast day it was. Around the country, in every parish and on Radio Éireann, bells tolled for the Angelus at noon and at six o'clock. It seemed to me the bells of the Good Shepard were always tolling, calling the faithful from their homes to come to church. And we went in our droves. There were devotions every evening in May and October. In between, there were Novenas, Benedictions, Forty Hours Adoration, Missions and Retreats. And then there were marriages, funerals and christenings as well as First Holy Communions and Confirmations. The Good Shepard was our second home.

It seems strange but I liked Lent, six weeks of fasting and abstinence in preparation for Easter. It started with Ash Wednesday. At morning Mass,

I paraded up to the altar rails and the priest would put his thumb into a bowl of ashes and put a daub on my forehead. Before I made my first Holy Communion, it was the only time I got to go to the altar and kneel in front of the priest. In those days, everyone would have a daub. You would see the daubed ones on the road, in the shops, queueing for buses. We were all Catholics. We were all one, united in our love of God, our priests and bishops.

Every Easter Saturday, our local Church was full for midnight Mass. It was a peculiar mix. Fervent devotees like my mother and myself would be in the church for an hour before, for a ceremony that would go on for up to two hours. Just before and after the Mass started, the men from the pubs would cram into the back of the church, smelling of drink and tobacco. The world of the profane entering into the sacred. But all was forgiven. All these people, leaving the houses and pubs of the parish, and traipsing up the Good Shepard in the dark. All coming together to celebrate the triumph of Jesus over death. There was hope for everyone.

My mother was devoted to the family, to my father, my sister Judy, my brother Maurice and me. In later, more difficult times, when Dad's career fell apart, she strove to keep the show on the road washing, cleaning, cooking, knitting, darning, weaving rugs, polishing the silver. She sacrificed herself, making do with a bowl of soup when the rest of us were given meat and potatoes. As a penitential practice, she slept in a bed with no sheets, just coarse woollen blankets. And she was the one who made sure that we went to Mass, Confession and Holy Communion. She was the one who called us in from play to pray.

And yet while she called us to prayer and made sure we went to Mass, Holy Communion and Confession, I don't remember my mother talking to me about her faith, about her love of God, or about her devotion to Our Lady and Blessed Martin. Everything was done in a good Catholic way but, beyond the prayers, little was said, except some well-worn adages that would come out in times of sadness or grief such as 'God willing', 'God bless', 'God works in mysterious ways', 'God does not close one door, but opens another', and when a child died 'God takes the good ones first'.

My father was a religious man, but he too never talked to me about God or Jesus. He never got excited about religion. He went to Mass on Sundays and dutifully dropped to his knees when my mother called us to say the rosary. He kept a bible beside his bed, but I never saw him read it. He was soft and quiet spoken. He never raised his voice, lost his temper. He did not speak badly of others. He was virtuous.

I was, then, brought up in a loving family which was enmeshed in a Catholic web of meaning. I should have been on the road to being a good Catholic man like my father. But slowly the holy spirit began to seep out of my being. The passion and enthusiasm for being Catholic began to sag. There was a sense that it was all a performance. It was about rules and regulations. There was little joy. Life was like one long penitential practice. It had to be endured and then, when it came to the end, the task was to die a good death, to suffer and bear pain in the same way that Christ had done on the cross.

It was like being a follower of some strange sport's team. People went to all the matches. They read about the panoply of saints and their performances. They festooned themselves in team scarves, jerseys and caps. But they never talked about their passion. It would seem that my mother was a passionate Catholic but, for her, there was a time to be pious, humble and Catholic and there was a time to indulge herself. The morning was dominated by going to Mass and the afternoon to reading and smoking. She liked *Woman, Woman's Way, The Reader's Digest*. She took particular delight in leafing through the *Sears* Catalogue that had been brought as a gift from America. She would sit on the couch in the sitting room, pulling on her *Craven A* cigarette, turning the pages of the enormous volume and gazing at images of clothes that she could never have. She also liked the exotic recipes in her women's magazines drooling over then while puffing on her cigarette.

When *The Sunday World* was first published in 1973. it caused a bit of a sensation as it nearly always had a scantily dressed buxom model on the front page and above it, the paper's slogan, 'Are you Getting it every Sunday'. In those later days, my mother would buy the Sunday papers after Mass and bring them with her into the local pub where she would have a gin and tonic before going home to cook lunch. I was surprised one Sunday when she arrived into the pub with a copy of the *Sunday World*. When I asked her why she had bought it she told me that, like everyone else, she enjoyed a bit of titillation.

If, like David Attenborough looking at the ants, it was possible to look down on what was happening then in Catholic Ireland, and all the toing and froing up and down, in and out of churches, what we would see is repetitive, ritual behaviour. I used to think that it was religious belief that created ritual behaviour. Now I think it is the other way round, or at least that without practice there is little belief. To invert and paraphrase the French philosopher Blaise Pascal, if you don't kneel and move your lips in prayer, you will not believe. If people don't gather, if they don't engage in shared rituals, there is a limited sense of belonging.

And when people do gather to engage in some shared ritual, we don't really know what they are thinking, let alone what they believe. We don't really know what they are feeling. It is only an approximate knowledge. But the important thing is that they have come together. It could be going to Mass on Sunday. It could be a family gathering to celebrate a birthday. It could be friends meeting in a pub. It is the ritual that creates a sense of belonging. It is the ritual that makes the occasion sacred. It is the ritual that creates and sustains shared values about what is important in being religious, being a family, being friends.

And sometimes I think that the engagement in Catholic rituals was a kind of performance. People like my mother went up and down to the Church to convince themselves and others that they were good Catholics. Putting all the time and effort into going to church was a demonstration of how much they believed. There was an element of putting on a public display for each other. They walked the walk together. They talked the talk. They made sacrifices. They engaged in practices that, effectively, cost them, in terms of giving up time and money and opportunities to enjoy themselves. They embodied piety and humility. These practices demonstrated that they were devoted followers of Christ.[45]

And it all created a sense of collective effervescence. It was the simple faith. No questioning, no debate, no public expression of doubt. And, for generations, it seemed the simple faith was rock solid. And in many ways, it was. But it was like a rock-hard eggshell that had no yolk of belief to sustain it. So, when cracks began to appear, there was no ideology, no way of talking and debating, to prevent the egg from falling to pieces.[46] It may be that for too many people, for too long, the practice had become perfunctory. People were going through the motions. The engagement in rituals was done out of a sense of doctrinal duty.

A Sacred Canopy

All during this time, from the 1950s well into the 1980s, there were signs of the faith everywhere. Every town and village had a large church. Priests, nuns and brothers paraded around in the clerical dress. There were crucifixes on the walls in schools, hospitals and welfare homes. In family homes, there were holy pictures, statues, sacred heart lamps, fonts for holy water and crucifixes, often over the parents' bed. People blessed themselves passing a Church. They wore medals, scapulars and badges. They carried their rosary beads in their pockets or handbags. They invoked God, Our Lady and the saints in their conversation. It was part and parcel of creating and maintaining the Catholic web of meaning, the wonderful, exotic, mysterious explanation of the meaning of life.

But there was a strong doctrinal side to being Catholic. This was the world of learning the catechism: the little green book that contained all the main teachings of the Church. Like every other child, it was drummed into me in school, relentlessly, day after day. Knowledge of the catechism was essential to receiving the sacrament of Confirmation and becoming a soldier of Christ. It had to be 'known off by heart'. It was a system of indoctrination and became the basis for the type of legalist-orthodoxy and a strict adherence to the rules and regulations of the Church that dominated being Catholic in Ireland.[47]

I am not sure to what extent official Church doctrine had much to do with being Catholic. I doubt many Catholics knew or thought about the fine details of Church teachings. I think that the theology, canon law and teachings of the Church are beyond most of the laity. It is a bit like a car. What happens under the bonnet is a mystery. Most people are happy to drive around in one, but few have any notion how it really works. They rely on mechanics. Similarly, with the Church, I suspect it is a minority of Catholics who know how the Church works in terms of theology and canon law. They get the main bits, that Jesus lived, that he performed miracles and that he rose from the dead. But how this fits together to create the superstructure of the Church and how it operates, is not just beyond them, but of little interest.

I must have said the Creed thousands of times. I knew it off by heart. Like many prayers, I chanted it without reflecting very much about what it meant. The idea of God as a father figure in heaven, looking down on earth and caring personally for every Catholic was easy to understand. But there were many things I just did not understand. Was Jesus part of God all along or did he become part of God after he died and was resurrected?

I used to think that St Patrick was a genius to use the shamrock to explain the mystery of there being three divine persons in the one God. I remember thinking to myself at the time that it was obvious; that three separate leaves could be part of the one stem. It is a metaphor for sameness and difference. Many are contained within a whole. All the different gods and spirits belonged to one whole.[48]

I felt relieved and grateful that St Patrick had converted the pagans. Looking back, I can see that the Christian crusade was to get people to move away from the multitude of spirits, gods and goddesses that were part of the landscape and to get them to think of God above looking down and deciding if they were good or bad.

But the reality was that I didn't get the Trinity. And this is why priests, nuns and brothers and a host of other religious specialists were like car mechanics. They knew how the system worked. They had the knowledge. Like the catechism, they asked the questions, and they gave the answers. They knew how God operated. When I asked a question, I got a pat answer which was often a repetition of something from the catechism. I never found out how it was, when he was dying on the cross, Jesus talked to God. But if he was God, was he talking to himself?

And there was the Holy Spirit. I never managed to figure out how he fitted in. I was told, but again never really understood how he was the one that enabled Jesus to be conceived in the womb of the Virgin Mary. He was the facilitator, the giver of life. When I was growing up, he was called the Holy Ghost and it seemed to me that he was more nebulous but at the same time, having made Mary pregnant, he was sensuous. He was all about feeling. You could think rationally of God the father, and Jesus the son, but you felt the spirit of the Holy Ghost. He was the one that invaded your being, your soul. He led you to the father and the son. But, again, given that they are all one, was he leading people to himself? But I like the idea that you don't know God so much as you feel him. When I was growing up there were loads of good Catholics who would be more attuned to 'him' and, when something good happened, would confidently announce that it was the power of the Holy Ghost, that he was leading me to God.

Being able to talk knowledgeably about this unsolvable mystery made priests, nuns and brothers superior. It took me a while to realise that talking knowledgeably about something, being in the know, is key to holding power over people, to symbolically dominating them. It is central to the power that clergy have over the laity, parents over children, teachers over students and, up to recently but increasingly contested, men over women. I know. You don't know. You are ignorant. Let me explain it to you. I know God, you don't. Let me explain 'him' to you. It is not that knowledge creates power. It is rather that those in power create a knowledge that you cannot access or understand but are forced to accept.

And then, in this Catholic world, to make things even more complicated, there was Our Lady. She, it appears, is the mother of God and this is because she gave birth to Jesus. For a long time when I was growing up, I used to think that the Immaculate Conception referred to this mysterious event. It took a while for me to realise that God could not have been born to a woman who was stained with original sin. So, from the very start, she was different from all other humans, because she was conceived and born without original sin. She was immaculate and therefore could give birth to God. And Jesus, being God could not have been conceived by a man, in this case Joseph, so Mary had to be made pregnant by the Holy Ghost. I became even more confused. Did this mean, I wondered, that God, as the Holy Ghost, became human and had sex with Mary which led to Jesus being conceived?

I sometimes think that this way of thinking infiltrated Catholic sex education. Sex was something that happened in marriage. Husbands and wives did not have to be told the facts of life. It was something strange and wonderful that happened in the middle of the night. It is a pity that instead of developing the wonderful mystery of life, of sex, love and beauty, of the sense of belonging to a whole, the Church wanted to nail everything down, to explain everything away.

Saints Above

It took me a long time to understand the complex Catholic world into which I was born. It was like a big Russian novel, full of wonderful characters. There was, of course, the devil and his cohort of fallen angels who were fought by the good angels. And then there were saints. I grew up in a world of saints. They were the celebrities of the Church. People would mention them in passing. Besides Our Lady, the big favourite, there was St Jude, St Therese of Lisieux and St Francis. And then there were saints that would be invoked for specific purposes. Like everyone else, my mother prayed to St Christopher before she, or a loved one, went on a journey. She would put a medal of St Christopher into the suitcase. If she lost something she would immediately say a prayer to St Anthony.

Besides saints, there was a panoply of holy people. My mother's favourite was Martin de Pores. A magazine came into the house once a month. It was devoted to him. Followers were asked to pray for his elevation to sainthood as he was only 'Blessed'. There was great celebration at home in 1962 when he was finally designated a saint. He was Peruvian. He is the patron saint of mixed-race people. His following in Ireland may seem strange, given that, at the time, it was almost completely white. But he was promoted by the Dominicans, who were a very popular and prominent religious order.

There are up to 10,000 saints. Many of them can be implored to cure illnesses or ailments such as gout or gallstones. There are others that can be asked to pass an exam, get a job, help with depression. There are saints for occupations such as bakers, and for people who are motorcyclists or chess players. And then there are saints who are linked to places. Ireland has St Patrick, St Columba and St Brigid.

Saints are part and parcel of magical thinking which is still a major feature not just of Irish Catholicism but of most religions.[49] The world is still, as it has always been, an enchanting, bewildering, mysterious place that is awesome and often frightening. The attempt to make being religious rational and reasonable, to confine it to a reading of sacred texts and scriptures has not succeeded. Despite the domination of reason and science, most human beings believe, or have an intuitive feeling, that the world is still full of spirits, forces, energies and Gods that can be invoked to change the course of events.[50]

As well as having saints that could be called on to intervene and turn events around, my mother had some prized relics that she kept hidden away. These were lent or given to people who were going through hard times. Once upon a time, she was given a small bottle of water from Lourdes. She used to put a small drop into her bath. I had no idea of this and one night she left the bottle on the side of the bath. I was next in for a bath and could not figure out what the little bottle was about and emptied it all into my bathwater. My mother was forlorn.

There is a rich tradition of magical-devotional religion in Ireland. In May 1979, I undertook a small study of the annual Nine Day Solemn Novena to Our Lady of Perpetual Succour in Limerick.[51] Novenas were very popular. The Limerick novena had become a major success. It had been started eight years previously by Fr Vincent Kavanagh a Redemptorist priest.

The scale of the operation was enormous. This was Catholic show business at its best. There were masses on all day and into the evening. The church was not big enough to hold the crowds, so a large marquee was erected in the grounds. An average of twenty thousand attended each day over the first eight days. On the final Sunday, there were 34,000.

Fr Kavanagh developed the model of the ceremony from the United States. He was keen to create a religious experience. He deliberately factored in a continuous rhythm of movement between standing, kneeling and sitting. The liturgy was built around traditional prayers and hymns, sermons, blessings of the sick and the reading of thanksgivings and petitions that people wrote on forms and submitted in boxes.

There were close to 20,000 petitions made during the Novena. These covered a variety of issues such as health, family problems, success in work or studies, financial problems and for the spread of the faith. Some people made donations with their petitions. While Fr Kavanagh would not tell me how much money was received, he insisted it was not very much.

The Church creates and stokes the fires of magical-devotional practice, but it often struggles to avoid them going wild and going beyond its jurisdiction. This is what happened with the Charismatic Renewal movement in the 1970s. The Church had difficulty keeping it within Catholic liturgy and theology. Folk masses and speaking in tongues were just about tolerated. The problem came when members of the laity started to hold prayer meetings in their houses. I once suggested to Fr Joe Dunn, my boss at the time and the producer of Radarc films, that the Charismatics were responding to the need for mysticism. In his slow, laconic tone of voice, he told me that the problem with mysticism was that it began in mist and ended in schism.

The Church, then, has to maintain a distinction between miracles, the curing of the sick, apparitions and other occasions of divine intervention which it propagates and blesses and those which become a threat to its power. It is a fine balance. What makes Catholicism and the Catholic Church different from Protestantism, is that it allows for and incorporates more magical thinking and practice.

The Church has regularly to put out devotional bush fires. In 1985, hundreds of thousands of people throughout Ireland gathered at grottos and statues of Our Lady, often at night, in the pouring rain, having travelled long distances. They prayed and sang. Many firmly believed that the statues moved, bled or cried.[52] There was a need for the Church to be understanding and supportive and yet it had to try and move what was, literally, happening outside the Church, back inside. The task for the Church is to feed the need for mystery, magic and enchantment, but in a controlled manner. When it does so, it can be very successful. There were many reasons why the Catholic Church became so powerful in Ireland, but one of them was the way it was able to blend the magical and the devotional with the legal and the orthodox.

It is hard to keep a lid on the yearning for magic, for cures and miracles. In the 1990s, Christina Gallagher established the House of Prayer on Achill Island in Mayo. The House was opened in 1993 by the Archbishop of Tuam, but soon the Church began to distance itself when Gallagher claimed to be a prophet, to have had visions of Our Lady and to have stigmata on her feet. These were followed by claims of miracle cures.

The official Church deemed Gallagher to be a Catholic in good standing, but it washed its hands of the enterprise when it eventually declared that the House of Prayer did not have its confidence. Gallagher received thousands of donations from the public, so much that she was able to live in a €4 million house in Dublin and buy houses for herself and her daughter in Mayo.

But the Church did not have a monopoly over magic. The culture in which I grew up was full of superstitions, folk-beliefs, faith-healing and lucky charms. People had lucky pennies, they hung horseshoes over doors, they would touch wood when they thought of some impending peril. My mother was particularly superstitious. She would remind us when it was Friday 13th. She would not walk under a ladder. She would not allow an umbrella to be opened in the house.

I inherited many of these beliefs and practices. When Aileen and I married in 1973 we rented a small flat. The previous owners had left a holy water font. Aileen would not let me throw it out. She felt it would be, as she put it, bad juju. There was a genuine fear of dark forces of evil. Aileen would not play with a Ouija board. She firmly believed that houses could be haunted. We did not talk about it much. It was just something she felt. There was something out there that could do you harm.

There was regular talk of the devil. When I was about ten years old, I overheard hushed discussions at the dining-room table about the time grand uncle Tom had performed an exorcism on a woman who had been possessed. Aunt Joan, Uncle Jack and Dad were trying to persuade him to write up an account of the event. It is a pity he didn't.

When we went on the annual school retreat to the Jesuits in Rathfarnham, we were presided over by a priest who, like grand uncle Tom, had pure white hair. He told us that, until five years previously, he had a shock of black hair and then, one night, the devil entered his bedroom. He spent hours trying to exorcise him from his soul. He succeeded. But in the morning when he looked in the mirror, he saw his hair had gone white.

People believed in fairies, banshees, leprechauns and ghosts. I never went to a fortune teller, but my aunt Maureen liked to 'read' the tea leaves at the bottom of my cup. There was a woman I knew who liked to read my palm. She also believed in horoscopes. She asked me what sign I was and when I told her I was a Capricorn she launched into a spiel about how it made so much sense to her and that it explained so much about my behaviour. She went on and on. I never told her that I had lied and that I was an Aquarian.

But the world is full of strange, inexplicable events. Long after I had stopped going to Mass or having much to do with institutional religion, I got ring worm. The treatment the doctor gave me did not work. Then I met Joan. She was deep into the mystical world. I had many friends like her. She told me about a faith-healer in Meath. It was miles away, but I went. She lived in a modern bungalow. She looked at the ringworm and then she went to a drawer and took out a crucifix. She asked me to say a Hail Mary as she moved the crucifix up and down my arm. I told her I didn't pray because I didn't believe in God. She said it did not matter. Within two weeks the ringworm was gone.

As we have seen, over the last five hundred years, there has been in Ireland, as elsewhere in the West, an inexorable rationalisation of every aspect of daily life. We are dominated by bureaucratic organisations. We are expected to behave in an orderly, predictable fashion. We look for and respect scientific explanations for events. We admire new technologies. We believe in progress. The result is that our world is less enchanted. We do not see events, whether tragic or miraculous as being the work of the devil or God. We compartmentalise magical thinking into books, films and games. Most of all we live in and between two worlds. One that is rational, scientific, predictable and controllable. The other world is mysterious, inexplicable and unpredictable. We believe in science, but we recognise our dependency on truth, beauty and goodness. They are vital to being human and to our survival, But they have no scientific explanation.[53]

Ireland is full of holy wells, special mountains, islands, lakes, trees and groves. There are mainly local sites that date back hundreds if not thousands of years. They are sacred spaces many of which have been coopted within Christianity. People go there for comfort, solace and consolation. It makes them feel good. It may well be that it is the persistence of these religious sites that makes Catholic Ireland different. Many of them were revived in the years after the Reformation. Visiting them, making pilgrimages, spending time praying, making votive offerings, became part of Catholic life. It became a cultural line of demarcation from Anglican Protestants.[54]

There is also a strong tradition of penitential practice. Every year, on the last Sunday in July, people gather to climb Croagh Patrick in Mayo. It can be seen as soulful work, an attempt to transcend the profane world of getting and spending. I think it is spiritual and transcendental to engage in practices that go back thousands of years, to pagan and Celtic times when the understanding of God or the spirit world were very different.

Catholic doctrine

When I finished my undergraduate degree in social science, my first job was as an interviewer on Micheál MacGréil's survey of prejudice and tolerance in Ireland. I then got promoted to being a research assistant on a social survey of religious beliefs, practices and values. It was, and probably still is, the largest social survey undertaken in Ireland. We conducted personal interviews with over 2,500 people throughout the country.[55]

The results showed that nine in ten Catholics, who then formed 95 per cent of the population, went to Mass at least once a week. This was matched by a very high level of belief. Nine in ten fully accepted belief in God, that the Church was founded by Christ for the salvation of 'man', and that Christ rose from the dead. They had no difficulty with these beliefs. There was a similar level of belief in transubstantiation (that during the consecration at Mass the bread and wine are turned into the actual body and blood of Christ) in the Immaculate Conception of Our Lady (that she was born without the stain of original sin), in her assumption into heaven, and that sins are forgiven in Confession.

At any level of analysis, this reflected an extraordinary level of orthodoxy among Catholics. It was as if these teachings were beyond doubt, beyond question. But there were indications that things were changing. Only two-thirds believed in papal infallibility and only half fully believed in hell and the devil.[56]

Perhaps the greatest indication of the level of devotion to the Church was that seven in ten people said that, if there was a clash, they would choose their religion over their occupation and, more significantly, half said they would choose their religion over their family. On reflection, it was perhaps a hypothetical question as the Church was so deeply embedded in family life that it would be hard to imagine them being separate and people having to choose between one or the other. However, there was a sense that many people, above all else, saw themselves not just as Catholics, but as highly committed ones.

This strong sense of identity reinforced the perception that the Church was something far greater than the state. I think that many politicians at the time would have agreed. The Church penetrated into every aspect of Irish society; into homes, schools, hospitals and universities; into voluntary groups, clubs and private organisations and many parts of the civil and public service. One in seven Catholics were members of Catholic lay voluntary groups. These included groups such as the Catholic Boy Scouts and Girl Guides, the National Federation of Youth Clubs, St Vincent de Paul and the Legion of Mary.[57]

My father's side of the family were central figures in this Catholic army. My aunt Joan played different roles. She held a high position in the Legion of Mary. She would spend her evenings writing long letters of support and encouragement to the people working abroad. I think she might have been director of the North American mission. It was part and parcel of keeping volunteers in tune with the ethos and mission of the Legion. At the end of tea on Sunday, she would sit at the table and talk animatedly about how well the Church was doing all over the world. About how many souls were being saved. She firmly believed that everyone's first allegiance must be to the Church and not the state. She was adamant that it was not a sin to avoid or evade tax as long as it was in a good cause.

She looked and dressed like a nun. She wasn't tall, but she was a big woman with a strong masculine face. She never talked about her past, but she had gone out to Argentina in the 1930s and stayed there for a number of years. When she returned to Ireland, she became a socialite. She rose to become head bookkeeper in the Irish National Insurance company. She was a member of Woodbrook golf club. And then there must have been some epiphany because suddenly she gave up her social life to become a nun.

Although she took full vows, she did not live in a religious community. It was rumoured that she was too forceful and independent minded for community life. So, she lived in the wider world. As well as the Legion, she was heavily involved in the Regina Coeli, a hostel for single mothers and distressed women, some of whom were prostitutes. It was mentioned in the Mother and Baby Home Commission Report as being one of the few homes that enabled mothers to keep their babies.

She was also involved in the Catholic Marriage Bureau. This was linked to her work in Regina Caeoli. She operated all over the country. Her activities brought about a bizarre event. At the end of every summer, Dad, Maurice and I used to go to Donegal to spend a week in a small hotel in Inver, Co. Donegal. We were joined by my uncle Jack and Aunt Joan.

Every year, Dad drove Aunt Joan over to a remote cottage in the middle of an enormous bog. Maurice and I went along for the ride. A farmer's wife had died suddenly a couple of years before and left him with three young children. Since he knew little about cooking, mending clothes and minding children, he needed a new wife, otherwise the children would have to be put in care. My Aunt Joan got to work and arranged a marriage between him and one of her Dublin prostitutes from the Regina Coeli. So, quite quickly, a young woman who made her living on the streets of Dublin, ended up in a cottage in the back of beyond.

Dad, Maurice and I would wait in the car while Aunt Joan went inside. Then, one year, we got invited in. There were now four children. We were given lemonade and biscuits. The cottage was tiny and barren; no carpet, a concrete floor, wooden chairs with cushions, a tin-topped table and a white electric stove. There was an earthiness to it all that was far away from the romantic image of Irish cottages portrayed in John Hinde picture postcards that were popular at the time.

The story reveals how the Church penetrated every aspect of Irish society, providing all sorts of social services. It was a way of keeping Ireland Catholic and caring. In some respects, the new farmer's wife may have been lucky. She could have ended up in a Magdalene laundry.

Despite all this bureaucratic charitable work, Aunt Joan oozed religious excitement and enchantment. Her eyes would light up when she talked about how the Holy Ghost was guiding her and the Church, that we were part of a wonderful, miraculous journey which I could join. But what was most remarkable about her was how she devoted her life to others. When my mother was going through a difficult period because of my father's drinking, Aunt Joan not only provided financial help but she would phone my mother every day, usually around eleven after my mother had come back from Mass, and they would talk.

When Aunt Joan died and we gathered around outside the Church after the funeral, a woman came up to my sister Judy and introduced herself and said that many years previously, she had been a hopeless alcoholic and that she was literally lying in a gutter one night when Aunt Joan came across her. She brought her to the hostel and then, for the next year or more, she talked to her and guided her away from drink. She said that if Aunt Joan had not come along that night and if she had not stayed with her, she would have been dead years ago.

My grand uncle Tom rose to become a Monseigneur and Vicar General. This was quite a major position as back in those days there were no auxiliary bishops in the diocese. Uncle Tom, as we called him, presided over the family like a Mafia boss. His name was mentioned in reverential terms. Everything had to be done his way. He had a good sense of humour and enjoyed a game of cards. Some Sunday evenings he came to our house. It was a big occasion. I was presented to him, and he would smile and pat my head.

He was a small, soft man with a warm smile. But he was, in effect, a general in the Roman Catholic army and everyone knew it. Like many of those who rose to a high rank in the Irish Church, he had trained in Rome where they had time to vet him. I never saw him without a collar. Despite having risen to the top, he never came across as being very religious, at least not in the same way as Aunt Joan. I never once heard him talking about God, Jesus or the Holy Ghost. He was not an exemplar of spirituality, more a loyal, dedicated officer. He was good at what he did. He achieved high status. He was a kind man but, on reflection, he was soulless. He was like someone who helps run a huge successful restaurant but rarely talks passionately about food.

Grand uncle Tom was one of Archbishop John Charles McQuaid's right-hand men. He was involved in the promotion of Catholic culture and there was mention of him being a member of Ríoghact, Maria Duce and the Catholic Cinema and Theatre Patron's Association – all right-wing Catholic groups dedicated to stopping the spread of Protestantism, Communism and Judaism. Their work would be gradually replaced by secretive organisations such the Knights of Columbanus and Opus Dei which had the aim of ensuring the maintenance of Catholic Ireland and ensuring that good Catholics obtained positions of power and influence.

Protestants were problematic. Someone like my grand uncle Tom would have seen them as a threat, a potential source of contamination. It was fine if they kept to themselves. It was when they infiltrated institutional spaces in which Catholics gathered – churches, schools, hospitals, welfare homes and so forth – then there was a problem. It was not a system of apartheid: it was more about keeping Catholics safe and pure.

The aim of the Church and its leaders was to make sure that anyone who rose to the top of any social field was a good Catholic and was deferential to the Church and its leaders. This meant being quiet, obedient, loyal, deferential, pious and humble. It meant embodying a way of being, a way of talking and presenting oneself, that created and maintained a Catholic mind and body. It was evidenced in the small, seemingly insignificant ways that, as in any army, members were always subservient to the greater good of the institution.

On the day of my grand uncle Tom's funeral, after he had said Mass, Archbishop McQuaid came to the parochial house. All our family lined up in a circle around the living room, Archbishop McQuaid entered, spoke a few words to Aunt Joan, and then began to go around the room. He said nothing and we all dropped on our knees as he held out his hand to kiss his ring. It was a blessing, but the power of the ring was magical.

I suspect that there are many others who have grown up in a traditional, orthodox religion in which orthodoxy is maintained through limiting and controlling what is said and done and how people perform and present themselves. It is central to symbolic domination. People embody the view of themselves presented by those in power. In Catholic Ireland, people learnt to present themselves as pious, humble and obedient.

The Catholic Church is like an exclusive club. Unless you are born and baptised a Catholic, it is difficult to become a member. People can join as adults, but it is a long and arduous process. It is not like taking up a new sport. People cannot start playing immediately. They have to learn the catechism and prepare themselves for the sacraments of baptism, eucharist and confirmation. Since they have not been socialised into being Catholic, they have to learn how to think, act and be Catholic.

I grew up on a small avenue in south Dublin. It was a calm place, part of the leafy suburbs. The avenue was dominated by a large old estate house. The house was divided into three large apartments. Fionnula and her parents lived in the upstairs, our family occupied the middle floor, and there was another family in the basement. There was also an annex. At the entrance from the main road, there was a gate lodge. The remaining families lived in bungalows that had been built on the old estate after the war. What was different was that although nine in ten of the population was Catholic, on our avenue three of the families were Protestant and there was one mixed marriage.

Protestants were all well-regarded, well-respected members of the community. Not only did they go to different churches, but they also went to different schools and mainly socialised with their Protestant friends and family. They had their own doctors, hospitals, social welfare organisations and, in wider society, their own shops and sports clubs. They played cricket and rugby. They belonged to a world that was set apart and different.

As children we played together: mostly on the small cul-de-sac avenue on which we lived but occasionally in our back gardens. It was a world of fine distinctions. There were class as well as religious differences. There was little interaction between neighbours in general, but even less so between Catholics and Protestants. My father invited one of the Protestant families in one Christmas, but they did not come.

The division between Catholics and Protestants was taken for granted. In comparison with Northern Ireland, the divisions on the avenue were trivial and, in some respects, almost ecumenical. But the mindset of difference was created and maintained by the Church. It was alright to interact in daily life and it was even alright for a Catholic to marry a Protestant as long as the children were brought up as Catholics. But it was not permissible to go to a Protestant Church, school or hospital. Maintaining the Catholic defence line was paramount.

The Church developed a unique way of keeping an eye on what was happening in every nook and cranny of Irish society. Its huge army of priests, nuns and brothers were able to see what was happening in every parish, school, hospital and welfare home. Priests were the most important. They visited homes and schools and, each year, sent in reports to the local bishop. The purpose of the visits was to keep an eye on the black sheep in the parish. In each parish, there were the blue policemen of the state and the black policemen of the Church. There is little knowledge of the extent to which they exchanged information, but the reality is that there was little that was not known about most people, particularly in rural Ireland.

Priests were the conduits of local information. As well as Church activities, they were often involved in other local interest groups and organisations, including farming groups, the GAA and other sports clubs. They became power brokers, putting in a good word for some, writing character references for others. Unlike the regular policemen, they could not fine those who went against the Church, but they could isolate and marginalise those who resisted or challenged their rule.

Fr Tony Flannery tells the story about how his mother had a run-in with her local parish priest when his sister decided to join a convent in an adjoining diocese. When his mother went to get the necessary certificate to allow her daughter to go, he was rude and said the daughter would be a small loss. A few weeks later, the priest challenged his mother in public as to why she was sending her daughter to a 'foreign' convent. Flannery does not say how his mother responded but it was obviously a significant event.

That might seem like a trivial little exchange in today's Ireland, but back in the early 1960s it was anything but trivial. That particular priest ruled the parish – which he was wont to refer to as 'his' parish – with a rod of iron, and to stand up to him could have negative consequences for any family. A word from the parish priest could seriously affect a young person's opportunities in life.[58]

Knowledge of who was doing what, with whom, when and where, was an important part of keeping people in control. It was informal, there was no centralised system and there were no detailed written records. Everything was in the heads of the clergy but, if needs be, this information could be quickly and easily gained. When I was Research Officer for the Church's Research and Development Committee, it was decided to bring together high-profile people from politics, the media and the world of business to give their opinions as to how the Catholic Church in Ireland should respond to the challenges of the modern world. I was at a meeting when several bishops reviewed the names of various potential members. What struck me was the way in which characters were assessed. A person's appropriateness would be discussed, the pros and cons of them being included. There might be a move towards acceptance and then there would be a casual comment from one of the bishops who, for example, might say of a well-known media personality 'I believe he sends his children to a Protestant school'. Gone. Of a politician, 'he has strange views on contraception'. Gone. Of a priest, 'I hear that he is often late on the altar.' Gone. But it also operated in subtle ways. There was mention of another character and, again, there was a discussion, positive things were said and then someone said, 'he comes across as having a chip on his shoulder'. And then someone commented, 'wasn't his father an alcoholic?' Once there was a flaw in the character, the candidacy was over.

Much of Patsy McGarry's memoir revolves around significant episodes within the Church during the last fifty years. These episodes reveal how Church leaders thought and operated and how they dealt with clerical sexual abuse. As the religious correspondent of *The Irish Times*, he was a powerful figure in terms of what stories were told and how he presented them. His memoir can be read as a personal story of the institutional clash between the Church and the media. McGarry knew the way the Church exercised its power.

In October 1999, he wrote an article that described how he had been at a national gathering of priests and how the majority present listened to various speakers but were reluctant to ask any questions. Cathal Daly, the former primate of All Ireland, wrote to McGarry and said that what he had written was 'like an obituary for the Catholic Church and good riddance.' McGarry was furious.

> I believed my card was being marked. I thought to myself, *this is how these guys operate behind the scenes*. Daly, by then, would have known everything about me – seed, breed and education at the junior seminary for Achonry's Catholic diocese, St Nathy's College, Ballaghaderren, where the then Bishop of Achonry, Tom Flynn, had taught me.[59]

Being sinful

I never really liked going to Confession. It may be that I never found a good confessor. Most of my confessions were confessions of the imagination, things I made up to get in and out as quickly as possible. The priest did not know me, and I did not know the priest. We were two people sitting in the dark, going through the ritual.

When my son Arron was about six, he was disappointed that, unlike many of his other friends, he was not making his First Holy Communion. I think he was also disappointed that there would not be a family celebration, that he would not be feted and given lots of money. He wanted to know why he couldn't just go along and join in. I told him that it was complicated. I decided not to go into the baptism bit and just told him that before going to receive, he would have had to go to Confession. I then had to explain to him that Confession was about telling the priest the things that he had done wrong, like telling lies. There was a short silence before he asked if he could tell the priest the things that I had done wrong. It was a perverse idea, but not perhaps as perverse as the idea of forcing a seven-year-old child into a dark confessional box to tell his sins to a priest. It was a unique and, on reflection, quite successful form of maintaining institutional discipline.[60]

In preparation for my confession, I was supposed to go through the ten commandments of God and the six commandments of the Church. These were part of the little green catechism mentioned earlier. I found it much easier to confess sins against the Church commandments. These had to do with going to Mass on Sundays, fasting and abstaining from meat (mainly Lent and Fridays), going to Confession at least once a year and receiving Holy Communion at Easter. It was easy enough to tell the priest that I had eaten meat on Fridays. There was another rule or commandment that said that you had to abstain from any food from midnight before receiving Holy Communion. There was another commandment which said that you had to contribute to the support of the Church which meant paying annual dues and having small change in your pocket for the collections at Mass. In terms of maintaining order and compliance among the laity, many of these regulations made good sense.

The ten commandments were much broader and archaic. They seemed more about how to live an ethical life in ancient Judea. Although they were regularly explained during sermons at Mass and in school, I could not understand how they were relevant for all time. I could see the point of honouring your parents, taking a day off from getting and spending to honour God, not killing, stealing, lying or committing adultery. But how do you misuse God's name? What is coveting your neighbour's wife, servant, ox or donkey? Could these be translated? Are there not some better commandments relevant to today?

When I was thirteen or fourteen, I went on a school retreat to the Jesuits in Rathfarnham. My father knew the Jesuits. I asked him if he knew of a priest that would be good to talk to. I didn't tell my father that I was genuinely worried that I was masturbating too often. I had, so to speak, been late finding myself and now that I had, I found it hard to let go. My mother became concerned about how I suddenly had taken to having long baths. I don't think any amount of holy water would have made a difference.

My father gave me the name of a priest. He told me, he was a good man and easy to talk to. And so it was that I presented myself to him in his room in Rathfarnham Castle. He was old. Older than my father. He had a shock of grey hair that contrasted with his red and purple face. But he was a gentle, genial soul. We talked about me and the family and then it came to the crunch. Was there anything troubling me. I began to blather about breasts, legs and lips and about exploring girls' bodies, of their hidden beauties and how I could not get these images out of my mind and how I was spilling seed all over the place. Like any good therapist, he let me prattle on and on. He never cried halt. And then, almost as if I was spent, I stopped and there was a silence.

For a few seconds, he said nothing and then he looked over at me and asked, 'Do you play rugby, Tom?' I told him I did. He then asked if

I was playing enough. I said probably not as I did not like it that much. He told me to try and play a bit more. It might help me stop playing with myself.

The more I went to confession, the more I realised that the main interest of priests was in the sixth commandment. I was forever being interrogated about my bad thoughts and whether I had given into them. Did I take pleasure? Was I interfering with myself? Were there nocturnal emissions? I did not realise it at the time, but as I knelt down in the dark and confessed my sexual sins, I was just another body caught in a process that had evolved and been perfected since the beginning of Christianity. It was, as the French philosopher Michel Foucault, described it, a way of instilling sex in bodies and making penitents aware of themselves as sexual subjects, of being constantly aware of it and then, through a process of confession of dragging the sexual serpent of desire and lust out of the body and, in doing so, healing it. The priest in the confession healed the penitent in the same way as a doctor healed a patient by identifying the infection and extracting it.[61]

The problem was that it became an empty performative ritual. I went through the motions of confession not to satisfy myself but the priest and Church doctrine. I would lie. When the priest asked if I had bad thoughts, I would tell him that I did and that I did give into them and that I did interfere with myself but, then, in order to get away with small penance, I would lie and say I prayed hard to stop myself. It was a religious charade, each of us playing our roles. Once I saw through it, I never went back. I stopped going to Mass unless I had to. When I did go, I didn't go up for Holy Communion. I did not believe that I was receiving the body and blood of Christ. But there was something else. At the back of my mind was the edict that those who received but did not believe would, when they died, go straight to hell.

The irony is that I wanted to confess the truth about myself. I would have loved to have had someone to talk to about all my raging passions, longings and desires. But there was no one to talk to. No counsellor. No therapist. I hoped that I would find someone who would help me understand my sexual feelings. I was part of a generation that did not have the language to talk about sex. It was a source of shame and embarrassment. Even the mention of the word was enough to make one blush.

Self-denial, sexual repression and fear

The success of any family, group, community or society is related to the ability of its members to sacrifice themselves for the common good. Catholic orthodoxy meant that family, community and the Church, were always more important than the individual. It meant a suppression of the self which, if successful in socialisation, led to self-repression. The 'I' became strangled by the 'we'. Children had to be taught not to talk or worst of all, boast about themselves. The 'I' was the devil. A pernicious serpent whose head had to be chopped off every time it was seen to emerge in any boy and girl. And to maintain discipline, any shaming or chastisement had to be performed publicly.

One Sunday evening, Aunt Dorrie came to tea. She wasn't really an aunt, just a cousin of my father, but in the extended family every one of the same age as my father and mother were either aunts or uncles. We were sitting around the big circular table in the dining room. I cannot remember how old I was, but I was a truculent, wilful boy subject to tantrums. After the summer salad, my mother brought over the Victoria sponge sandwich cake that had been sitting on top of the sideboard. The middle of the cake was laden with raspberry jam and thick fresh cream. My mother put the cake in front of her and started cutting slices.

Aunt Dorrie was served first. I knew that being the youngest, I would be served last. I thought that this was unfair. I could not restrain myself and blurted out 'I want cake'. My mother was dismayed with this behaviour and putting on her cold, dry face, she turned to me and asked in a slow voice 'And who is this I that is doing the wanting?' It was a line that she repeated on and off over the years.[62]

The culture of self-denial meant not being fussy. There was no such thing as having likes and dislikes. It was a culture of refusing offers of hospitality, of not putting people to any trouble and, only after being pressed repeatedly, eventually accepting gratefully anything that was offered.

This culture of self-denial reached into the higher echelons of society. Most professional people, which in those days meant men, were educated by the Catholic Church and, at least publicly, embraced its ethos. My father was an architect who seems to have specialised in designing churches around Ireland. He was part of a cadre of professional men who embraced the Catholic ethos of being humble and docile. It was a sin to seek wealth, to be ambitious and self-promoting. It was important to play down any success as unsought and unexpected. It was part and parcel of being virtuous. For a long time, it was worthwhile for professional people like my father, as well as businessmen and politicians, to be in good standing with the Catholic Church. It was like being in the same club. People had the same disposition, the same lifestyle. Every year during Lent, he organised a two-day retreat for architects in the Jesuit house in Milltown Park. Up to fifty attended. Many of them would meet beforehand in O'Brien's pub in Leeson St and retire back there when the retreat was over.

The logic and practice of self-denial and self-deprecation is linked to the practice of belittling and putting people down. In the Catholic culture of modern Ireland, the less one practised self-deprecation, the more likely one was to be belittled. To understand belittling, we have to understand what was said by mothers, fathers, teachers, friends, neighbours and colleagues that undermined, demeaned and demoralized those who were thought to have 'lost the run of themselves', 'got too big for their boots' and therefore needed 'the wind taken out of their sails' and 'to be taken down a peg or two'. It is important to realise how these practices became the norm of everyday life in homes, schools, pubs and ordinary social encounters.

'Josling', 'pulling people's legs,' 'taking the piss' became embedded in Irish culture. It became second nature. It may have seemed harmless, but it was a tactic used to maintain social order, to keep people in tow, to keep them in tune.[63] The aim was to break the spirit of those who rose above their station in life. As an old lonely bachelor shepherd told the American anthropologist Nancy Scheper-Hughes: 'They broke our spirits, and now look at us old, timid and afraid to try anything new. Fear that's the Golden Rule we were reared by.'[64]

As suggested earlier, belittling was a form of external constraint: it is something that was exercised over an individual by others. However, the best form of social control is internal self-restraint when people control themselves. In Ireland, internalised self-restraint manifested itself in practices of self-denial and self-deprecation. This, in turn, was linked to the tactic of putting oneself down, telling stories about foolish things said and done, the ability to laugh at oneself.

It is important to emphasise that these tactics of maintaining orthodoxy were not unique to Ireland. They were to be found in many rural societies and working-class cultures. Indeed, there is evidence to suggest that ridicule and shaming were strategies used in human groups tens of thousands of years ago as a means of preventing bullying and maintaining social equality.[65] However, as in many other aspects of social life, what happened in Ireland may not be different from what happened in other Western societies, it is just that it was more extreme. The practices of belittling and self-denial penetrated deeply into social life and into the minds and bodies of Irish people.

It is important, then, to see that the culture of self-denial was not just about being virtuous. It was central to maintaining orthodoxy and social control. It was ingrained in the body, in the ways people saw, understood and presented themselves. It was manifested in the way emotions were controlled and displayed. It was embedded in social interaction, in the ways people created and maintained webs of meaning. Most of all, perhaps, it was revealed in the sense of humour. There is a way in which the Irish make each other laugh and feel at ease with each other. To attain recognition and status in a group, it is often necessary to get other people to laugh at you. And so, as part of a credibility display to convince people that you don't take yourself seriously, it is good to make a fool of yourself.

Many years ago, I was on a beach in the Greek island of Mykonos. It was midday and the sun worshiping was at its height. There were long horizontal lines of bronzing bodies reaching up from the edge of the sea, each of them placed in the middle of their bright beach towels. I became aware of Irish voices. A small group of originally pale white but now red-skinned young men arrived, hung-over, loud and boisterous. They were going to go snorkelling. I watched in disbelief as the first of them started to walk towards the sea. He had made the mistake of putting on his flippers before setting off to the water. His attempts to navigate a path through the line of pristine sunworshippers failed miserably. He was spraying sand over their bronzed bodies. There were angry shouts in various languages. The final straw was reached when he stumbled and fell onto the back of a German woman. She and her partner rose and shouted at him. This led to a kind of brainwave. He started to walk backwards. But he fell again. There was another brainwave. This time he took the flippers off and walked down to the sea. All the time, his friends and many others, including myself, were in convulsions of laughter.

Again, I am not arguing that this was a uniquely Irish event. I think it could have happened elsewhere. It is rather that it is more pervasive and runs deeper in the Irish mind and body. And I think it relates to a Catholic culture and it is part and parcel of Irish Catholics feeling at home with each other, feeling attached and attuned, enjoying themselves among their own kind. This way of being, of expressing oneself is, I believe, part of a collective consciousness that was developed over generations. It has its roots in the way Irish people practised religion. It has, however, become separated from institutional religion. Once the gates of censorship were opened, once media, the market and the forces of globalisation began to seep into bedrooms, homes and bodies, the Church's ability to maintain doctrinal orthodoxy among the laity began to disappear. However, while the power of the institutional Church has faded, the culture of self-denial and humility and the sense of humour, has remained.

The messages of self-expression and fulfilment are everywhere. They are now embedded in everyday conversations; in the way people talk about themselves. It is the theme of self-help books. It is the dominant discourse in social media, in radio and television. It is the ideology of the liberal individualism, of the market and consumerism. There are signs of the new faith everywhere. On the inside of the pants that I am wearing at the moment, there is a patch sewn into the cloth on which there is an embroidered message: 'Take it easy. You're happy'.

Sexual Repression

The culture of self-denial, the repression of the ego, was linked to the repression of instinct and everything to do with sex. Again, it was not that sex was not repressed elsewhere around the world, it was the way it was repressed among Irish Catholics, the way reached into every individual and became the greatest sin of all. And this, of course, meant that instead of being just a normal part of human life, as it had been for thousands of years, it was in the bodies, hearts and minds, but never on the lips, of Irish Catholics.[66] When it entered innocent young bodies, it led to hysteria.

I was probably about 4 or 5 years old. I was in a next-door neighbour's garden. It was an early summer's day, and a tent had been put up for us to play in and around. I was playing with Fionnuala. We were both in 'low babies'. The kindergarten was in the upstairs part of the old estate house in which we lived.

It was common in those days to leave children alone and unaccompanied for long periods. Like many children of that age, we began to play doctors and nurses. I cannot remember the order of events but at one stage I got to be the doctor and was examining Fionnuala. I was quite thorough. She was lying on her back. I had a stick that I was using as a stethoscope. I had moved from her head, down to over her chest and on down to her 'private parts'. She was lifting off her panties when the woman who was supposed to be supervising us, looked into the tent and screamed in horror. She was completely flustered and began crying. I don't remember her hitting me. But she dragged me away from my examination, shouting at me to go home, all the time consoling Fionnuala.

The next day, after the mid-morning break, the head of the kindergarten came into the classroom. There was a short discussion with my teacher. After the head left, the teacher took a deep breath and announced that she had something important to say. She called out my name and told me to come to the top of the class. As I stood beside her, she declared that 'this boy' had done something so shameful, so bad, so evil, that she could not tell them what it was. It was something that children in Africa would never dream of doing – there was a collection box on the teacher's table that had a small black baby on top and which nodded up and down when a coin was put into the box. I had to apologise to the class. I don't remember crying. I think I must have been in shock. But I remember the incident vividly. I have often wondered if that was my first step towards understanding sexual repression.

Sometimes I think that Freud was right; repressed sex explains a great deal of human behaviour. It is a life force, an instinct that had to be disciplined and controlled. Down through the ages, what makes human societies and groups different and successful are the ways in which they limited and repressed sex. Unless it was controlled, families and kinship groups could not have survived, wealth could not have been inherited, the trust between strangers could not have been developed, trade would have been stymied, and the type of sophisticated interdependence that makes world capitalism and globalisation possible could not have emerged. What makes Ireland different, perhaps what makes any society different, is the way that it deals with sex.

Throughout most societies today and throughout history, the confinement of sex to marriage was attained in and through religious practice and belief. It was tied into the interest in maintaining private property from one generation to the next. Religions provided the moral means. For a long time in Ireland, as elsewhere, sex was controlled through regulating marriage. Only those who married could, so to speak, have safe sex, in that they could have sexual intercourse without being censured. For most others, it was a risky, fearful business. For young women it was a game of roulette. If a woman had sex outside marriage, she might be able to persuade the young man to marry her. But if she became pregnant, the stakes suddenly became higher. If the man didn't commit to marriage, if he absconded, she could be incarcerated in some mother and baby home or in a Magdalene laundry. While this fear began to die out in the 1970s, the last Magdalene laundry in Ireland did not close until 1996.

What happened in the nineteenth century in the rest of the West was that sex moved away from the control of priests and began to be talked about, written about, examined, and researched by a new cadre of lay experts such as psychologists, anthropologists and sociologists. Now we have a multitude of therapists and counsellors helping us tell the truth about ourselves.

In the last century, throughout most of the West, there were new discourses about sex, new ways of understanding and appreciating its role in society and personal development. In Ireland, it remained within the language of Catholic bishops, priests and theologians. Even when doctors used medical discourse to discuss sex, it was under the umbrella of Church teaching. The Church ran the hospitals in which doctors trained and worked. It was the same in other fields. Whereas in other Western societies, sex was being written about and studied by scientists and sociologists in the nineteenth century, it was more than a hundred years later before anything similar happened in Ireland. In the late 1980s, I produced a research proposal to study sex. I gave it to Conor Ward, my head of department, a professor and priest. I did not hear back for a few weeks and then one day, I met him in the corridor and asked him if he had had a chance to read it. He said nothing for a while and then, looking at me askance, asked me if it would not be more worthwhile to study the unemployed. It was not until he retired that I got to do some research and teach a course on the sociology of sex.

Oliver J. Flanagan, a well-known T. D. and Minster from rural Ireland during the 1960s and 70s, once remarked that 'sex never came to Ireland until Telefís Éireann went on the air.'[67] In some respects, he was right. Sex was on everyone's mind. It was the biggest source of shame and public humiliation. In other parts of the West, as well as being the subject of public debate, it began to be explored in the arts, particularly literature, theatre and film. In Catholic Ireland, it had to be suppressed. Sex was seen as a bit like Covid, if not monitored, controlled and isolated, it could rampage through the community. It would lead to moral decay and, eventually, the complete disintegration of society. Consequently, whenever sex reared its ugly head, whenever symptoms manifested themselves, particularly in women, it had to be rooted out.

So, to go beyond Freud, to understand how I have come to be the way I am, I have to understand my sexual make-up. But I would argue that to do this, it is necessary to see myself as part of a society that was deeply sexually repressed. It was because it was so repressed, it could not be recognised or talked about. My awkwardness, embarrassment, blushing, giggling were part of a wider culture of repression. And this was one of the reasons why sexual abuse of women and children went on in plain sight without being seen.

It is not a coincidence that most religions have taken a very cautious if not antithetical attitude to passionate love and sex. It can tear families and communities apart. It can cause havoc with inheritance. It can lead people to abandon their religion and the churches, sects and groups to which they belong. This was one of the main reasons that the Church introduced celibacy and why, for centuries, it made out that being celibate was what made priests, nuns and brothers closer to God. Of course, the main reason celibacy was introduced was to ensure that after a priest died, any property involved remained in the hands of the Church and was not passed on to a wife or children.

The problem with Catholic Ireland was that priests, let alone bishops, were rarely if ever able to tell the sexual truth about themselves. In the aftermath of Vatican II, there were, in the 1970s, hundreds of chapters, meetings and retreats among priests, nuns and brothers to enable them to talk about themselves and their vocations. I wonder did anyone of them ask, what must have been on many of their minds, how they were dealing with their vows of celibacy. How did they deal with their sexual longings and fantasies? I suspect it was the elephant in the room but, nobody was willing or able to see it. They, who were so good at extracting confessions from the laity, found it impossible to confess themselves. Maybe it is another example of credibility enhancing display. They had to live the lie that celibacy was not an issue. They had to live the lie that it was not a problem. It was the cross that they had chosen and had to bear, at least publicly.

When I was working in the Research and Development Unit, my first boss was Fr Jim Lennon. He was a kind, genial man who was well-liked. Jim was considerate and generous. He was devoted to the Church. He was good company. Aileen and I began to go bird watching and walking with him. He had a car, and it was great to get out of Dublin and into the Wicklow mountains. The advantage of Aileen coming along was that we did not talk work. And we certainly did not talk about matters of faith. He was a Roman soldier. I accepted that. I never thought he would abuse his position.

We lost contact with Jim when he returned to be a parish priest in Drogheda. Soon after, he was appointed bishop. To celebrate his elevation, he invited Aileen and I to go for a walk one Sunday along the beach in Baltray and then to go back to his house for lunch. The lunch took place in a palatial dining room at a table that could have seated a dozen comfortably. We were served by his fawning, devoted housekeeper. It was all rather formal. Although he did not drink, he always provided a good bottle of wine. After Aileen and I left and were walking back to our car, Aileen burst out laughing. 'You'll never guess?' 'What,' I asked. She said that when she was following me out the door, she turned to thank him and to kiss him on the cheek. But Jim was having none of that. As Aileen came close to him, he leaned into her, brought his hand behind her head and drew her into him, kissed her on the lips and forced his tongue into her mouth.

Given the very small number of celibates in the Irish population (approx.00002%), they are, in terms of a normal distribution, very unusual. On this basis, they could be said to be very different or even sexually 'queer'. However, for generations, they were paragons of virtue. They were, ostensibly, able to control and repress their sexual desires. This is what qualified them to teach the laity, the vast majority of the population, about sex. And it is odd, or queer that, for so long and still to this day, the majority of the population who were heterosexual, were willing to hand over the instruction of what it was to be sexual, to men and women who, ostensibly, did not engage in sexual activities and tried to purge themselves of sexual desire. It is a bit like someone who does not play or listen to music, deciding what good music was, and when, where and how it should be played and enjoyed.

Fear

My Aunt Joan was deluded. She could not see that the devotion to the Church that she longed for could not succeed because the Church had become an empire of repression. The Church was a patriarchal, totalitarian regime. Fear was everywhere, mainly in schools but also in many homes where sexually repressed men gave vent to their anger by abusing. The main fear was that if you did not obey the commandments of God and the Church, you would go to hell for all eternity. This was backed up by the fear of punishment and social exclusion if you broke the rules.

As I grew up, being a nice boy from a good family, meant that I had little or no contact with the guards. But, from a young age, I had a fear of priests, of the men in black. When the priests were not swanning around the altar in their finery, they were parading around the parish in their black suits, black shirts and small white collars. They were powerful figures, God's representatives on earth. And they knew it. They were saluted and greeted. It was an honour to be in their company. It was something that I learnt quite young. When I was about eight years old, I was walking with a friend down a road beside the Good Shepard Church. Four priests lived on the road. My friend and I were jostling and laughing, and we did not notice Fr Hanlon pass by. We did not salute him. We did not stop and bow and say 'hello father'. A couple of seconds after he had passed, I got a clatter from his hand across the back of my head. 'Pay more respect the next time you pass a priest' he bellowed.

I think this was the attraction of becoming a priest, or indeed a nun or brother. The level of deference, honour and respect they attained was astounding. They generated a sense of awe. They lived different lives. They were set apart from the rest of us. They were sacred. We, on the other hand, lived in the profane world. We were contaminated by sin.

Sometimes I think I might have been serenely happy as a child if I had not lived in the state of fear generated by the Church. I never feared my mother, or my father. Neither of them hit me, not once in my whole life. My mother kept a bamboo cane in the hall in a stand along with umbrellas. She regularly threatened to use it, but she never did. My father never even threatened to hit me. He detested violence.

And yet they sent me to the De La Salle brothers who beat me on a daily basis. I was not alone. Almost everyone got beaten. It was a fee-paying school, but beating children was no worse than beating a dog. It had to be done. 'Spare the rod and spoil the child.' The less sadistic of the brothers used to say before the beating started: 'This hurts me more than it hurts you.' I often thought of saying 'Then let me beat you.' But I never did.

And slowly, day after day, the religious ecstasy and enchantment of my early childhood changed, slowly but surely, to fear and resentment. I began to detest these brothers and everything that they stood for. I hated the way they instilled fear; their well-honed regime of terror. I hated being beaten for making mistakes, for not knowing the right answers, for not praying loud enough, for blotting my copy book, for laughing, for being happy. It seemed that I could be beaten for anything, at any time, without warning.

We had Brother Bernard, for five years, from second to sixth class. Every year we hoped that we would get another brother, someone younger, less brutal, less senile. But no. The sight of him still sends shivers of loathing down my body. He was tall and thin. He might have only been in his fifties or sixties but the short white hair around his bald head, probably made him look older than he was.

The curiosity about sex created vivid imaginations. One Halloween I was sitting in the front row of the large class. It was time to be brave and naughty, to gain honour and respect among my classmates. I tore off a piece from my copy book and wrote 'Don't kiss your girlfriend tonight there is danger under her lips.' It got back as far as Michael Flaherty whose roaring laugh brought the attention of Bernard. He grabbed the piece of paper. He wanted to know who had written such filth. I was fingered. He took out his leather and started to wallop my hands. Suddenly he stopped. He realised that this was beyond the normal offence and decided he would have to call in the Headmaster, Brother Florence who we nicknamed Flory.

A couple of minutes later, they both stormed back into the classroom. Flory grabbed me by the ear and pulled me down the stairs into his office. He was ranting. He could not contain his rage. He fumbled for the cane behind the door. He was a small fat man. He lashed into me. He was sweating heavily. The lashing and running up and down the stairs had taken their toll. He stopped for a breather. It was my moment of salvation. He gasped. 'How could you write such a thing.' 'A boy from High School told me,' I said. It was a Protestant school.

I had played a religious card. It worked like magic. It was a complete lie, but he believed me. Another innocent Catholic boy had been contaminated by the Protestants. It was the only obvious explanation. He calmed down. He did not apologise or forgive me. Instead, he talked about keeping bad company.

Catholic enforcement

In 1970, the De La Salle brothers in Ireland had 452 members in 35 different houses. In terms of numbers, they were second behind the Irish Christian Brothers who had 1,196 members and who operated from 110 houses. There were eight other orders of brothers, but they were small, only adding another thousand members overall. Altogether there were 2,534 brothers, which is slightly less than the estimated 2,800 GPs in Ireland today.[68]

The brothers were a small part of the enormous Catholic army. In 1970, there were 3,944 diocesan clergy, 7,946 religious order priests and 18,662 nuns, giving an overall total of 33,086. Even allowing for it being an all-Ireland number, it is almost equivalent to the present number of teachers in the Republic of Ireland.

The development and maintenance of this army of men and women depended on an annual recruitment drive. Vocations had to be obtained each year. The main sources were the schools run by the priests, nuns and brothers. They were able to cultivate boys and girls who were deemed to be likely candidates. But there were also recruitment officers. These were specialists who would go around the schools and give talks about what their orders did and how a religious life was a good one.[69]

There was a social class dimension to the recruitment. Orders of Brothers were the bottom rung in the institutional Church. They were forced to recruit among the working class and small farmers. It would have been similar among some of the orders of nuns, particularly the Sisters of Mercy who, in 1970, were by far the largest order with 5,430 members. But Diocesan priests, male religious orders and many orders of nuns, could recruit among urban bourgeoisie and larger farmers. Among these classes it was also an honour to have a son or daughter as a priest or nun.

The level of attraction to becoming a priest, nun or brother was very high until the 1960s. In some respects, it was a career that was much sought after. For many, it was like joining the civil service. And such was the level of attraction that dioceses and religious orders could choose top-class candidates, those with good honours in their Leaving Certificate examination, who could have gone to university and become professionals. Becoming a priest, nun or brother ensured status for oneself and for one's family.

Mothers were a key ingredient in creating vocations. Women who married were expected to stay at home and have large families. This was what was encouraged by the Catholic Church and written into the Constitution and, in the case of working in the civil service, written into law. The status of women in the community became defined in terms of being a good mother who raised good Catholic children. When a woman complied, she was blessed by the priest. Her standing within the community was enhanced when a son became a priest or a daughter a nun. There was a symbiotic relationship. Mothers blessed the Church with vocations and they, in return, were blessed by the Church.[70]

Such was the success of mothers and of recruiting officers that the number of vocations grew steadily throughout the last century. It reached a peak in 1966 when, across all categories of priests, nuns and brothers, there were 1,409 vocations. More than one third of these were the 592 girls who joined an order of nuns.[71]

But Irish society had begun to change. The state began to distance itself from the Church's view of what it was to live a good life. It began to encourage consumption. Irish people began to open up to the West, new ideas and travel. For me, this was reflected in the numbers watching television, listening to popular music and following new trends in fashion. It was a culture of self-expression and indulgence which was very different from the culture of self-denial in which I had grown up. But the biggest change of all was among women.

Among the bourgeoisie, particularly in towns and cities, women began to distance themselves from the Church's image of what it was to be a good woman. They began to see themselves as having careers other than being mothers with large families. More importantly, their mothers encouraged them not to do as they had done.[72] The change was well under way by the late 1960s; the publication in 1968 of *Humane Vitae* (which forbade artificial contraception) accelerated the process. The clamour for contraception, for women to be able to limit and control fertility, to have sex, either inside or outside of marriage, was beginning. Women became increasingly alienated from the Church. Mothers became less interested in and committed to passing on the faith to their children.

It did not take long for vocations to decline. It was the key indicator that something dramatic was happening. Within thirty years the number of vocations had become a trickle of what it had been. By 1996, it had declined to 111. There was only one vocation to the brothers. There were only 19 to orders of sisters – down from 592 in 1966. Ten years later, the number of vocations to all forms of religious life had fallen to 53. Priests, nuns and brothers became old. The average age of a diocesan priest is now over 70 years old.

Masquerading

When I began my degree in Social Science in University College Dublin, I wanted to find out why I had become the way I was. I wanted to move away from a more psychological explanation that focused on my personal quirks and focus more on issues such as gender, class, ethnicity and, of course, religion. With a couple of minor exceptions, I learnt very little during my undergraduate years that helped me answer my question. It was a very Catholic education. In my first year, the introductory course on philosophy was given by Desmond Connell, a future Archbishop of Dublin. There were some challenging lectures. Denys Turner, who became a professor of historical theology, lectured on existentialism and Paddy Masterson, although a passionate believer in God, taught us about atheism.

We did not do sociology until second year. The course on Marxism was given by James Kavanagh, a future Dublin bishop. He was the professor and head of the department. He was replaced by Conor Ward a priest whose book *Priests and People* was central to him being appointed. There was a lecture course on ethics, again given by a priest Fr Bertie Crowe. The course was unashamedly Catholic. Fr Crowe announced at the outset that he would show that sex outside marriage, contraception and abortion were always morally wrong. But there was a course on sociological theory given by an American, Don Bennett. He was an inspiration. Not only was he an atheist, but he was also a committed anarchist.

I toyed with anarchism for a while. I went to a couple of meetings and subscribed to the Black Flag magazine. Anarchists did not go in for the type of strenuous ideological debates that characterised the wannabe Marxists. It seemed to me that Marxism was a type of theology in which people were divided on the extent of economic determinism and the role of the state. For me, it seemed to mirror debates about God and the role of the Church. Anarchists had this wonderful notion that we did not need churches or states. If people managed to divest themselves of these institutions, and private property, they could live in harmony.

All the time that I was engaging in these thoughts, sharing them with friends in pubs drinking pints of stout and sitting on floors smoking joints, there was a strong sense of us being outsiders, of not being part of the Catholic system that dominated social and political life. We were the young pretenders, too afraid to lift our heads above the parapet, to openly resist and challenge the Catholic powers that be.

When I began my job in the Research and Development Unit, I worked in offices above Veritas, the Catholic bookshop in the centre of Dublin. It was an old ramshackle building full of various small Church management organisations. As well as the Research and Development Unit, there was one in charge of promoting vocations, another supporting the management of primary schools, another one for secondary schools. There was also Trócaire, in charge of development aid and, finally, Intercom, which produced an in-house magazine for diocesan priests. All these agencies were new creations. They emerged from Vatican II and were part of a new process where the bishops started working together rather than looking after their own diocese. It was a belated attempt to create a new way of running the empire. The forces of the media and the market were already knocking at the door.

The offices were managed by priests. There was a regular coming and going of priests, nuns and brothers as well as members of the laity, to attend meetings. It was a happy place to work. There was no tension because all the lay people who worked there were devoted to the Church. The priests had charisma. They were celebrities. There were many young women who worked in the offices. They giggled, fawned over and teased the priests who would happily laugh along, reach out, catch and tickle them. It was a strange, seemingly innocent, form of affection.

As soon as I started working, Aileen and I got married. We wanted to live together to have sex without fear and condemnation. We had a small flat on the top floor of a small house in Terenure on the south side of the city. In the first year, there were regular, unannounced calls to the house from one of the local curates. Since there were several Jews living in the area, I developed this tactic of apologising and saying that I was of a different religious persuasion. However, one day I came home from work and there was a priest sitting at the kitchen table. We chatted for a while and then he announced abruptly: 'Aileen tells me you're an atheist'.

I cursed her under my breath, mumbled, and said I was not sure what I was. The topic of conversation changed to sport. It was a summer evening in June and Aileen had been watching Wimbledon. He asked if the young Swede Borg was going to win. I mumbled again all the time thinking how could I rid myself of this priest?

And then he came out with the question I had dreaded: 'Do you mind me asking what you work at Tom?' I quaked. I could lie, but then I thought maybe he knows already. Maybe he has been sent to check me out. I told him I did survey work and that I was doing a survey for the Church on religious beliefs and practices. He said that he had not heard of the survey, but that it must be very important work. I said it was. There was some more chit-chat. But all I remember is feeling very awkward and embarrassed and hoping that he would leave.

For weeks after I went over and over the encounter. Had it happened by accident? Was he just a friendly curate doing his rounds, perhaps hearing from neighbours that there was a new young couple who had moved into the upstairs flat at No. 18, and that he thought he would reach out to us? Or had someone made a phone call and had a word in his ear? Even if it was pure chance, what was the possibility of him telling the Parish Priest what he had encountered on his pastoral visitations: that there was a young atheist doing research for the Church and the PP telling someone else and word eventually getting back to my boss Jim Lennon.

The need to personally resist and challenge the power of the Church came to a head when Aileen became pregnant in 1978. We announced before Christmas that the baby would not be baptised. That Christmas, there was tension in the air. My mother and father said nothing, but my brother Maurice was not happy. He was living at home with my sister Judy. When Aileen and I called over on Christmas morning, there was a show-down. Maurice was supposed to be going to Mass. I accepted his unusual offer that I would go with him. I suspected something was afoot. Instead of going to the church, we withdrew to the family garage, which was down the avenue, hidden away from the house. There was little chance of us being disturbed. It was a cold, damp, unlit, decaying space that was hardly ever used. Maurice had prepared for the occasion. There was a bottle of whiskey and two glasses. He poured two large ones. As we sipped our drinks, he told me that the baby had to be baptised. He looked me in the eye and told me that if we didn't baptise the baby, it would break Mum's heart. I loved him and I knew that he was not being selfish. He just wanted us to be a happy family. I told him that I realised it would be difficult, but that the hypocrisy had to stop. I asked him if he was ever going to tell Mum that he did not go to Mass. He did not answer the question. He wanted to know what was to be lost by going along with Mum's wishes and, more importantly, what right I had to bring the curtains down, and why it had to be now.

It was during this time that I began to realise the power of the Catholic Church in Ireland. It was a power that nobody questioned let alone set out to describe and analyse. Most sociologists who wrote about religion did so from a functional perspective. Religion was the source of the values and beliefs that created social order. This was the view held in most sociology departments. There were a growing number of Marxists in Trinity, but there was nothing in Marxist theory that would help explain how the Church came to be, and remained, so powerful.

I spent most of my academic life trying to understand the role of the Catholic Church in Irish society. It has helped me understand how I have come to be the way I am. The legacies of my Catholic upbringing, of the power of the Church in everyday life, and in social and political life, have reached into my mind, body and soul, into how I see and understand myself and the meaning of life.

I used to think that the Church held a monopoly over morality in Ireland. I then began to realise that it also held a monopoly over spirituality, over the ways in which we try to reach out beyond the material conditions of our lives. More recently, I have begun to think that the Church, like many other institutional religions, has held a monopoly over our whole understanding of what it is to be religious.

Symbolic Domination

When we think of power, we often think of the power of the state and of global corporations. The state has the power to extract taxes and punish and imprison those who don't obey its laws. The wealthy dominate by their control of resources and employment. But there is another form of power. It is the ability to get people to accept what is proclaimed as true, to have a monopoly over the meaning of life and morality. For generations what was declared by the Catholic Church in Ireland was unquestioned and unchallenged. It was the key element in the cultural air that people breathed.[73]

The symbols of Church power were everywhere. Priests, nuns and brothers paraded throughout the country in their clerical dress. Towns and villages were dominated by churches, schools, hospitals and welfare homes which were full of Catholic iconography. It was represented in the way people talked, walked and presented themselves. It was a way of being, a mentality, that reached into every crevice of society, and into the hearts, minds and bodies of individuals. For the vast majority of people at that time, there was only one way of being religious.

This symbolic power is best represented by the images of political leaders going on bended knee before bishops to kiss their rings. It was reinforced for many years by the supplicant and submissive ways that politicians deferred to bishops and priests and the way people in the media were reluctant to criticise or challenge the Church. Symbolic domination reaches a peak when those who are dominated cannot challenge or resist the dominators, when to do so would be unthinkable. It becomes violent when it becomes absolute and when those who are dominated accept and embody the definitions of themselves by the dominator. This is what happens in abusive relations when victims are led to believe that they are at fault. It was what happened to women for generations; they were held to blame for sexual disorder. We can understand how this happened in Ireland by focusing on the extremes. It is often through the pathological, that we can understand the normal. And it is often through stories that we can understand how the Church's monopoly over truth and morality operated in Ireland. Personal and local stories can reveal a universal truth.

In 1945, Peggy McCarthy became pregnant.[74] She was 25 years old and lived and worked in Listowel in Co. Kerry. She was single and attended the local dance hall. She became pregnant. Her boyfriend disappeared to England. On the 10 February 1946, she went into labour at her home. She was attended by her mother and a local midwife. But complications set in. Peggy was in agony. It was necessary to for her to go to the hospital in Listowel. John Guerin, a local hackney driver brought her to the hospital. That was when her nightmare began. Even though the nun who ran the hospital saw that Peggy was in mortal danger, she refused to admit her as she was not married. It was not just against the policy of the Order of Nuns that ran the hospital, it was against Kerry County Council regulations.

Guerin then brought Peggy to the County Hospital in Tralee which was 16 miles away. Again, she was refused entry because she was not married. Guerin was directed to the hospital in Killarney, a further 20 miles away, as it was the only hospital that would treat women who were pregnant outside of marriage. It is not clear whether Peggy McCarthy made it to Killarney hospital or ended up giving birth at the side of the road. What is known is that she died shortly after her daughter Breda was born.

When Guerin brought her body back to the local parish Church in Listowel, he found the gates were locked. The door of the chapel in the local convent was also locked. Canon Patrick Brennan, the local parish priest, had decreed that she could not have a Catholic funeral and could not be buried in the consecrated ground of the local graveyard.

Even though he was technically contravening the canon law of the Church, he was an all-powerful figure and, up to then, few people were willing to challenge him. People were in awe of him. A participant in the radio documentary that was made about the case, said that when the Canon attended the local mart, farmers would kneel in the gutter and excrement of the cattle and bless themselves as he passed by.

The family, friends and local parishioners who had gathered at the Church in Listowel were incensed at the Canon's actions. Guerin and others broke through the locked gates of the Church. There was a confrontation. After negotiations a compromise was reached, and Peggy McCarthy's body was brought to the small chapel beside the hospital in Listowel where previously she had been refused entry. The compromise was that Peggy could be waked in the chapel, but she would not be given a funeral Mass. But the Canon agreed to let her be buried in the local graveyard.

Like many tyrants before him, Canon Brennan may have felt that he needed to lay down the law. He needed to make an example out of Peggy McCarthy. There was no room for compassion or forgiveness. Local people said that the first nun who refused to admit Peggy and the Canon later regretted her actions.

Breda was brought up by her grandparents. She was told that she was their child. She has a mild intellectual disability. When her grandmother died in 1964, a local priest decreed that she should be incarcerated in a Magdalene Laundry. She lived in Magdalene laundries until they closed. However, she had become institutionalised and now lives in a religious home in Dublin. When on a trip back to Listowel, she visited her grandparents' grave and saw Peggy's name inscribed on the tombstone, she told her companion who accompanied her that she knew that Peggy was her mother.

The story reveals the rules and mind-set that the Catholc Church had created by the middle of the last century. Almost every Catholic, everywhere, was expected to follow the laws of the Church. The opposition by Guerin and the other parishioners was exceptional. But this exception proves how strong the rule was maintained. There are very few other stories of opposition to the power of the Church.

It was a form of ideological control. The success of the regime was that while the Church could not impose fines, it could not send people to jail, it still managed to maintain obedience. As well as awe, deference and reverence, priests knew that, having moral control, they could undermine and damage the reputation of a member of the laity. This 'fear' factor worked best, and survived longest, in rural areas where family, kinship and community formed the basis of society. For many priests, the ability to dominate and control in the community, to meet little or no opposition, was as addictive as it was for men, particularly fathers in families.

The story of what happened to Peggy McCarthy reveals the way in which the Catholic Church and the state colluded to dominate, symbolically and physically, Irish society in the twentieth century. This collusion operated in schools and social welfare homes which were funded by the state but run within a Catholic ethos. The strength of that ethos was evident in the physical violence perpetrated on Peggy McCarthy. But the collusion was also evident in the way in which her daughter Breda had to share the shame of her mother and be incarcerated in an institution for 'fallen women' when the only thing that was wrong with her was that she had a mild disability. The story shows that when symbolic domination becomes absolute; evil things can happen to the innocent.

The story also reveals that when it comes to understanding the relationship between the Catholic Church and the state in modern Ireland, we need to go beyond describing the occasions and ways in which the Church influenced or directed the state's public policy, particularly in relation to the fields of family, health, education and social welfare. It is far more fruitful to examine the relationship in terms of the ways in which the Catholic Church symbolically dominated the state. The Church legitimated, or 'blessed', the state as long as it did not undermine its position in these fields. The Church was able to protect its interests by preventing civil servants, administrators and politicians, from saying or doing anything that was contrary to its interests. Anything that was contrary to Church ethos and doctrine entered not just the realm of the unsayable, it was beyond the realm of thought. The Church had developed a stranglehold on sex. It was unmentionable. There was no language to express sexual feelings and emotions. There was no language to express abuse.

There are many other stories that reveal the extent to which the Church sought to control sex and, in particular, women during the twentieth century. In February 1984, the state's Employment Appeals Tribunal upheld the right of an order of nuns who owned a school, to sack Eileen Flynn a teacher because she was living with a married man and had become pregnant. One of the nuns testified to the tribunal that Flynn had 'flaunted' her pregnancy and did not try to hide it or to redeem herself. The Tribunal upheld the dismissal on the grounds that Eileen Flynn's lifestyle was repugnant to the nuns' values. In giving his judgement, Justice Noel Ryan said: 'In other places women are condemned to death for this sort of offence. They are not Christians in the Far East. I do not agree with this, of course. Here people take a very serious view of this, and it is idle to shut one's eyes to it.'[75]

Turning a Blind Eye

Power can make us say and do strange things. It can make us see things that do not exist, and it can prevent us from seeing what is in front of our eyes. Each generation is told of Hans Christian Andersen's tale about the emperor who, having been hoodwinked into buying super-fine clothes that nobody could see, walked around naked. For members of his entourage to maintain their positions, they had to 'see' and praise the clothes that did not exist. They had to live the lie. The make-believe continued until an 'innocent' child blurted out the naked truth.

The tale of the emperor with no clothes is a reminder of collective delusion – people see things that are not there – UFOs, apparitions, statues moving and so forth. And, on the other hand, people cannot see what is in front of their eyes. People can live in denial. We use adages such as 'nobody saw the elephant in the kitchen' to remind ourselves how easy it is for people to 'turn a blind eye'. The tale of the emperor is also a tale about power and how powerful people, organisations and institutions can make us oblivious to reality. It is a story about how power dominates and corrupts. It is a funny story, but the reality is that, when people turn a blind eye, morality can easily be undermined, and innocent lives can be destroyed. What gives the story about the emperor a nice twist is that it was the innocence of a little child which broke the bubble of denial. However, it generally takes enormous courage and conviction to be a whistle-blower.

We all live with lies, some bigger and more important than others. We are persuaded – and we persuade ourselves – that we are thin when we are fat, that we are sober when we are drunk, that we are poor when we are rich.

When power is close to being absolute, people will not see children being taken away by fathers, uncles, priests and brothers to be sexually abused. In the face of such power, then, people quickly sink into living with lies and denying the truth. They cannot ask questions. They cannot draw attention to the elephant in the room. They are afraid to rock the boat. They fear that the very structures of security, comfort and reward, in which they have been cocooned, may come tumbling down. They might lose everything.

A good example of ideological control was the case of Dr Michael Neary. He was a consultant obstetrician and gynaecologist at Our Lady of Lourdes Hospital in Drogheda. It had a strong Catholic ethos: sterilisation was not allowed and there was no access to contraception. Neary was well-respected, busy and popular. Over the years, there had been complaints that he had been carrying out a high number of peripartum hysterectomies – the removal of a womb within six weeks of a woman giving birth. Eventually a whistle-blower was listened to and, in 2003, Neary was suspended. Following a court case, Neary was found guilty of professional misconduct and was struck off the General Register of Medical Practitioners. A formal inquiry was established under Judge Maureen Harding Clark. It reported in 2006.[76]

The report found that the number of hysterectomies performed by Neary and his colleagues over twenty-five years was ten times higher than in other maternity units in Ireland. So how did it happen that so many highly educated, professional people seemed oblivious to what was happening? They could not see the elephant in the room. How did the removal of women's wombs around the time of birth come to be seen as routine? Was this another example of women being dominated by a patriarchal medical discourse and practice? Would there have been the same blindness around Drogheda if these women had had a leg removed and were hobbling about on crutches? The reality is that the experiences of the women were personal and confidential and, consequently, hidden from each other and the public. But what is most disconcerting is that the vast majority of those who participated in or witnessed the regular removal of wombs, said or did nothing. The inquiry found that during his twenty-five-year term few people – patients, their families or GPs, his fellow obstetricians, junior doctors, anaesthetists, surgical nurses, midwives, pathologists and technicians, matrons and sisters – ever complained about Neary's practice. He was able to prevent them from questioning him.

The report concluded that it was a story 'set in a time of unquestioning submission to authority'. It was also related to the culture of the hospital, 'which operated by a separate and unique set of rules and was accountable to a religious community rather than to objective medical standards.' In other words, people were so embedded in the culture that they could not question what was going on. 'It was inconceivable to the doctors and most of the midwives who so often assisted him [Neary] that the hysterectomies on young women were anything more than bad luck.'

But there was more going on than culture and bad luck and it helps us understand the ways in which the power of the Catholic Church was maintained. Neary and his colleagues had a major say in the appointment, retention and promotion of many of those who worked in the hospital. Consultants could and did get nurses transferred. Such was the level of fear that over the years, Neary was able to discipline his colleagues to accept his views and obey his commands without criticism or resistance. It took an outsider, who had not been indoctrinated in this disciplinary system, to 'see' what was going on and to challenge him and the nuns who ran the hospital.

It is hard to disassociate Neary's attitude to women from that of the Catholic Church. Priests, bishops and theologians had no problem dictating what should happen to women when it came to fertility. I got a glimpse of this in 1982 when I had lunch with Fr Dougan. He was then the Professor of Political Science and Sociology in University College Galway. We were talking about symphysiotomies. He was completely in favour of them. Breaking a woman's pelvic bone was, he said, not a major trauma. It didn't do her any harm and then she was able to have as many children as she liked. It was as if women and children were some sort of reserve army who suffered collateral damage on the Church's journey to create a Catholic society.[77]

The Church developed and encouraged a culture of turning a blind eye to what happened to innocent young boys and girls in homes around Ireland who were abused by their fathers, uncles and brothers. It encouraged a culture in which nothing was said when a young woman who became pregnant outside of marriage, often because of sexual abuse, was quietly taken away and put in a Magdalene laundry or mother and baby home. It was able to persuade people to accept and say nothing about the system of incarcerating innocent young children in industrial and reformatory schools in which they were mentally, physically and sexually abused. Little was said when children were ferociously and regularly beaten in schools. Little was said when good teachers, nurses and whoever else worked under the control of the Church were dismissed or did not have their appointments renewed when they resisted or challenged the Church.[78] Nothing was said because the Church had persuaded people that what it and its officials did was in their best interests. It was in the common good. The Church was a sacred institution beyond question.

The ability to silence critics and challengers in wider society was no different from what was happening within the Church. Priests, nuns and brothers quickly learnt that to survive they had to maintain unquestioning loyalty and obedience. Whatever else, the institutional Church had to be protected against all threats. Members would be supported, even if they were abusers, as long as they remained loyal and obedient to the institution. The concern was to root out ideological dissidents and troublemakers rather than abusers. To do this there was a need for information to be shared. In a regime of fear, when a priest could be silenced or transferred very quickly, it must have been hard to know who to trust.

In such a regime there is no court of justice, no way of correcting bad reports about oneself, and the methods of maintaining reports were subtle. Mostly they were by word of mouth: there were few written reports. As we saw earlier in relation to making appointments to a Church committee, all that was needed was a remark to be passed. Catholic Ireland was one large informal gossip machine. There were trusted sources. Comments about people and what they said and did could be remembered and, when needed, used against them.

We can gain an understanding from this tactic of the overall strategy by which the Church was able to maintain information about the comings and goings, deeds and misdeeds, of Catholics throughout the country. One imagines that information gained at local level could be made available, if requested, to those working in other dioceses. And most people knew how this informal system of control worked and perhaps lived in fear of being reported. One never knew who would say what to whom. Any total organisation that is built on maintaining a total ideology needs to be constantly fed information about deviations from the norm. In many respects, the Catholic Church in Ireland developed a system of surveillance which was extensive but because it was informal, soft and subtle it was hard to identify and document and could be easily denied.

Even though I had been researching the power and influence of the Church in Irish society for many years, I did not see through what was happening. Such was the power of the Church, it was difficult to say anything critical about it as an institution or about the priests, nuns and brothers that worked in it. Fr James McNamee, a paedophile priest built a swimming pool in his back garden as a means of attracting in young boys so that he could abuse them in a hut built for that purpose. Most of the parishioners thought he was a lovely man who did wonderful things for the children of the parish. It was probably the adoration parents had for McNamee which prevented the children from being able to tell them about his evil ways.[79]

In the 1980s, I took part in an RTÉ television programme in which there was an item about youth education. One of the participants was a young priest. He waltzed into the studios in his clerical dress and dark sunglasses. He was overweight, sweaty and smelt of strong cologne. He spoke authoritatively about the great work that he was doing to help disadvantaged youth. Years later he was exposed as a skilled paedophile who used to collect young boys from their parents, bring them back to his house, abuse and rape them, and then leave them home. And nothing was said. Nothing could be said. He was a sacred man. He was Fr Seán Fortune. He was a curate in the diocese of Ferns. He turned out to be one of the more depraved paedophile priests in the country.[80]

Who knew what, where and when? Did people not see what was happening? Did they not suspect what was going on behind closed doors? Did nobody think for a second that there was something wrong when a priest takes a young child into a room, closes the door and then sometime later the child emerges distraught and crying? The reality is that not only was it happening in presbyteries, schools and other institutional buildings, not only was it being done by priests and brothers, but it was also being done in family homes by fathers, uncles, brothers and friends. It was all part of a patriarchal system presided over and blessed by the Church.

There were suspicions but, again, nothing could be said. It was too awful to think about. Some of those in power, like Bishop Larry Ryan, realised that it was happening but did not think that being abused would do much harm, that it would have any life-lasting effects. But did he think that all that was happening was a bit of fondling, maybe a bit of groping? Sure it happened to us all. It happened to me. It was part and parcel of dealing with celibates, with the sexually repressed. A De La Salle brother liked to rub his hand up and down my thigh as he helped me with my irregular Latin verbs.

Marie Keenan did some insightful, innovative research on paedophile priests which shone a light on the mentality of some priests at the time.[81] She argued that it was the impossibility of priests trying to embody a perfect celibate clerical masculinity that led many of them to rationalise the most unacceptable behaviours. They used and abused children to maintain the image of themselves as being good priests. In some respects, children became a means for the priests to maintain their vocation, their image and, in the grand scheme of the things, the mission and glory of the Church. They were worth it and there was a reserve army of children to be used.

A Church out of tune

When I was growing up, there were pictures and stories of the enormous crowds that came out in Dublin in 1932 for the Eucharistic Congress. It was a celebration of Catholic Ireland. A coming-out party that went on for five days. There was a great deal of mass hysteria in Europe at the time. The Pope did not come, but he sent a papal legate. I suspect that other than being a major general in the Roman army, most people had no idea who he was, but he was revered. This had nothing to do with charisma. It was an adoration of the Church and all things Catholic. There were masses in the Phoenix Park, first for men, then for women and finally for children with hundreds of thousands attending each day. My grand uncle Tom was one of the organisers. He talked about the event for years after. I remember the way his eyes lit up, the way he savoured recounting favourite moments.

When Pope John Paul II came in 1979, the country went into another paroxysm of Catholic delight. More than 2.5 million people, over two-thirds of the population, gathered to sing and pray at different events around the country. Over a million gathered in the Phoenix Park in Dublin on the first day and then hundreds of thousands attended masses in Galway, Limerick, Mayo and Louth. My former boss, Jim Lennon was one of the key organisers of the Mass in Louth.

There are times when it feels good to be part of a greater whole. A feeling of complete togetherness. A collective consciousness that leads to a commitment to each other; of all for one and one for all. If it was possible to harness the energy, the sense of collective well-being, that was created during the pope's visit then, surely, it would be possible for this enormous army of Catholic souls to conquer the world.

There was a hope that somehow the Pope's visit would help turn the tide. That there would be a return to the Church. And for a while it looked like that. There was a temporary increase in vocations and in 1983 two-thirds of the electorate voted to make abortion unconstitutional. But the sense of bonding and belonging, of everyone being united and happy to be Catholic, was fading. The tide of modernity was too strong. It had seeped into the hearts, minds and bodies of Catholic men, women and children. They were happy to celebrate, but they did not want to go back to those days of being pious, humble and pure. They wanted to embrace a culture of self-expression and fulfilment, of not living in fear, of not being afraid to be happy. The papal visit in 1979 was the last hurrah for devotional Catholicism. When Pope Francis came in 2018, only 150, 000 went to the Mass in the Phoenix Park. It could have been the weather. It could have been the furore in the media in advance of the visit about the way the Church dealt with clerical child sexual abuse. It was probably that popes no longer have the charisma they once had.

The clerical child sex abuse scandals severely damaged the reputation of the Church, particularly in the way in which it seemed more interested in covering up crimes, in protecting criminals, in protecting its reputation and vested interests rather than admitting to and atoning for the life-long damage it caused to innocent children and vulnerable young women. The Church, and its bishops and priests, went from being sacred cows that could not be questioned or challenged, into pariahs who had to be rooted out by the media and castigated by the state. The sense of honour and respect that Catholics had for the Church and the clergy began to dissipate. Commitment could no longer be attained through doctrine and the enforcement of rules, especially in relation to sexuality, marriage and fertility control.

Increasingly the laity began to see priests not as leaders and preachers, let alone as moral policemen that had to be obeyed, but as service providers who perform services at important life-transition events such as birth, marriage and death and family celebrations such as First Holy Communion and Confirmation. These have become more family than Church events. But it is because they are traditional, because they revolve around rituals, inherited ways of performing, they create a sense of belonging that is sacred.

It would seem that many Catholics in Ireland still feel attuned with each other but distant from the institutional Church and its teachings, liturgies, rules and regulations. They are happy to have the priest preside but, increasingly, they want to put their own personal stamp on the occasion. They might like the tradition. They might like the local church in which they were brought up; the sense of awe. But they also want to do and say things, to play music, sing songs and give speeches, that may be outside the traditional liturgy. The more priests enforce the rules, the more they are in danger of becoming less attuned to the needs and interests of the laity. This is perhaps why, less than half of marriages now take place in a Catholic Church.

Grand uncle Tom used to say that one of the great things about being Catholic was that no matter where you went in the world, you were able to go into Mass in any church and it would be the same everywhere, the same liturgy in Latin, the priest facing the altar and chanting out the prayers. There was a sense of global belonging, Catholics everywhere united in practice and belief.

The changes brought in after Vatican II, with the priest facing the people and the prayers in English, diminished the sense of awe, mystery and enchantment. The priest was no longer looking up to God but out into the faces of the people. It must have seemed that this would create a greater collective consciousness; that the laity would connect more with the priest and the liturgy. But the reality is that, although the readings are in English, the prose is often arcane. Take, for example, a reading for Sunday, 3 July 2022.

> Rejoice with Jerusalem, and be glad with her, all you that love her: rejoice for joy with her, all you that mourn for her. That you may suck and be filled with the breasts of her consolations: that you may milk out, and flow with delights, from the abundance of her glory.[82]

I suspect that for most Catholics this reading would make as much sense if it was in Latin. But the scriptures are sacred. They cannot be changed. And this is where the divide between the priest and the laity takes place. The scriptures only begin to make sense when they are interpreted by the priest. The laity need to be guided. The priest is an expert. He is the one who knows the message hidden in the readings. His job is to interpret the reading and make it meaningful. The consequence of all this, maybe not consciously, is that it has the long-term effect which is intended. It has the effectt of reproducing the power of the priest. The one who knows having to explain to those who don't know. A form of mansplaining.[83]

This is reflected in the Fr Seán Sheehy affair. He gave a sermon in Listowel on 30 October 2022.[84] It was an old-fashioned sermon with references to sin, Satan and hell. He referred to the scripture readings and used them to decipher God's will. His tone was loud and dogmatic like that of a rampaging evangelist. It may have been an approach he developed during his time in the USA. Sheehy seems to have concentrated on the first reading from Wisdom 11. 22–122.

> But you (Lord) have mercy on all, because you can do all things; and you overlook people's sins that they may repent. . . . Therefore you rebuke offenders little by little, warn them and remind them of the sins they are committing, that they may abandon their wickedness and believe in you, O LORD![85]

He began by saying that sin was rampant in Ireland. It was seen in the legislation of governments, in the promotion of abortion, in the lunatic approach of transgenderism and in the promotion of sex between couples of the same sex. He went on towards the end to castigate the free distribution of contraceptives to young people saying that it promoted promiscuity. He intimated that there was no hope for those who engaged in such behaviour. Sinners had to be reminded that they were on their way to hell. Sinners would find out the day they died that it was not him but God who was saying these things. People he pronounced 'had to be protected from Satan and all his wiles and ways.'

The sermon wàs divisive. It was reported that some members of the congregation got up and left. As they did, they were derided by Fr Sheehy. Speaking afterward, he accepted that at the end of the sermon, members of the congregation got up and left but, he said, other parishioners not only stayed, but applauded him.

The more priests follow a hard-line doctrinaire position, the more likely it is to alienate cultural Catholics who go to Mass more for the experience and less for the preaching. The following day, Ray Browne, the bishop of

Kerry, rebuked Fr Sheehy and apologised to those who were offended by the sermon. He said that 'the views expressed do not represent the Christian position. The homily at a regular weekend parish Mass is not appropriate for such issues to be spoken of in such terms.'[86] He did not explain the difference, if any, between a Catholic and Christian position.

In the national media coverage in the following days, Fr Sheehy questioned the bishop for issuing the apology saying that everything he had said was in line with the scriptures and Church teaching. He claimed that Bishop Browne was 'muzzling the truth to appease the people.'[87]

The problem for the Church is how, in an increasingly non-institutional approach to being religious, can it proclaim its teachings without offending people or, worse still, alienating them. There are many mortal sins, such as sex outside marriage, the use of contraceptives, divorce and gay relationships, that are problematic to preach about. It probably makes matters worse when Fr Sheehy reminded everyone that sinners are in danger of going to hell. It is an indication of how times have changed when sin and hell can no longer be mentioned in sermons, for fear that they may cause offense.

All power to the Church

For most of the nineteenth and twentieth centuries, the Church acted less as a voluntary and more as a compulsory organisation. The laity was obliged to follow its rules and regulations. It was detrimental to one's life chances to criticise let alone challenge the Church. Everyone knew what happened to Noël Browne, the young socialist who had tried to take on the Catholic Church in 1951 by providing health services for mothers. The Church declared that this was state interference in the family. For many, Browne was a cultural hero, but the majority saw him as a hot-head, a maverick who refused to play the game. Not only did the Catholic Church defeat him, it strangled his reputation.[88] One of the consequences was that there was an unwillingness, to criticise the Church. It was a sacred cow.

Moral Monopoly emerged from my dissertation. When it was first published in 1987, it received praise in some quarters but was condemned in others. Mary Kenny wrote in *The Irish Press* that it was a 'sneering, insulting and often vulgar attack on the Catholic Church in Ireland'. I was invited onto the Rodney Rice show on RTÉ radio 1 on Saturday morning. One of the panellists was John Kelly, a highly regarded Fine Gael T. D. who was a constitutional lawyer as well as a former Minister and Attorney General. He objected to me claiming that the Catholic Church was an institution that was primarily interested in maintaining its own power and that priests were moral policemen. He said the Church had no interest in power and that priests were welcomed with open arms any time they visited a home.

When the programme finished, the other panellists gathered together with Rodney Rice. They were regular contributors to the media. It was my first time on national radio. I stood a while thinking that someone would say something to me. That I would be included. But no. I decided to leave and said I would be on my way. They looked over and said goodbye. It was not a deliberate attempt to exclude. It was probably not even conscious. I think John Kelly may have felt sorry for me, that he thought that I had been brainwashed when I was doing my PhD in America. That I had been contaminated.

I had an experience of priestly visitation later that year. My son Luke died some months after the publication, suddenly and tragically. He fell out of the babysitter's arms as she came down the stairs and hit his head on the stone floor at the bottom. He was put on a life support machine. For two days after the accident, Aileen and I tried to come to terms with the fact that he was going to die. Family and friends flooded into the house. We sat on the couch in the living room. There were stunned, long intense silences and mutterings mixed with tears. There was little to be said and everything to be felt. At the end of the second day, we decided to go into the hospital the following morning, to turn off the life-support machine, and say goodbye.

We were in shock. People were coming and going and then, sometime after we made the decision, Aileen's sister Maura came up to us and said the local parish priest had arrived. I did not know him. We had only moved into the area the previous year. We did not go to Mass, we had no connection with the Church.

He swept into the room and introduced himself to us and gave us his sympathies. He went and stood with his back to the fire. It was a commanding presence. I suspect he felt it was his duty to say a few words. And so, he started to talk about Gods' mysterious ways and how difficult it is to make sense of a tragedy like this. He went on to say that only the previous week he had heard of a woman in Ballyfermot who was out walking with her two young children in a pram and that a car had mounted the footpath and taken the pram out in front of her. But there was comfort in knowing that they were, like Luke, in heaven with God.

As he told the story, I sat gobsmacked. I didn't want him to stay. I got up and said it was very good of him to call but that we were exhausted. He said a few more words and we left the room together. As we got to the hall door, he was still talking. I opened the door. I thanked him again and said that we were not practising anymore. He said nothing. I was still seething. Then I blurted out that I had written a book about the power of the Catholic Church in Ireland. He turned to me, put his hand on my shoulder and said 'I know, we won't hold that against you, Tom.'

I think on reflection that he was simply doing what he had always done. He had heard of the tragedy, and he felt compelled to come and offer his condolences, to reach out and do whatever he could to assuage our grief. He was not condescending. He was genuine. He would have been shocked if he had been told that maybe he should not have displayed himself, that he should have been quieter and humbler. But that is what happens when people in power don't critically reflect, when they live in a bubble in which people defer to and fawn over them. The Church was in decline, but priests were still seen as sacred, and many thought they were doing good and certainly meant no harm. It is no different from some men who think that there is nothing offensive in remarking about women's looks, whistling at them, tickling and fondling them, or patting them on the bottom. They think that the women might feel honoured by the attention they are getting.

It is difficult for priests to transcend their institutional role. The more priests try to be themselves, the more they tell the truth about themselves, the more they run the risk of getting offside with their bishops, their fellow priest and more orthodox members of the laity. In a new age of memoirs, of trying to confess the truth about oneself, there is a notable absence of priests writing honestly and openly about themselves, particularly in terms of their beliefs and their sins. It is difficult for them to change from being confessors to confessing.[89]

The more the priests are seen as different, as dogmatic and triumphalist, the more, particularly in an age of woke culture, they come across as pompous and arrogant. In the same way that men have had to critically reflect about the ways in which they dominate women, priests have to reflect on the ways they dominate the laity, particularly women, children and members of minorities such as LGBTQ+. To do this, the Church needs to critically reflect on how it operates as a dogmatic, hierarchal, patriarchal institution and how this is embedded in its theology and cannon law. And, at an individual level, priests need to reflect on the ways in which they may symbolically dominate people, particularly women.

But can the old order change? Two hundred years ago, the laity needed the Church to become self-disciplined, modern and civilised. Today it is more a service provider that gives meaning and sanctity to major life events. The Church is no longer a means for the laity to attain salvation or honour, respect and power. Many of the Church's teachings and liturgies are out of sync with the beliefs, practices and interests of the laity. Increasingly, people don't want the traditional services that the Church provides; they want to create their own services, their own ways of celebrating and mourning, their own sense of mystery and enchantment.

There is, then, a problem between trying to appease the laity while at the same time, being evangelical, and preaching the doctrine of the Church. It would seem that what binds the more than 1.4 billion Catholics around the world is that they believe that they have the same fundamental beliefs about God, about Jesus, and the Church being the true interpreter of the gospels and the path to salvation. Ostensibly, this is what makes Catholics feel the same. As in any other organisation, there are rules and regulations to be followed. The problem for the Church is when people, who see and understand themselves as members, don't follow the rules.[90]

For example, people around the world can play a sport like golf, soccer or rugby because they follow the rules. At a higher level, you cannot be a good citizen if you don't obey state law. So, what happens when Catholics do not obey Church or God's laws? Increasingly there is little that can be done. The Church used to rely on the threat of eternal damnation. Now it has to rely on creating a sense of sentimental attachment. The only thing that keeps many Catholics attached to the Church is identity, tradition and a feeling of belonging. They may get this from going to Mass and attending funerals, marriages and other services. But I think it has little to do with doctrine and following rules.

Breaking free

Such was the level of colonisation by the Church of the religious field, that it took me many years to realise that not being Catholic does not mean that I am not religious. I continually search for the meaning of life. I struggle to live a good life. I am as attached and attuned to those I love and care for as much as any good Catholic. I am as bewildered and enchanted by the beauty and mystery of life as theologians, prophets and mystics. Over many years, I have tried to transcend the taken-for-granted ways in which I see and understand myself. It is this continual search for truth and meaning, of pushing myself in different directions, of trying to find my soul, of trying to find God, which is an essential part of being religious.

I used to think of transcendence as an overwhelming mystical experience that was powerful enough to cause a rupture in the way someone saw and understood the world. It was as if a light had been shone on their life that revealed a startling new truth, something which had been hidden. And with this light, the world which had until then been unquestioned and taken-for-granted, melted into air.

Most traditional religions have a story about transcendence whether it was Moses on the mount, St Paul on the road to Damascus, the appearance of the Archangel Gabriel to Mohammad, or the moment of enlightenment of Siddhartha Gautauma in which he saw through the meaning of the cosmos and became Buddha.

I think most transcendental experiences take place because people feel stuck in ways of being that are unfulfilling. They begin to search. They change their rituals and routines. They create the conditions necessary for transformation. They go into a desert, on a pilgrimage to a sacred place, to the top of a mountain. They make demands on themselves.

In her book *Haven*, Emma Donoghue gives a vivid description of three monks journeying to, and then trying to live on, Skellig Michael off the coast of Kerry.[91] The early Irish monks developed a range of penitential practices that were designed to help them achieve transcendence. They would incarcerate themselves in cells, sometimes for months.

The search for transcendence through penitential practice became part of Irish religious culture. People may not withdraw from the world or mortify their bodies, but they fast and abstain and go on pilgrimages. Each year, thousands of people climb Croagh Patrick, some in bare feet. Others go to St Patrick's Purgatory on Lough Derg in Donegal where they fast for 36 hours – taking just black tea and toast – and walk around rock beds in their bare feet. And although institutional religion is in decline in the West, over 350,000 people, many of whom might not call themselves Christian, walked the Camino de Santiago in the north of Spain.

Again, this brings into focus the thin line between what is religious and non-religious. Walking the Camino has echoes of religious behaviour, of achieving some spiritual awareness, whereas running a marathon does not. Similarly, fasting and abstaining during Lent is seen as religious, whereas doing so in January is not. It seems obvious that the monks who went to live on Skellig Michael were being religious, but what about someone going to live on some other remote island off the west coast of Ireland looking for peace and quiet?

We might say that there must be some notion of God, of saving one's soul, or self-transcendence or spirituality for it to be understood as religious. But the notion of there being a God only emerged in the second era of religion. Were people in the first era of religion, in hunting and gathering societies, not religious? Are people today who search for transcendence in nature, love, art, music, literature, dance or drugs not religious? These are difficult questions. There is often a thin line between religious ecstasy and getting high, between mindfulness and mindlessness. Much depends on the time and circumstances and the intentions and motivations of the individuals.

In many respects, my early search for transcendence, was sincere but perhaps a little pathetic. I was desperate to go beyond the Catholic system that had invaded my being. During my last two years in school, when I was about sixteen years old, I began to question the meaning of life, not in school, but with my friend Tom Hobson. We sought out new ideas, new music. He was the one to turn me on to Van Morrison. He was passionate about plants. But they did not work for me. What we agreed on, however, was the need for a new mysticism, some way of being in touch with the world, with nature, that was beyond reason and science. In those early days, we dreamed of getting high. But cannabis was impossible to get. One evening, when his parents were away for the night, we made do with a bottle of cough mixture which contained lots of codeine. I feel asleep on his parent's bed and woke up to find I had coughed up my share of the bottle and most of my stomach over the family poodle who had fallen asleep in my lap. The next morning there was a frantic washing and brushing of the dog before his parents came home.

But in our search for transcendence, we also read. Our main inspiration was Herman Hess. We eventually got onto *Steppenwolf, Damien* and *The Glass Bead Game*, but we started with *Narcissus and Goldmund*. It is an existential story of two young men in a medieval monastery, Narcissus, a newly qualified teacher, is dedicated to an ascetic, intellectual life as a means of finding God. Goldmund a gifted student is a dreamer. Goldmund has a transcendent moment, an epiphany, when, one day, he wanders from the monastery and encounters a gypsy woman with whom he makes wonderful love. He tells Narcissus and decides to leave the monastery and search for the meaning of life by wandering in the wider world.

There are vivid descriptions of Goldmund becoming enveloped in luscious forests. Peasants befriend him. He encounters numerous women on his journey who attract, excite and intrigue him. He is taken in by a knight and falls in love with one of his daughters, but the knight does not trust him and sends him on his way. He kills a man in a fight. He encounters a beautiful sculpture of the Madonna which inspires him. He goes to the city where the carver lives and working under him, becomes a successful carver himself. But he cannot settle down and moves on. He gets caught up in an outbreak of the plague. He meets more women. At the end, he is caught in the rooms of a count's wife and is about to be hung, when Narcissus comes to his rescue.

What, if anything, has this got to do with being religious? Everything. Hesse was dealing with transcendence. Narcissus tries to find the meaning of life within the confines of a cloister, through reason and ritual. Goldmund goes out and enters into the raw, sensuous, unpredictable, emotionally upheaving world. He tries to find meaning through sex and art. But, at the end, transcendence comes through their friendship. Out of two human beings meeting by chance, emerges a new understanding of what it is to be human, to be alive, to embrace the ambiguous, uncertainty of living in a void and trying to create a centre. Trying to create and recreate meaning, over and over, again and again.

For Tom and me, Hesse became a prophet. We were a pair of Goldmunds trying to transcend the narrow confines of the home and school in which our parents and the De La Salle brothers felt secure. We did not belong to any Church or sect. But we were searching. We were trying to enter the world, to feel and embrace it. We were trying to be spiritual and mystical. In all of this, we were very much being religious.

I didn't meet a gypsy girl, but I did meet Aileen. She was sixteen. I was eighteen. Falling in love is a religious experience. It has little to do with reason and everything to do with being human and a part of nature and, maybe, a sense of being in God. As in other forms of love, something emerged between us that was neither me nor Aileen. It transcended us both. Two became one. Aileen became a sculptress. Her early sculptures were an attempt to re-present and re-imagine shapes found in nature. Everything she saw and experienced in the woods that surrounded her home, belonged to her. There was a way of knowing and understanding nature that was beyond words. Where does religion end and art begin? Or maybe it is the other way round? Where does art end and religion begin?

Transcendence revolves around a new way of being in the world, of seeing and understanding oneself and others differently. It is a transformation of the self. A rebirthing. This is what happens when people are converted. They begin a new life. It is what happens when someone becomes a member of a sect or Church, or if they join a religious order. Transcendence is a feeling because it involves an embodiment of a different way of being. It happens when someone gives up a web of meaning, a way of being, which has become such a part of themselves that they are reluctant, unwilling or unable to let go.

In the 1970s, as members of the cannabis smoking community we felt we were stuck in the mud of Catholic Ireland, weighed down by the rules and regulations of narrow-minded parents, priests and politicians. On summer nights we sat and stared at the stars in search of transcendence. It was awesome and there was a strong sense of being in harmony with each other and the cosmos, but, in no way did we see ourselves as being religious. Indeed, there was a curiosity and apprehension about those who did not take to the weed and went down a religious route, mainly towards forms of Buddhism. It was kind of quaint but weird. I used to go to the Buttery in Trinity College to get cannabis. There was one dealer who gave up smoking weed as he had 'found the knowledge'. I wondered then if it was possible to get the same sense of ecstasy without smoking pot or taking drugs.

Then there was Gerry Griffin, a friend from school. He became very involved in Transcendental Meditation. I wondered would the high from chanting a mantra be anything like being stoned. And there was my cousin John Inglis who caused his and my aunt Joan endless worry when he joined the Guru Marahaj Ji (The Devine Light Mission) sect. Aunt Joan pleaded with me to go to the community house in which he was living and to talk some sense into him. I went and John, who was always genial and gentle, sat and talked with me with his enchanting beatific smile and kept saying he was very happy and not to worry about him. I speculated when I left if the rumour was true that they were all having mad sex with each other.

There was a moral panic about new religious movements, of children being captivated and brainwashed 'by some Eastern nonsense' and being turned against 'their' religion. There were regular stories in the media which led to questions being asked in the Dáil.[92] The most famous were a group of latter-day hippy types who took over an island off the Donegal coast. Locals said they could hear wild screams from the island as the members chanted and indeed did scream to let go tension. They became known as The Screamers. Again, there were rumours that they too were having wild sex.

Originally, there was a close relationship between religion and sex. It was only with the rise of Abrahamic religions based on individual salvation that a tension emerged. And this tension was exacerbated with the emergence of priestly chastity.[93] The importance of maintaining chastity as a means of maintaining solidarity among priests and members of religious orders was transferred to the laity. As we saw earlier, sex, lust and desire were seen as the greatest threats to family, community and social order in Ireland. They had to be controlled and, when necessary, rigorously and ruthlessly punished. The history of Ireland is littered with sexually transgressive individuals who were excluded and incarcerated.[94]

There is a thin line between transgression and transcendence. For the early Christian monks and mystics, transcendence often revolved around what they did with their bodies, particularly in relation to mortification and controlling sexual desire. The history of the West can be understood as the emergence of new ways of governing bodies through confinement, exclusion and punishment. But the most successful of all was the control of sex. When he died in 1984, the French philosopher Michel Foucault had published three of his proposed six volume history of sexuality.[95]

Like many others, Foucault recognised that while he continually searched for truth, he knew he would never find 'the' truth, or any one whole, absolute truth. But, at the same time, he recognised the need to continually transcend the taken-for-granted ways in which we 'know' the world. Taking a long-term historical perspective, he argued that people are always caught in discourses not of their own choosing. These discourses frame the way they see and understand the world.[96]

Like many others of my generation, my attempts at being spiritual, were part of a struggle to divest myself of the Catholic discourse into which I was socialised. I grew up in an era in which everything about the meaning of life was framed by priests and theologians. Life was seen as a struggle between God and our natural instincts, the most basic of which was sex, The obsession that the Church had with sex meant that if you wanted to speak a new truth about yourself you had to be transgressive. You had to abandon the Catholic discourse that saw sex as sinful and demeaning and see and embrace sex as joyous and fulfilling. It was a dangerous enterprise. For generations the Church had enforced its discourse. It had established a very effective regime of discipline and punishment. Those who transgressed were shamed and shunned and, if necessary, separated out and put into penal institutions.

The question was how, other than identifying, describing and analysing their influence, could discourses be transcended. Since their power was inscribed in bodily practices, one way to break free from the mould was to engage in transgressive acts. While Foucault was a dedicated philosopher, he recognised the need to transcend existing forms of knowledge by being physically transgressive. Being an openly gay man in Paris in the 1970s was, in its own way, transgressive. But he went further. He started going to California where he frequented gay bath houses and took acid.[97] This was less about doing philosophy and more about being spiritual. It was about finding one's soul through new experiences, through engaging in transgressive practices. 'We will call 'spirituality', then, the set of these researches, ascetic exercises, etc., which are not for knowledge but for the subject, for the subject's very being, the price to be paid for access to the truth.'[98]

I took acid a few times. It was part of an attempt to see, and more importantly, feel the world differently. It was enveloping. Something quite mundane, an object, could appear wonderful as if I had not noticed its beauty before. Other objects could seem strange. People's faces were fascinating. I was often mesmerised by the way their mouths moved, the contours of their skin and the way their eyes lit up, more than by what they said. And then there was the intensity of colours of anything from a banana to a flower. At night I could sit and look at the stars for ages. If anyone had said that these attempts at trying to search for meaning, truth and love were attempts at attaining transcendence and were, therefore, being religious, I would have laughed at them.

Charisma

Transcendence revolves around transgressing limits, around going beyond the taken for granted, of trying to see how we are pinned down by discourses and practices into which we were born and socialised. We are dominated by tradition; inherited, unquestioned ways of being, saying and doing that become bound into rules and regulations.

In each age, there have been those who have risen and challenged traditions and existing rules and regulations. They do and say different things. They have no power other than the force of their personality, but their actions and words have a resonance with the changing times, with the needs and interests of people. They have a strong message, and they create an emotional connection. Such charismatic leaders have no coercive power. They have to rely on capturing the zeitgeist of the times. People are drawn to shamans, gurus and prophets and follow their lead because they are convinced that they have extraordinary powers or qualities. Under the influence of charismatic authority, people give up tradition and are often willing to break existing codes, rules and laws.[99]

Charismatic authority is based on the ability of a leader to get people to see and go beyond existing ways of thinking and being, to break free of the chains of tradition and law in which they are bound up. But because charismatic leadership is more emotional than rational, it is unpredictable. Why some leaders emerge rather than others depends on the existing social conditions; generally it is a time of upheaval. Much depends on the ability of the leader to say and do wonderful things, to be heroic and inspiring.

We think of great charismatic leaders like Jesus, Mohammad, Buddha and Gandhi. They overturned traditions and challenged and resisted existing laws and ways of being and thinking.

I sometimes hope for some new prophet or messiah that would shine a new light on the world and help the vast majority of us transcend the taken-for-granted ways in which we understand the meaning of life and help us live ecologically sustainable lives. A messiah who would inspire people, especially the wealthy, to give up wanting, getting, spending and, instead, try to live a more quiet, simple, humble life that revolves around loving and caring and living more in harmony with nature.

Charismatic leaders can also be dangerous and evil, particularly when they believe in their own rhetoric. It is because humans are emotional, because they can become angry and alienated, that they believe that there is a saviour, someone with extraordinary qualities, that can lead them to the promised land. We are all vulnerable particularly in times of stress and upheaval. We think we can discern the good guys, the prophets, from the zealots and fanatics. But it is not easy. There are many religious and political leaders who specialise in stirring emotions, who rant, rave and demonise.[100] In 1978, over 900 Americans, including children, members of a sect called the People's Temple died in a mass murder-suicide pact in a jungle settlement in South America. They were led by Rev. Jim Jones. And then there was Hitler.

But, as suggested earlier, there is a thin divide between charismatic authority and symbolic domination. Sometimes charisma has less to do with the individual and more to do with the office they hold. Popes and other religious leaders have a certain charisma that is independent of who they are. Bishop Eamon Casey, Fr Micheal Cleary and Fr Seán Fortune combined their personal charisma with the charisma that comes from the office they held from being priests. For much of the last two hundred years, there was a charisma, an authority that came with just being a priest.[101]

This is why we need to be vigilant in the ways in which we are symbolically dominated and easily led astray. Many years ago, way before I had started doing my yoga tree postures, I used to lead sessions in adult learning as part of a Diploma in Development Studies. There were about twenty students, most of them from Africa and Asia. Every year I began the first session by entering the class late when everyone else was gathered. Without any greeting or announcement, I told them they had to do an exercise. I told them to close their eyes and stand still and then they had to try and stand on one foot. They would fail but they had to keep trying.

Once they had closed their eyes, I left the room. I stood outside for about five minutes before going back in. Some had their eyes open, but others were still trying to stand on one foot. I asked them to sit back down at their desks. I asked them what they had learned. After much discussion, I suggested that perhaps the main thing to be learnt was about power, about how easy it was for me to dominate and for them to allow themselves to be dominated. But this domination was based on emotion. There was a fear of what might happen if they disobeyed and a sense of shame of being the odd-one-out.

I had come into the room. They did not know me. They assumed that I was there to teach them and that because I had been blessed by the College, that what I was doing was for their benefit. And so, within seconds, I had symbolically and physically dominated them. They accepted my commands, my definition of the situation, my truth. I suggested to them that if they were to be engaged in any struggle to increase freedom and emancipation, they had to realise that anything they said and did, could lead to docile acceptance, to a lack of questioning and therefore, perhaps unconsciously, to dominating the very people they thought they might be trying to help.

It is necessary, then, to be always vigilant and realise that as much as we can be inspired by people who are able to embody and transform the zeitgeist, who can lead us into new ways of thinking and being, we can also be easily hoodwinked by charlatans. What makes the task of 'seeing through' people and their arguments is that they often appear so rational and meaningful. Indeed, it may well be that the notion that there will always be progress, always better ways of doing things, always new technologies that will solve our problems, may be a false God. On the other hand, we need equally to be wary of the prophets of doom, those who gain attention and following by proclaiming that the apocalypse is coming.

If, as I have argued, being religious, and possessing charismatic appeal, are rooted in emotions, then we are drawn back into the fundamental question about the relationship between reason and religion.[102] Much of religion is rooted in feelings of enchantment, belonging, wonder and mystery. These are fundamental aspects to being human and have substantial consequences. We know that emotions and reason are not natural bedfellows.

Falling in love is perhaps a universal feeling. It can be overwhelming, but it is not always reasonable. It can lead people to give up wealth and power, to lose face, to travel to the ends of the earth or, tragically, to hurt, maim and murder people.

Millions of people have done things out of love and compassion, including giving up their lives for a cause, which may seem irrational. That is why we ask people who are overwhelmed by emotion to be reasonable. While we laugh at the follies of people in love, we are scared by the antics of those who hate. And we know how quickly the flames of hatred can turn into a conflagration that burns anyone and everyone in its path.

This is why we cannot let go of reason. There has to be a reality check. We can be overwhelmed by experience and emotion, they can bring us together, but they can also drive us apart. We have to be able to be reasonable about our experiences, beliefs and practices. We can be inspired by love, beauty, nature, wonder and mystery, we can have intense feelings and experiences that motivate us to love and care, but they have to be subject to the rigours of reason, debate and justification.

The argument is simple. Human beings were religious before they became reasonable. They were enchanted and mesmerised by their environment. They developed rituals and language to become attuned with each other. They found ways of questioning and transcending their ways of being. With the development of reason, they became critically reflective of the ways in which they were religious.

Science and reason can provide an understanding and explanation of life. They can help us describe, analyse and control our world, but they cannot provide meaning. It is through transcending themselves as individuals and becoming members of a group that humans develop meaning. There is no scientific way of doing this. Being religious revolves around feelings of mystery and enchantment.

How these feelings are generated does not have to be reasonable, indeed in some sense feelings and experiences are often unreasonable. But the development of reason means that there is a moral responsibility to be able to understand, explain and justify one's feelings and emotions when they impact on others. And, if religion is founded on emotions, then there is a need for people to defend and justify their way of being religious when it effects or impinges on others. It is not enough to justify that I did something by saying that I was angry. Nor is it enough to say that my actions are justified by religious experiences, beliefs and practices.

Reason has impacted on every area of social life, including religion. We can see the world as an enchanting, mysterious, magical place and we can engage in whatever rituals and practices that maintain that experience. They can be spiritually and morally uplifting. But once they enter the public sphere, once they impact on other people's lives beyond the members of a group, sect or church, they have to be subject to reason, to debate and discussion. Unless we find a balance between being religious and being reasonable, there is always the danger of uncontrolled, demonic power.

Good apples in a crumbling barrel

Like many separated people who were once in love, I have a complex and ambivalent relation with the Church. I was deeply attached and committed to all things Catholic for the first twelve years of my life. I was caught up in a heaven of hope and beauty which was at the same time, an empire of obedience, discipline, punishment and fear. I have met many inspiring, loving people who, like my aunt Joan, are devoted to the Church. Most of them are caring people, many of them providing essential services for little or no reward, other than recognition and respect. I doubt many see themselves as Roman soldiers. And that is a problem: many cannot announce to themselves, to others in private and, least of all publicly, their doubts, ambiguities, and disbeliefs. Some leave quietly. Those who stay have to remain obedient and tow the institutional line.

The Catholic Church continually fails to critique its own power. The Church may have helped Irish people gain political freedom and become educated and civilised, but what it has not investigated openly and honestly is how the system of hierarchy, obedience, celibacy and silence operated, how it led to absolute power and tyranny and, at the same time, to a whole host of perversions.

I have come to detest the arrogance, pomposity and power of the Church and so I tend to see people who are part of the Church system as Roman soldiers. I detest the way it operates. In many ways it is like any multinational company that is primarily interested in reproducing and developing its power. I detest the way its ethos and teachings still prevail in many if not most schools, hospitals and welfare organisations. And yet, even after writing *Moral Monopoly*, I was happy to send my daughter Olwen to be taught by the Dominican nuns in Muckross Park, a secondary school that Aileen had attended. Like many others of my generation, when it comes to being Catholic, I am fluid, ambiguous, inconsistent and contradictory.

This was all too evident when it came to Aileen's death and funeral. She had lived with an aggressive cancer for nearly three years. In the end, she died quickly. I had made no preparations for her funeral. She wanted to be buried with our son Luke and so cremation was not a possibility. There was also the question of finding a venue that was beautiful and enchanting, but big enough for all those who would want to attend. There was only one, the church down the road in Rathgar in which I had only been a few times in my life, mostly for funerals.

I turned to my good friend Fr Raphael Gallagher. Raphael may be a Roman soldier, but he is a lovely man. I was blessed; he was living in Rome but happened to be back home for a week attending a conference. He stepped in and organised everything. He talked to the local parish priest and then when we got the okay, he sat down with me, and we designed the small removal service for the night before and then the funeral Mass the next day. There was a mixture of readings, songs, homilies and memories. Raphael's task was to ensure that what took place reflected my desires, that it was a celebration of Aileen, and yet, at the same time, fulfilled the doctrinal demands of the Mass as a sacrament. And so there it goes. I bitch and scream about the Church but, when in need, reach out to it for help.

A few years ago, I had the opportunity to talk with some priests from a rural diocese. There were about forty of them. We gathered in a local hotel and before going up to the conference room they met and chatted among themselves. Most of them were dressed in grey or black. A few wore clerical collars. They were all about seventy years old. Some were quiet, others exuberant. If they had not been dressed in clerical clothes, they could have been taken as a bunch of seniors on a day out. There was great camaraderie. At one level, it was an organisational meeting. But at another level these men belonged to an organisation like no other. They had given up their lives for it.

We sat around in a large circle. There was one woman amongst us. She was a pastoral assistant. She and other members of the diocesan pastoral team had taken on visiting the sick and elderly: many of the priests found this difficult to do on top of their normal everyday duties. It soon became obvious that she was the heart and soul of the group of priests. She kept referring to them affectionately as 'the lads'. She knew them all by name. She was devoted to them, and they had a fondness for her. The priest who had organised the meeting introduced me and then he called on the pastoral assistant to bring them all together. She spoke softly and eloquently and asked them to be mindful of the day ahead and to let go their anxieties. She laced her words with some Christian reflections but otherwise it could have been a mindfulness session among any organisational employees. I got the impression that they knew and accepted that she was their spiritual leader.

After they all introduced and said something about themselves, I talked about the Church and what it meant to be Catholic in contemporary Ireland. This was followed by small group discussions. I joined a couple of them. There was a quiet sense of despair, that the world that they knew and the roles that they had in that world, had changed utterly. They felt out of place with the younger laity. Many felt that they were just servants, running events for people who did not believe but liked the venue and the occasion.

My memory of that meeting is of a group of elderly men caught offside by history. The great enterprise that they had bought into, had given up their lives for, was falling to pieces around them. They felt that they had little or no authority. They reminded me of old bachelor farmers who had devoted their lives to looking after the farm and their mothers while the other siblings lived the life of Reilly.

As suggested earlier, the main problem for many priests is that, quite rapidly, they have gone from being honoured, respected, revered and even adored, to becoming servants to a laity that does not engage in many Church sacraments and rituals and does not believe very much in its teachings. One of the priests told the story of how a woman came up to him before a Christening and said that while she was quite happy to go along with the service and become the child's godmother, she had no intention of seeing that the child would be brought up a good Catholic.

Religious reformation

The first era of being religious which, I have argued, lasted for tens of thousands of years, emerged from people coming together to chant, dance and sing and to do so, not for any other reason, not out of any other interest, than creating a sense of belonging. From the very beginning, what made humans different was their ability to bond together, to develop new sensibilities, to look out and care for each other. The second era was the institutionalisation of religion. This began over two and a half thousand years ago and was linked to the development of reason, science and technology. The colonisation of the religious field led to the development of religious specialists, of doctrines and dogmas and convictions by adherents that their religion is 'the' truth, that they were not just different but morally superior.

Again, the music analogy helps. Imagine a group of people saying that they had found the one, true and only way of making music, let's say for example classical music, and that all other music was just noise. Over time they become more emboldened and proclaim that listening to anything other than, for example classical music was a form of heresy and contamination. And so, to maintain the purity of the music, people could only marry those who played and listened to classical music. Children had to go to schools in which there was only classical music which they had to learn to listen to and play.

In many parts of the world today, there is an institutionally enforced religious fundamentalism that makes anything that took place in Catholic Ireland look mild. In Ireland, as elsewhere in the West, religious freedom is seen as a human right. The melting away of the power of institutional religion, has allowed hundreds of different religious flowers to grow. It is an era of religious cosmopolitanism in which differences in the ways of being religious are recognised, understood and appreciated. This third era is one of creatively mixing and matching, of bringing together different religious traditions and mixing them with more contemporary ways of being spiritual.

Gladys Ganiel has described and analysed the transformations that are taking place in post-Catholic Ireland. She sees significant changes in the way people are being religious outside of the Church. In this era of extra-institutional religion, there is less certainty and more ambiguity. Religious expression is more diverse and individualised. There is a new market of ideas, beliefs and rituals with the result that all sorts of religious flowers are beginning to bloom.[103]

The question is how prolific they are. I think there is, as I have argued, evidence of people throwing out the religious baby with the institutional Catholic bathwater. Such was the hegemony of the Catholic Church, that most people who abandon its teachings and practices, have no appetite for seeking out new ways of being religious. Having listened to the one institutional song for so long, they have decided that they are amusical. It would seem that the majority of former Catholics in Ireland make little or no effort to explore new ways of being spiritual, of coming together to share the beauties and mysteries of life, to develop rituals that enhance their feeling of bonding, belonging and enchantment. I think this may be a symptom of post-religious colonisation.

In my study the *Meanings of Life*, I met very few former Catholics who were creative in their ways of being religious. There was one exception. Joan Gallagher was raised as a Catholic but no longer believed in God. However, she believed in a spiritual realm, something other than material being. She was a member of a group of seven women who developed what she called an 'earth-based spirituality'. They had no core beliefs. When they met, about once a month, they engaged in rituals. They started by invoking the spirits which they labelled 'north, south, east and west'. They then went into drumming, chanting and moving, creating what she called a 'natural flow'. They also had a 'cleansing ritual' that used herbs such as sage and rosemary mixed with ordinary or blessed water. They celebrated Celtic festivals, particularly Brigid's day in February and they would often go out and celebrate the solstices in winter and summer.[104]

We could label this as a form of 'new age religion'. It has many of the ingredients we associate with religion. There is a coming together, to celebrate and create a sense of enchantment. There is a sense of reaching out to a realm beyond reason. The ritual creates a sense of collective effervescence that creates a collective consciousness. It makes use of traditional religious elements such as feast days and holy water. There seems to be some shared belief, but these are not clearly stated and are nothing close to doctrine. In the beginning, there must have been a very definite sense that they were transcending existing religious discourse and practice, that they were creating a new path to being attuned with each other; creating a sense of enchantment and an appreciation of nature.

It is hard to know how many groups there are like this in Ireland. But the numbers are small. The 2022 Census indicated that there were about 7,102 people who described themselves as spiritualist, pagan or pantheist.[105] There are, for example, a number of neo-pagan groups which like Joan Gallagher's group, celebrate Celtic traditions. And then there are those who belong to groups that are oriented towards witchcraft and druids that embrace numerous spirits and are oriented towards nature. Again, it is important to remember that until the emergence of the second era of institutional religion, these groups and their rituals and beliefs would have been the dominant forms of being religious. In other words, aspects of the third era of being religious, that is the post-institutional, seem to resemble some of the aspects of the first era which dominated for thousands of years before religions formed into churches, theologies and doctrines.

It is easy to understand these groups and individuals as being religious. There may be no reference to God or gods, but there is a sense of the members seeing themselves as belonging to some whole. Maybe this realm of being could be called super-natural? There are attempts to recognise, respect and revere the mysterious, enchanting beauty of the world to which they belong. This is done through symbols and rituals which become sacred and set apart from the ordinary perfunctory routines of everyday life.[106]

Are these the ingredients necessary to make it a form of religious behaviour? This brings me back to where I began. If six women stand in a space and do yoga exercises, are they not being religious? The difference may be that for Joan Gallagher's group, the rituals are an end in themselves. They are, so to speak, a pure form of religious behaviour. In the yoga class, the end is not so much about developing a new understanding and appreciation of nature, a new way of being in the world, but of being fit and healthy. There is no attempt to create a sense of awe and wonderment. There is no sense of them worshipping anything other than themselves as individuals. There is little or no collective effervescence; little or no collective consciousness other than participating in a commercial service. But it seems to me that doing yoga can, more generally, be seen as being religious. There may be little enchantment or attunement, but there can be a desire to transcend the getting, spending and controlling of everyday life.

The same might be said for meditation and mindfulness. If someone sits at the end of their garden concentrating on breathing, trying to empty their minds and just be in the world, is this religious behaviour? Or, again, is it more a means towards other ends? It may be that what makes it religious is that the orientation is towards letting go of the self that has become inhabited by the everyday and becoming calm and still and trying to become one with nature. I would argue that all of these can be seen as forms of transcendence, of seeking new ways of being spiritual and mystical and, therefore, of being religious.

There is a long tradition within the history of religion and philosophy that revolves around detachment, of trying to free oneself from the trials, tribulations and temptations of the material world. It ranges for Buddhism, to Stoicism to the other-worldly lives of Irish monks. In some respects, the culture of self-denial that I wrote about earlier, was part of this tradition. The way to self-transcendence was not through pleasure but rather asceticism, penance and a mortification of the body. I think any attempt at disengaging from the media, market and consumption combined with attempts to reconnect with nature and each other are core elements of a reformation of religion. This necessitates, a re-examination and a re-evaluation of the ways of being religious which revolve around recognising and appreciating the way people transcend themselves, the ways they become and remain attuned with each other and how they see and engage with the splendour, beauty and harmony of nature. It has much less to do with our own salvation in the next world, in heaven, purgatory or hell, and far more to do with becoming immersed, attached and attuned to nature. That if there is a God, we will not find 'him' except in and through nature.

The problem is how to find God when we live in environments in which we are increasingly distant from nature. Over the last ten thousand years, since we have begun to live in human-made environments and to be able to master and control so much of our world, the whole realm of what it is to be enchanted and connected to God and nature has changed dramatically. We now live in a world in which enchantment, wonderment and awe come less from nature and more from human creations, from fantastic constructions, computer technology and digital media, from films, games and theme parks.[107]

CHAPTER 3

A New Era of Being Religious

Attunement

For thousands of years, rituals were a key factor in maintaining a sense of collective consciousness among bands of hunter-gatherers, first in clans and tribes and, then, in the last three thousand years, in towns and villages. Among tribes, the rituals often involved long preparations, decorating the face and the body, dressing up in colourful clothes, using sacred objects and then, chanting and praying. Special foods would be prepared. There was alcohol and drugs. These rituals could be to celebrate rites of passage, seasons of the year or times of mourning; they were part and parcel of being human. Their purpose was to create a sense of emotional excitement, an effervescence, that broke through the necessities and demands of the everyday. It was engagement in collective rituals that created a sense of bonding and belonging which, in turn, created a shared sense of knowing the world, of caring for members, and with that, a sense of recognising appropriate and inappropriate behaviour, of what was right and wrong.[108] There is a circular reinforcing process at work. Collective consciousness creates rituals which create collective effervescence which, in turn, recreates collective consciousness which creates a collective conscience about what is right and wrong.

Without these rituals, without these ways of the individual surrendering to the group, family or community, without some emotional fervour of collective effervescence, it would be difficult to maintain group cohesion. Engaging in collective rituals builds and rebuilds a sense of belonging which is emotional and non-rational and predates and has little to do with theology, dogma and doctrine.[109]

The argument is simple. Whenever people gather to celebrate being a group, whether it is family or friends; when the aim is, first and foremost, to celebrate their existence as a group, when personal interests and material gain is not just secondary but seen as detrimental to the group, they are being religious. When members of a family, group or community come together, when they talk, eat, drink, sing and dance, they are being religious. There are codes, mostly soft and informal, about what can be said and done. These rituals give rise to emotions. People laugh and cry, rejoice and mourn.[110]

There may be those who argue that this has nothing to do with religion. These deniers are mostly religious leaders, bishops, theologians, priests and other specialists. They may argue that because there is no mention of God or gods, or supernatural spirits, because there is no church or theology, these celebrations have nothing to do with religion. Indeed, some would argue that to suggest that they are religious is sacrilegious. And yet it might seem ludicrous to say that a singsong in a pub is not musical, preparing a meal for friends is not cooking or a group going for a cycle is not a sport.

I would maintain that in many group gatherings and celebrations, there is a manifestation of a collective spirit. Something emerges that is beyond each individual member. Something that reaffirms them as being part of a collective, whole. Something that helps them realise that they are not alone, they are trees that are part of a wood that lives, breaths together, in which all the elements are interdependent.

The collective consciousness that emerges as part of a group is sacred. The sense of bonding, the whole which emerges, is more than the sum of individual members. Each individual member of the group is unique and so is the whole that they create. McGilchrist argues that the harmony between the one and the many is central not just to human being but to everything.

> The coming together of sameness and difference makes relation possible; and, if, as I believe, everything exists *only in relation*, this 'coming together' must be essential – at the very ground of – all there is. Harmony is the instantiation, not just of sameness and difference, but of a special creative relationship between them: in an excess of either it disappears into mere unison or mere discord.[111]

The feeling of bonding that comes from being a member of family, group or community may be universal. It exists in other species, but it would seem that it is stronger among primates when it becomes emotional and, with the development of symbols, language and rituals, strongest among humans. It would seem to have emerged as part and parcel of a system of mutual care and protection within groups. It is also a mechanism of social differentiation. 'We' belong to this group, 'we' are connected. 'Ye' belong to a different group and 'we' recognise that 'ye' are also connected. Each new generation is socialised into this way of thinking. It creates a strong sense of belonging not just among a tribe or clan but of being part of a wider society. As much as each individual in a group is different to other members, so too are groups within the social whole.

There are strong residues of this form of social classification in contemporary society, particularly rural Ireland. Individuals are identified as belonging to an extended family, for example the O'Tooles, and these would be identified as Catholic or Protestant and coming from a particular village or townland in a county. Families are also labelled as belonging to a political party. And, in rural Ireland there are pubs that are classified according to religion, class and political party.[112]

Collective effervescence

When tens of thousands of people gather to celebrate, for whatever reason, it can create a sense of euphoria and excitement. Endorphins are released. There is a sense of ecstasy. The largest gatherings in the world tend to be religious. Over two million Muslims go to Mecca every year for Hajj. In India, every six years, 20 million Hindus gather for the Maha Kumbh Mela Hindu festival on the banks of the river Ganges near Allahabad. Every twelve years, 120 million gather.

I suspect that among the millions of Catholics that came out to be with Pope John Paul II in 1979, there was a sense of being united of, literally singing from the same hymn sheet, as if they were one enormous happy family. With the force of collective energy, there is a potential for participants to act in unison and, possibly, to change the way they live their lives. It would seem, however, that the effect and sense of bonding of large gatherings does not last long. Once people go back home, they return to the same webs of meaning, to the same ways of being and thinking. The social divisions of class, race, ethnicity, religion and gender return to their default setting.

It is the same when tens of thousands of people go to a big concert or sporting event. There is a sense of euphoria, a collective high. But the sense of being one and the same quickly wears off. There are, of course, exceptions. There have been many mass gatherings that have been central to people changing their outlook and way of being. The Nuremberg rallies are, unfortunately, a classic example.

The question is that, given we are living in an age of individualism, outside of music and sports events, there are few mass gatherings that create a sense of bonding and belonging, let alone instil a lasting sense of common purpose and commitment. Is it possible for people to be roused and energised, to transcend their individual interests and concerns and seek to live a life in harmony with each other outside of these arenas?

There may be a logical contradiction at the heart of this. In cosmopolitan society what is sacred, what everyone is committed to, is the right of individuals to pursue what they see as the good life, to attain health, happiness and salvation, however they decide to look for it. This means that although I may strongly disagree with your beliefs, commitments, rituals and way of living, I recognise you have the right to live as you like as long as it does not impinge on my rights. And, of course, vice versa.

One of the consequences of this third era of being religious is that there can be a fear of engaging in rituals that may diminish or undermine self-interest. There is a fear of surrendering to the whole. It may be suffocating. Letting go and giving into the 'We' threatens to overwhelm the individual, the sacred 'I'.[113] In effect, this is what happened during the reign of the Catholic Church in Ireland: the commitment to the 'We' strangled the 'I'. But being religious has moved away from being dogmatic and fundamentalist to being open, democratic and cosmopolitan.[114] It is about being inclusive, recognising and accepting different orientations, identities, tastes and preferences and that these could be fluid and dynamic.

This seems contrary to the idea of community, that religion and being religious, revolves around individuals subsuming themselves within a great social whole. I have already suggested that collective consciousness, a sense of bonding, emerges through losing oneself to the group and that this is attained by engaging in collective rituals. So, then, is it possible for individuals to generate collective effervescence when they have fundamentally different beliefs? I think it is, because fundamentally belief – what goes on in the minds of those who gather together – is secondary to engaging in the ritual.

Every year, towards the end of summer, tens of thousands of people gather in the Nevada desert for the Burning Man festival.[115] A makeshift city is created and dismantled each year. It is an artistic celebration of life and death. People dress up. There are light shows and art installations. There is a Temple of Tears and people come with notes, photos, memorabilia and, sometimes, the ashes of loved ones who have died. At the end the Temple is burnt to the ground. Participants talk about the strong sense of community and connectivity. And participants come back. In 2019, three-quarters of the participants had been to previous burns.

What makes the festival a unique ritual is that while there are shared ideals and expectations about how people should behave – rules of etiquette that need to be followed to attain recognition, acceptance and status – there is no doctrine and there is no authority. There is a strong sense of community and, over the years, a strong sense of tradition. Only 5 per cent of the burners see themselves as religious but almost half say they are spiritual. There is a definite sense of the place being sacred. There is a general rule at the end of the festival of participants removing all matter that would be out of place. Another rule is that there is no market, no buying, selling or trading. People give and share. It is a gift economy. There is a sense of the festival being almost a professionally designed spiritual event.

Larry Harvey, one of the co-founders of the festival, studied anthropology, psychology and sociology. He wrote: 'Beyond the dogmas, creeds and metaphysical ideas of religion, there is immediate experience. It is from this primal world, that faith arises . . . . The human urge to make events, objects, actions, and personalities sacred is protean.'[116]

Perhaps it goes beyond this. If ritual is central to attunement, then maybe belief, especially doctrine and dogma, is not just secondary but irrelevant. It does not matter what is going through people's minds. It does not matter if their beliefs are similar or if they are held strongly or weakly. What matters is that through ritual, people develop a sense of bonding.

Sport as a new religion?

In the West, the largest gatherings of people that take place weekly are in sportsgrounds. This raises the issue of the extent to which sport has become the new religion. It used to be said that a family that prays together stays together. What seems to be happening in many families and among many friends is that members talk less about religion and engage less in religious rituals and spend more time watching, talking about and going to sporting events. The teams they support have become their totems. They have their emblems and wear their badges, scarves, caps and shirts. The members of the teams are revered, almost like gods. Again, returning to the notion of cosmopolitanism, while most supporters accept that other people have their teams and gods and respect their choice, there are some xenophobic fans, particularly where there are long-term rivalries, who go from chanting and taunting opposition supporters, to attacking them.

In many ways, the closest connection between religion and sport is in relation to clan and tribal identities. In hunter-gatherer societies social identity came from belonging to tribes and clans. One might belong to a tribe of the air, and within that, to the clan of the eagles. This identity and sense of belonging has little to do with spirits or gods. It is a form of social differentiation. In sport, it could be said that some people belong to the tribe of soccer and, within that, for example, to Manchester United. I can be a follower of Manchester United, have shirts, scarves and emblems of the team and meet up with other tribal and clan members to watch and discuss players and matches. This produces a sense of bonding. The talk, the songs, the chants become part of a liturgy that makes the team sacred.

Over the last two hundred years, particularly in the West, sport has seeped into people's consciousness, into their interests and concerns and what they talk about. It used to be that everyday life was based around religious time and space. The religious year was broken into different times, Lent, Easter, Advent, Feast Days and so forth. The religious day was broken up into different activities, morning and night prayers, stopping at noon and six o'clock to say the Angelus, and saying the rosary. Homes were full of religious icons, crucifixes, statues, holy pictures, holy water fonts and Sacred Heart lamps. Many people still do all of this. However, for ever increasing numbers of people the year is broken into sporting events and fixtures.

In the last fifty years, family life revolves more around sport than religion. It could be that now it is a family that plays and follows sports together that stays together.[117] And it may well be that in some families, sport time takes precedence over family time. It used to be that if religious beliefs, values and practices clashed with family, religion took precedence.[118] Increasingly it may well be that if there is a clash between sport and family time, sport takes precedence.

For many people, sport has become a quasi-religious activity that fills the gap left in social life by participation in institutional religion. For someone like my mother, being actively involved in the Church, created a sense of belonging, of being a member of a community. Going to the local church and participating in the myriads of Catholic rituals, chanting prayers and singing hymns, created a collective effervescence that is perhaps little different from soccer fans attending matches in their stadia. Sport generates its own rituals, rites of passages, myths and sense of sacredness and the possibility of self-transcendence. Sport is not just spectacular, it is extraordinary and, like religion, a suspension of ordinary time. People come to watch the gods playing against each other. But while players may be seen and treated as sporting gods, there is nothing that is supernatural or transcendental about them. Many successful soccer players, to whom fans are devoted, bless themselves and look up to the heavens when they go out onto the pitch to play. They may be gods, but the difference is that in times of trouble nobody prays to them.

Sport could, then, be seen as a form of collective consciousness, of creating a strong sense of bonding and belonging that could be seen as spiritual. It is time out from the profane world of commitment, work and strife. It is about collective exhilaration. Sport has become an important metaphor for understanding and appreciating the ups and downs, the excitements, disappointments and vagaries of life. It creates noble, heroic figures who become exemplars of character, who generate honour and respect. It develops an appreciation for competition, for playing by the rules, winning and losing. It has become a model for living a good life, for being fit and active. Fit, healthy, sporty bodies generate honour and respect. They have become a form of secular salvation, a sign of being one of the saved in the same way that pious, humble, puritan bodies were previously a sign of being one of the saved. As a form of symbolic capital, fitness blesses and legitimates other forms of capital in a manner similar to the way that religious capital previously blessed the accumulation of other forms of capital.[119]

It is easy to imagine supporters of teams, especially season-ticket holders who sit together, who meet and talk and maybe travel to away games, as somehow glued together. It may well be that any gender, class, religious, political race or ethnic divisions are transcended for those hours. And it may well be that this feeling of belonging and attachment is as fleeting and ineffectual as it is among the congregation at many Masses.

Sport may, then, fulfil many of the functions of religion, but to what extent do sport clubs constitute a moral community? Members may engage in the same rituals and have similar values and beliefs, but is that sense of community as strong as a family or small group of friends in which there is a moral obligation and commitment to look out for, care and defend other members?

In Ireland, there is plenty of evidence that the GAA has taken over many of the functions that were previously fulfilled by the Catholic Church. The GAA is deeply embedded in everyday life in every parish in Ireland. There is still a symbiotic relationship between the two, but there is a sense that the bonding that exists within the GAA community, which is often referred to as a family, is strong and deep. There are intense rivalries at local and county level, but there is also an enormous sense of identity, bonding and belonging that is fostered in schools and families. People now live in GAA, as opposed to, Catholic Church time and space. In the latter half of the twentieth century, enormous stadia that hold tens of thousands of people were built throughout the country and local parish teams have substantial clubs that are central to parish life.

Belonging

Humans can delude themselves that they are superior to any other species. They believe that because of reason, science and technology, they are able to dominate and control nature. No other species seems so close. And yet, it may be that it is because of a lack of collective consciousness as a species, a lack of being able to bond together to ensure our own survival, that we are doomed to annihilation. We know from science, and we know intuitively, that we are responsible for the climate breakdown and that we are destroying ourselves, but we cannot come together to change the way we behave. We are possessed by the drive for power, control and self-interest.

Consider, for example, the daddy longlegs that live in a cave on the Colorado river in Texas. Every evening in an act of collective survival, they come together to defeat the predatory bats who also live in the cave. The daddy longlegs live along the walls of the cave near the entrance. Their enemy, thousands of bats, live deep within the cave. As the sun sets, the bats erupt from within, a deadly cloud of attackers, heading out into the night in search of mosquitos and other insects including daddy longlegs. The hundreds and thousands of daddy longlegs would be an easy feast for the bats. But this does not happen. Once the bats begin to stir, the daddy longlegs come together and move in and out, pulsating as if they were one large organism. The second that the bats are gone, the daddy longlegs stop pulsating. Meanwhile, outside, the mosquitos and other insects, flying about on their own, are easily picked off by the bats. It is a story of emergence, of how something can come out of nothing; of how individuals can come together and form a collective being that overcomes adversity and defeats a common enemy. Many species have developed this ability to act collectively. Bees and ants are perhaps the best examples, but we can see it in the way flocks of birds fly in unison through the sky, each changing direction far quicker and more seamlessly than the most skilled air pilots.

As with monkeys and apes, the larger the number in the group, the greater the difficulty of individuals maintaining good bonds and communication. A group of friends will know each other's personalities, foibles, strengths, interests, cares and concerns. Most of us will have maybe up to four or five friends who are intimate confidants. They are close friends. Then there are maybe fifteen good friends and maybe fifty people who could be called friends. The more members in the group, the less the level of bonding and sense of attunement to each other. After friends, there may be colleagues, neighbours, members of a club or association or parish who are known through personal interaction. After acquaintances there are perhaps hundreds of people who are recognised or known by name, but little else. There would be little knowledge of their social and personal circumstances let alone their cares and concerns. In this way, while there was a sense of unity among the people who came out to be with John Paul II in 1979, it was fleeting and shallow. In many respects, the level of solidarity is like the feeling of belonging to the Irish nation that, in daily life, is more imagined than real. But it is a latent feeling that, when the nation is under threat or attack, can be a real potent force.[120]

Robin Dunbar argues that in some respects, humans are very similar to monkeys and apes. As we saw earlier, humans have lived in groups for more than a hundred thousand years, primarily as a means of protecting themselves from attack by predators or neighbouring bands of hunter-gatherers. By living in proximity, group members developed a sense of attachment. They tried not to lose contact with each other. They, literally, stayed in touch. This meant developing a web of meaning that revolved around mutual care such as mothers looking out for each other and caring for each other's offspring. It involved grooming, searching through each other's hair and bodies for ticks, nits and other invaders.[121] The grooming became a ritual. There was a time for hunting and gathering and there was a time for grooming, for grunting and groaning which, later, became laughing, singing and dancing which, later became speech and symbols that developed into language, which thousands of years later became reason and science. But from the beginning, the fundamental part of human being, was about bonding and belonging.

What makes the group strong is that every member knows, understands and, often despite their limitations and failings, puts up with other members. They know their quirks and habits. It was this mutual care and consideration, being with and thinking of the other that enabled the human brain to grow. Group members became mindful of each other. The group developed a mentality of one for all and all for one. Over thousands of years, a natural size of group evolved which enabled this sense of belonging and mindfulness to be maintained. Dunbar argues that it has remained at between 100 and 200, with an average of 150. This is still the case despite the development of communications technology.[122] This relates to the size of our brain. There is a limit to the amount of people with whom we can be intimate and emotionally close. The reason for these divisions is that maintaining a sense of bonding requires time and effort and it is done on the basis of reciprocity. Family and friends are there for each other.

Research indicates that this is the way most humans lived up to the Industrial Revolution. Even in early city states and later in towns and cities, there was a tendency for people to live in small neighbourhoods. Dunbar argues that this optimal size for human groups extends to congregations. The optimal size for a parish, he suggests is 150. This is what one priest can manage. After that it requires a team of priests. But the plateau for there to be any sense of being a parish is 300.[123] In many respects, this is similar to the way armies are structured around squads, platoons and companies.

The size of the group also relates to the extent to which members can engage in rituals which create and sustain a sense of belonging and mutual commitment. Members need to be able to witness each other's participation in rituals, the energy and commitment they bring and the sacrifices they make to sustain the group. Group loyalty and attachment is sustained by credibility enhancing displays through which members convince themselves and others of their commitment. In all of this, it is what is done that is probably more important than what is said.

Belonging within groups

I have argued that family rituals are religious. They were once enmeshed in Catholic Church rituals. Increasingly they are becoming separated. There is a similarity to family rituals everywhere. Members gather to eat, drink and chat, to celebrate, mourn and collaborate. There is no liturgy. There is no supernatural element, no stated collective belief, no shared definition of the meaning of life, no enforced rules about what it is to live a good life. It could be said that family events are close to what humans have been doing for thousands of years.

Indeed, in contemporary family rituals, there is an element of ancestor worship. Former members are remembered, and stories told about them. There may be photos that serve as reminders. And within the rituals, there are often formal moments to sacralise the occasion. Members are called to attention and a speech is made in honour of the one that is being elevated and celebrated.

The deepest and most enduring form of bonding, belonging and attunement to one another is between a couple who have lived together for a number of years. I have been living with Carol for over twelve years. I think we are the same as billions of couples who live together. We have our rituals and routines, repeated ways of saying and doing thing that create a sense of bonding. Again, I sometimes think that we are like sophisticated ants that rely on our emotional antenna. We monitor, read and assess each other's feelings. We say and do things to keep our delicate web of meaning intact. We are aware of each other's anxieties, cares, concerns and responsibilities. We live in each other's space. At the same time, I have only an approximate knowledge of what she is thinking and feeling.[124]

Our sense of bonding revolves around small rituals, of things that are said and done to maintain the sense of attachment, bonding and belonging, of sighs, smiles and laughter. Most important of all, it revolves around touch, around hugs and kisses, dancing and making love. When we are out of sync, it is evident in looks and touches, in what is said and done and not said and done. There is a myriad of signals, of non-verbal forms of communication, that reveal our emotional disposition and the extent that we are in or out of tune.

And if we become out of tune, we have developed an ability to talk things through, to describe and share our thoughts and feelings. Our attunement does not take place spontaneously. It requires a conscious effort. It means being aware of differences and inequalities, of being aware of the ways in which we dominate each other.

It may be possible that I could live at the same time with another woman, or man, and have such a deep level of intimacy. But I doubt it and the reality is that throughout the world today, and throughout history, most couples live as an item. Making love is hard work.

I can see and read these signals with close family members and friends. It takes years of intimacy to develop and maintain the ability to read and understand the other. The knowledge I have of them has been developed over many years. It is an intimate knowledge that comes through having spent time together.

The more we see rituals that create and maintain love as sacred, the greater the chance of liberating religion from institutions, from bishops and priests, from doctrine and dogma. There is also a need to protect this sacred love from the profane world of the state, the market and the media. There is, as mentioned, a limit to the number of people we can love, to whom we can be attached and attuned. However, unless the times and places in which people can love are protected, there is a danger that they will be colonised. Love is sacred. And this is why families are sacred. It is within families that love is created and maintained.

I think I am like many other people in that the people I care for most are members of my family. I 're-member' them on a daily basis. I feel connected to them through the chains of events and the memories we have created. We share thoughts, images and experiences. The sharing of these becomes a ritual which, in turn, becomes part of a family tradition that, over time, becomes sacred.[125]

The question is to what extent the love that is learnt in families can be extended to larger groups. Has this always been a problem with human societies? Can the sense of bonding and belonging, of care and commitment, that emerges with clans and tribes, be extended to members of other clans and tribes? I think it is possible to develop a level of care, concern and attunement among strangers. It is the story of the Good Samaritan in the Gospels. There is a sense of bonding that comes from being a fellow human being. These experiences can be profoundly fulfilling and life-enhancing. There are, for example, thousands of people who work for non-religious voluntary groups that involve reaching out to strangers, to those who are in need or distress or who are overwhelmed by some crisis. In many respects, this giving of oneself to a stranger is profoundly religious.[126]

I think I have some sense of attachment not just with family and friends, or with Catholics and Irish people, but with people in general. I have an understanding of the frailties and foibles of others, of what it is to be human. I get this through all the stories that are told in the media, in literature, in conversations, books, films and songs. I think, or rather hope, that this latent attunement between fellow human beings could somehow come to fruition to tackle the climate breakdown. But I think for this to happen, we need to redevelop our connection with other species, to develop an awareness of our interdependence.

I also have only a very vague understanding of what it is like to be another animal living in nature. There was a time, less than a few hundred years ago, when the vast majority of humans lived in relative harmony with nature and other species, but the rationalisation of the world, science and technology, have sent us down a different track. We have become obsessed with ourselves, with power, domination and control. I think it is possible to backtrack, to transcend the conditions of our existence, but it will need a new understanding of the meaning of life and what it means to live morally.

Touch

What makes humans different from apes and monkeys is symbolic life, language and reflective consciousness. These emerged through a division of labour. While some went out and hunted and gathered, others stayed in the group sharing tasks, nurturing and caring for each other. This led to an extended childhood in which children learnt language and how to talk and communicate. All of this was a slow process of evolution over thousands of years. As well as language, humans began to develop symbols, like the ones found in caves in France that date back 50,000 years. There is also evidence that they developed death rituals which suggests that they may have conceived of some form of afterlife.

The great leap forward came with the move from hunting and gathering to farming. Not only did group size increase but food surpluses enabled the development of specialisms. Some became warriors who devoted themselves to defending and attacking other groups. Some became medicine men, necromancers, shamans and druids who devoted themselves to maintaining bonds. This was the first era of religion.

It seems that the development of symbols and language as a form of communication began to dominate over touch. It is impossible to think of apes and monkeys being in groups, sitting around together and not touching each other. And yet among humans over the last ten thousand years, it is easy to imagine them being together, as in ancient Greece, and debating and discussing the issues of the day without touching one another. Today there is a strict etiquette about who can touch whom, when, where and how. And yet it seems to me that you cannot wipe out tens of thousands of years of development. There is still a deep yearning to touch, be hugged, caressed and fondled.

When I was young, I would wait until my father was sitting in his armchair across from the television and I would sit on the arm and ask him for a back scratch. He always agreed and I would loosen my shirt and vest from behind and his large hand would go up and down my back his nails delicately scratching the surface. Nothing was ever said. We would just watch whatever was on the television. It was a soothing experience that I have sought out over the years. It is something that took a while for Carol to get into, but now she regularly gives me massages, head and back scratches while I sit on the floor in front of the couch when we are watching television.

Touching and feeling each other is fundamental to being human. What Carol does is reverting back to what humans did in groups over thousands of years. The philosopher, Richard Kearney points out that touch is vital for well-being. Our skin is the wiretap into our brains. It alleviates anxiety, bolsters the immune system, lowers blood pressure, helps with sleep and digestion, and wards off colds and infections.[127] Touch is what links minds and bodies. It is the soul of our being. The irony is that while we live in an era in which care of the body, the obsession with being fit, healthy and beautiful, the body itself has become so sacred that, like a piece of art, it can only be observed. It is a mortal sin to touch.

And yet, Kearney argues, touch is the primary way in which humans communicate. Being open to touching and feeling is essential if we are to enhance our being in the world, to develop our sense of taste, smell, sound and vision. If we are, as he puts it, to come to our senses. He argues, however, that instead of becoming more physically connected, humans are becoming absorbed by the phones, tablets and devices that they hold on to. The retreat into on-line gaming is reducing the amount of time of physical play. The solitary eye becomes the source of one-way sensationalism.[128] He recognises the enormous benefits of digital technology, but argues that it is leading to, what he calls, increasing 'excarnation' in which humans touching each other has become increasingly difficult, awkward and politically incorrect. The tragedy is that we have externalised our bodies. They have become objects of concern. We have, as Kearney suggests, become obsessed with our bodies in disembodied ways.[129]

The exception to all this is the touching that takes place between parents and children, particularly between mothers and babies. What I liked most about being a father was the freedom to be able to play with my children, everything from hugging, to tickling to rough and tumble games. There was a gap then until Isla and Faye, my two granddaughters, arrived. I fear that if people saw the games my partner Carol and I played with them, there would be many who would tell us to act our age as we reverted to childish antics.

Touching, embracing, hugging, fondling and kissing are important ways of maintaining attachment. Couples do it. Parents do it. And friends do it, but mainly on special occasions and often quite perfunctorily. The strict codes are about who can touch who, particularly between men and women but also with children, in what circumstances touch can take place and, if permissible, how it should be done. I grew up in a society in which children and women were regularly, openly and unapologetically manhandled by men. Like the rest of the West, we have become more civilised. But there is a danger that the less we touch, the less we become attuned.[130]

It is no coincidence that as touch diminished, there was a rise in the ownership of pets. Nowadays, if people want to touch, pet and fondle, they get a cat or dog. It is not a bad way of creating endorphins and there is plenty of evidence to show that having a pet is linked to better physical and mental health.[131] There are times when I am with my dog Missy, when she greets me effusively on my return home, when she comes into my study and climbs up on my chair looking for affection, that I stop what I am doing, and I stroke and pat her, and she licks my hand. And then there is the excitement of us going out into the world together, to explore the local lane. I feel attuned with her. It is enchanting and it may well be spiritual.

The most exquisite form of touch is sex. It must be the most pleasurable and fulfilling way of generating endorphins. I have had sex regularly throughout my life, unfortunately mostly with myself. The pleasure is small. It is like eating a biscuit when I'm hungry or a glass of water when I'm thirsty. Although masturbation is probably as old as religion, it did not become an issue, a cause of religious or medical debate, until the beginning of the 18th century.[132] It is still a taboo subject in polite Irish society. It remains in the realm of the private and the personal.

The German sociologist Max Weber pointed out that in most societies religion and sex are antithetical.[133] My interest in overcoming my colonisation by the Catholic Church involved trying to overcome its teachings of when, where, how, with whom and for what purpose I could have sex. I grew up in a culture in which having sex was confined to marriage, in which the main intention was supposedly to procreate and in which anything other than the missionary position was inappropriate. I like to think that I have been successful, that I am liberal and open to all forms of sexual expression, but I think I am as repressed as most Catholic men of my generation.

When I was coming of age in the 1960s, the *Kama Sutra* was highly sought after. It described in words and graphics a world of sex that was beyond the Irish imagination. It was a celebration of the joys of sex, of taking pleasure in being erotic, of exploring different ways, different positions, in which arousal could be developed and maintained. Needless to say, it was banned in Ireland. I have no idea what reasons were given. I imagine that there being no mention of marriage and procreation was a problem. And there were all sorts of positions for intercourse beyond the missionary one which was favoured by the Church because there was less chance of precious semen being lost.

A number of years ago, I visited the Khajuraho temples in India. There are about twenty of them dotted around a three-acre site. These Hindu and Jain temples are large, some of them the size of a cathedral. They have no interiors and are characterised by the detailed carvings on the exterior walls. The carvings depict scenes from everyday life, scenes of work, family, play, dancing and art. About ten per cent of the carvings show explicit sexual and erotic scenes, mostly love making couples in various positions. Being sexual was seen as sacred.

The really interesting question is to what extent, and how, humans can regain the sense of touch and return to forms of sexuality that were prevalent up to a thousand years ago and what role religion might play in this. It may well be that we have to let go of patriarchal, institutional religion and return to more pagan forms in which nature and fertility were worshipped.

Being enchanted

There are sights, sounds, places and events that create a sense of awe and beauty that can be enveloping if not overwhelming. For me, these experiences are central to being religious. They are a reminder that religion begins with emotion with an intuitive feeling that there is something else, some whole, some cosmic consciousness.

As mentioned, one of the most enchanting places in the world are the caves of Lascuax in France with their amazing artworks. They contain detailed coloured drawings mostly of animals that date from about 30,000 years ago. Similar art works have been discovered in caves around the world. The cave paintings can be seen as part and parcel of the development of reflective self-consciousness, of the externalisation and symbolisation of the natural world within which humans were evolving. They are a reflection of the enchanting, mysterious world in which they were living. They capture the inexplicable, beautiful wonders of the world.[134]

There is a commonality. Only a small proportion of the drawings were of fellow humans. Almost all were depictions of the animals, bison, horses, aurochs and deer, many of whom they hunted. What was the intention of the cave painters? It could have been a practical exercise: externalising and depicting the animals with which they lived so as to better understand and learn how to get meat and, at the same time, how to avoid becoming meat. Or maybe it had more to do with meaning, of symbolising the world as a means of understanding and appreciating the mystery of life. Maybe it was the creation of an enchanting spectacle and people came there to learn to paint and to depict scenes that become animated in the light of a fire as the flickers of flame danced on the ceiling. I can imagine the sense of awe that was created when these flickering images were accompanied by the sounds of chanting and drumming. Maybe this sense of enchantment was enhanced by eating the psychedelic mushrooms they found growing wild. And all of this created feelings of effervescence that were central to them bonding.[135]

The caves were part of the first era of religion. Over the next 30,000 years, humans created similar spaces for, it would appear, no other reason than to symbolically recreate the enchantment of the world. They spent years and vast fortunes creating temples, churches, mosques and synagogues. I still get shivers of enchantment when I enter these sacred places. They are enormous reservoirs of reverence and emotion. They are places in which people have been sad, happy and ecstatic. Places that have created a collective effervescence. Places that have created a sense of beauty and harmony.

People, many of whom might profess to being secular, go there for the experience, to be inspired by the wonders and mysteries of life. And it is easy to think that because there are so few new churches and temples being built, that this is evidence of the demise of religion. I am not so sure. I think that many town centres, shopping malls and sports' stadia have become places to which people go to be enchanted as well as night clubs, galleries and concert halls, restaurants, cafés and pubs. One of the small revolutions in Ireland was in the 1960s when young people found enchantment and wonder in the dancehalls, most of which were bleak, concrete structures, that mushroomed all over the country.

The search for enchantment, to be somewhere magical, to be captivated and overwhelmed, to feel part of something greater than oneself, is at the heart of being religious. We are used to associating these feelings with traditional, religious sites. But wherever people gather and lose themselves to music, dance and chanting and, thereby, to each other, and the more often they do this, and the more it becomes ritualised and forms a tradition, the more it becomes religious. And it is in this sense, that as much as people can make a heaven out of hell, something that seems plain and drab, can become magical. Add some lighting and music, and maybe some drugs, and the most innocuous concrete structure can be a magical theatre in which people lose themselves.

It seems to me that one of the major revolutions taking place today is a greater recognition of the sacredness of nature. That whatever feelings of enchantment we get from being in sacred places, nothing compares to being in nature. The beauty and the power of nature can be awesome, mesmerising and overwhelming. It is something that is appreciated from early childhood. It is an intense experience. It is something that is learnt but not taught. As mentioned earlier, I grew up in a large old estate house that had an enormous well-organised, beautiful garden that my father had created. It had lawns surrounded by flowerbeds, vegetable and fruit plots. Around the edge of the garden, there were enormous cedar trees, some of them fifty feet tall.

I tried to climb them all, but some were impossible as they were too dense. But there were four which became favourites. There was a great sense of achievement and excitement reaching the top and being able to look down over the other houses and gardens of the avenue. The lawn was also surrounded by an array of apple and pear trees. Again, some of these were more climbable than others. There was a large Bramley apple tree that was my favourite. It was in the bottom right-hand corner of the lawn. Beside it there was a small orange pippin that produced large, luscious apples and beside it a conference pear that often got so laden with fruit that the branches would reach down to the lawn. The Bramley produced the best cooking apples but that was not why it was my favourite. As I climbed towards the top, three branches came together to form a kind of armchair.

There was little to see from the armchair, but I liked to be there. I cannot remember when or why the habit began, but I would often climb up and sit in the armchair. It was my sanctuary within paradise. I cannot remember how long I sat there. I cannot remember my thoughts. I do remember storming out of the house and sitting in the tree after a row with my mother. I remember vowing never to go back into the house again. To never go back to her. I have no idea how long I lasted. I was caught in time and space, but I was a wilful child. When I think of myself then, I like the idea that somehow the tree was aware of my presence. That somehow the tree felt me. That there was some connection. It is, of course, magical thinking. It is a bit like thinking about God. But the difference was that in that tree, God was not external. I was in the tree and the tree was in me.[136]

Magical thinking

We might yearn to be more attuned to the world of nature and to live in an enchanted world, but we would find it very difficult to live a life that was even close to the palaeolithic man described by Charles Foster. It may be full of wonder, but it would be a much more unpredictable, fearful and violent world. Outside of war, over the last two and a half thousand years, the world has become, a much more reasonable and civilised place. This is not just because science and technology has brought more control but, as we saw earlier, there has been a rationalisation of almost every aspect of everyday life in the worlds of economics and politics, in organisational life and in wider society.[137] The decline in magical thinking can be linked to the decline in fear of the supernatural. The notion of hell and a wrathful, punishing God is disappearing.

Max Weber developed the concept of 'the iron cage of rationalism' to describe the disenchantment of the world.[138] Reason and science frame how we see and understand the world. They have been central to our interest in mastering and controlling the environment and creating social order. We don't expect nature to be reasonable, but we don't like it when people behave unreasonably in interpersonal relations, particularly in bureaucratic organisations. Even in the Catholic Church there is, as we saw earlier, a time and place for magical thinking.

But I am not sure if the world has become as disenchanted as Weber believed. The enchanted world of magic and miracles often sits alongside the world of reason and science. There is a time to be magical and a time to be rational. For some people there is little or no contradiction operating in systems that have very different logics. Reasonable people believe that it is bad luck to walk under a ladder, that bad things happen on Friday the 13th or if they see a black cat crossing their path.

I don't think of myself as engaging in superstitious, magical thought. But when Aileen was dying, I discovered that it was a way of thinking and being that, regardless of my attempts, enveloped me. I became obsessed with magpies. They seem to have always been a part of my life. We grew up together. I was socialised into their logic. 'One for sorrow, Two for joy.' It went on: 'three for a girl, four for a boy.' The rhyme goes on up to 'eight for heaven, nine for hell and ten for the devil's own self.' But in the folklore in which I was immersed, it was always whether there were one or two. I think it was my mother who first introduced me to them, telling me that it was a magpie who had stolen her ring. My uncle Bryan was obsessed with them. He told me that one day, in a desperate attempt to see a second magpie, he had driven his car into the ditch.

When Aileen got ill, the magpies and their illogical, magical world began to dominate me. In those dark days of deep despair, I was weak and vulnerable. I was desperate to see good omens. I remember vividly one bright June morning, when I cycled into Mount Carmel hospital, there was a sole magpie right below Aileen's bedroom window. It stood there proud, majestic with a cool disdain for me. I am certain that every morning I went into see Aileen, it was there, casually hopping around in the early morning sunlight, as if it knew it was a bad omen and took delight in stalking me. All those mornings, afternoons and evenings while Aileen struggled to come to terms with her cancer and the prospect of death, the magpie strutted its stuff on the lawn beneath her.

Six hours before she died, as she grimaced and struggled to avoid slipping off the crevice into the abyss of death, I found it hard to know what to say. I sang 'Some Enchanted Evening'. She complained that she could not dance. I felt the need to keep talking. I told her that she was beginning a journey down through the beautiful garden she had created, that it was full of beauty and that at the end there was a gate and that if she went through the gate, I would soon follow after her.

It was magical thinking. Did I believe in it? Not really. Did I hope it was true? Yes. Did Aileen? I don't know. I don't think so. She believed in some spiritual world, that somehow our energy or souls did not die with our bodies. But, like many things when it comes to being religious, there was no coherency to her thinking.

Aileen had peculiar beliefs. She did not believe in God or life after death, but she did believe in spirits and that a person's spirit lingered on earth, particularly in the places they had lived, long after their death. In the year before she died, she was put in contact with a shaman. She arranged for him to come to our house. I arranged to be away. When I returned, she told me that he was not what she had expected. He was in the army. He had trained with American Indians.

He undertook a complete investigation of the house and found that there were bad spirits in the far side of our bedroom that would have to be cast out. He was coming back the following week to do this. He told Aileen that he would have to meet me. I presume he thought I might be the source of the bad spirits. I was very reluctant, but I agreed.

When he arrived, there was nothing much different about him. He was in his late thirties, tall and well-built. The only thing that was different was that he had intense, piercing, light blue eyes that could have belonged to an animal. Aileen had told me that, as with her, he would need to sniff me out. And so, shortly after he arrived, he got me to stand still in the middle of the living room. He walked towards me slowly, staring into my eyes. He came right up to my face and then he began sniffing. He started with my face. There was no chanting, just his heavy breathing. He moved down around my chest and down around my arms. When he got to my waist, he dropped down on his hands and knees and went down my legs to my feet. He then moved in behind me and went up my back. When he was done, he announced that I was clean and went up to clear out the bad spirits in the bedroom.

I am not sure to what extent magical thinking enhances our ability to connect with nature and God. It may well be that the more we are just in the world, and not trying to master and control it, the more we are open to the type of magical thinking that was intrinsic to the way our ancestors lived in the world. There is a fine line between magical thinking and our inherited, intuitive knowledge of nature.[139] Both have a disposition to being open to the world, to uncertainty and not knowing, rather than wanting to be precise and definite, to being able to master and control. We tend to think of animism and seeing nature and the world as alive with spirits not just as outdated, but unacceptable. There is a naïve belief that the puzzle of why things are the way they are, will eventually be solved by science. But animism is not false. It is rather a way of seeing and being in nature, as seeing ourselves as part of some mysterious whole, rather than detached from it.[140]

CHAPTER 4

God and Nature

The question of God

For tens of thousands of years, the idea that there is a supernatural realm beyond the material reality in which we operate, has been central to being religious, to the meaning of life and how to live a good life. It has been central to the way in which people know and understand each other and the world in which they live. But what exactly people believe, and how much it influences how they live their lives, varies enormously. While there is a growing minority that believe that God is a figment of our imagination, there are billions of people, the vast majority of the world's population, who firmly believe that God exists.

The hope that there is something beyond the mundane problems of everyday life, remains at the core of what it is to be human.[141] It is reflected in the innocent question of children of what happens when people die, and it is reflected in the simple question that has puzzled philosophers as to why there is something rather than nothing. The notion of what God is varies across cultures and changes over time. The notion of there being one omnipotent God is a recent development. It may well be that, with the climate breakdown and a concern for our being in nature, there will be a return to animism in the third era of being religious.

I am ambiguous about God. My belief is unpredictable. It is weak one moment, strong the next. I am full of contradictions. I don't believe that when I die, I will be with God in heaven. Neither will I be with Luke and Aileen or all the people I love and have loved. I like the idea of heaven being a perfect, blissful space in which good people, and I would think of myself as one of them, are united with all those they have loved. But I think it is unreasonable. It is magical thinking.

My ambiguity about God is reflected in whether or not to use the word God as a means of putting a name on that which is so mysterious, enormous and significant and, yet, ineffable. It is trying to name that which cannot be named, but only felt and intuited. Instead of using the term God, I could use Nature, the Whole, the Cosmos, the Eternal. Over the last two and a half thousand years, God has become the most used name. The problem is that putting a name on something, necessarily, limits and controls understanding. It implies that everyone is agreed about what God is. And yet, for me, God cannot be defined. It is an intuition and feeling. My feeling of what God is, is different from yours, in the same way that my consciousness of reality is not the same as yours.

During the second era of being religious, the concept of God was colonised by institutional religions. The God into which I was socialised was a very Catholic one. It was a very patriarchal, judgemental, interventionist entity. God decided who, after death, would live a blissful, eternal life in heaven and who would suffer eternal pain in hell. Although my conception of God is very different, I have decided to use the term, not just because it is the most common, but also because I want to connect with the billions of believers whose conception of God is different from mine.

I don't believe in heaven or hell, but I do believe I am part of something extraordinary. That there is some force, some presence, some whole, of which I am a part. For humans, this whole has always been, and will always be, a mystery. The beauty and the wonder of the world is that, although billions of words have been written about the nature of the Cosmos, the whole or God, nobody *really* knows. The reality is that God, if that is what we call the whole, is not known rationally but felt. It is an intuitive knowledge.

And this is what makes the God question so fundamental and problematic. The notion of what the whole is and who knows the whole, has been one of the driving forces of history. It has brought people together, created joy and happiness but, at the same time, almost inevitably, it has created division, hatred, conflict and war.

For a long time, my speculation about the nature of the whole revolved around the big bang when, it would seem, everything began. Leaving aside the issue of how something could emerge from nothing, the notion of the big bang is a mystery. Speculative science suggests that if it had happened a fraction of a second earlier or later, we would not be here today. Our universe would have collapsed. I find this mind boggling. Surely, the universe, this reality in which we are immersed, could not have emerged by pure chance?[142] And then, there is the idea that there could be millions of other universes as well as our own. So, whatever the whole is, whatever God is, goes way beyond my conception of time and space.

As well as going back in time and out into space, I sometimes turn inwards and try to imagine my own being. I see myself as having a definite existence. This involves a physical body that extends in space and time and a mind that is self-conscious, that thinks, imagines and reasons. I see myself as just a tiny, momentary, miniscule particle that emerged as part of the big bang. And yet, this tiny particle is made of millions of billions of cells that are made up of billions of atoms which, in turn, are made up of billions of infinitesimally smaller particles. If I think from the viewpoint of one of these particles, my body would be the size of a galaxy, and the pimple on my nose the size of a planet.

I try to imagine a cell in my body. It is part of a complex flux. It depends on trillions of other cells that have come together to be me. Like every other cell, it has a purpose.[143] I then make a leap and imagine all these cells somehow being aware that they are part of some enormous whole that is me. But try as they might, they can only gain an approximate knowledge of me. They do not have the senses, the attributes, to decipher the nature of this body of which they are a part.[144] In some respects, I think that these cells are like humans. They are imperfect. They do not live in harmony. There is a battle for self-realisation. Some cells are dangerous. If they become dominant, they will kill me.

So, all the molecules and cells which compose me are busily going about their business inside of me and I am unaware of their existence. And yet, they are in me as much as I am in them. There are ongoing births and deaths of these molecules and cells which will, eventually, lead to my decline and death. This is no different from the birth and death of all finite things from cells to stars to galaxies and universes. I have this feeling that if these cells could see, understand and know me, that they would be astounded. I suspect that, like me and nature, they would have no idea that they were part of some whole, some infinite being. I am beyond their imagination. But I exist. The whole, call it God, is beyond my imagination, but the whole exists.

The issue of God or the whole is embedded in the notion of consciousness which itself is a mystery.[145] I know that I am conscious as I know you are conscious, but I have no real idea of your consciousness, of your sense of self, your sense of the world. I suggested above that cells may be conscious. I think what makes me different is that I am conscious of being conscious. I am self-conscious. I can reflect about being conscious, but cells cannot.

I have some very fuzzy ideas about how self-consciousness emerged among human beings. I think the answer lies in language, symbols and rituals. People came together and celebrated being part of this mysterious whole. This bound them together and led them to speculate about the nature of the whole of which they were a part. They began to name the world, and they began to classify the mysterious forces of nature into spirits and gods. It was only a matter of time before this self-consciousness not only made humans feel different from other species, but superior.

Are the ants, like the ones David Attenborough was looking at, in some way conscious? We can say that they act instinctively, but it seems to me that they are very conscious of each other. And then what of plants? They have some form of communication, but are they conscious of each other and, if so, how does this consciousness relate to human consciousness? And then I get all confused when it comes to feelings. When did they emerge? I can accept that animals have feelings. But do plants? And then, how do feelings relate to consciousness and being part of something else, call it nature, God, the eternal, the cosmos?

The realistic or scientific view of existence is that the emergence of consciousness was nothing more than a random collision of atoms. I myself, you the reader, all of us and everything that exists, is a random emergence from the big bang. This was the conclusion of Lucretius, a Roman poet who lived in the first century CE. The notion that 'there is no end or purpose to existence, only ceaseless creation and destruction, governed entirely by chance,' can be seen as either very deterministic and pessimistic or liberating.[146] The problem for me is that this materialist perspective does not explain how consciousness and non-material entities such as love, truth, goodness and beauty, emerged.[147]

The philosopher Phillip Goff holds that consciousness did not emerge over time but that it has always been there. It is eternal. It is in everything. The universe is conscious. Cells are conscious, as are rocks. Human consciousness is part of this consciousness. This is a traditional panpsychist position. But Goff goes further and argues that the universe is purposeful. Every cell in my body has a purpose. Up to now, we have linked this purpose to an all-knowing, all-powerful, transcendent God who created the universe. The task, as Goff sees it, is to transcend this way of thinking of God as external and transcendental and, through forms of communal spirituality, become open to this cosmic purpose. He is optimistic. 'My hope is that cosmic purposivism may point to a new optimism in human potential, a faith not based on dogmatic certainties but on a humble and open exploration of an unfolding purpose we don't yet fully understand.'[148]

The purpose of life, then, could be to become attuned with the cosmos. To go with the flow of time and space and accept we are insignificant. I can see that my existence came about because, at one tiny, arbitrary moment in time, one of the million sperms of my father's made it up into my mother's womb and fertilised one of the millions of her eggs. Like the universe itself, if my conception had been a millisecond earlier or later, I might not be here today or, at least, it would be a different me. This is humbling. I often think of myself as being at the centre of the universe but, in reality, I am just an arbitrary moment. And yet, I think Goff is right, I think the universe has a purpose, as do I.

In some respects, I think the purpose in my life is to try to transcend my understanding of nature, my connection with it, and my way of being in the world. It is like being on an ever-ending road. I know I will never come to an end, that I will never find an answer. And yet, for me, searching for the truth, trying to tell the truth about myself, and being true to myself, is part of who I am. I am trying to find a solution to an unsolvable problem. I am like a character in a Beckett play. I go on searching, reading, writing, looking, examining, peering into the grass, trees and hedgerows, bathing in the light between the clouds. It is this continual search for truth, for transcendence, which is spiritual and religious.[149]

There are times when I think there is little between atheists and theists. For many atheists, since there is no God, there is no beginning and there is no end. For many theists like me, since God is infinite and whole, there can have been no beginning and there can be no end. Everything is, has been and will always be part of this eternal whole. Whatever this whole is, the world in which we live is full of mystery and paradox.

There is conflict and violence, but there is also shared meaning. We value that which is good, true and beautiful.[150] Whether one is a theist or atheist, it is this mysterious whole, that should be our greatest treasure, our highest shared value.

Towards the end of *The Matter with Things*, Iain McGilchrist emphasises the need to redevelop a sense of the sacred. He accepts that most of our notions of what is sacred have come from religious traditions. So, the task is to learn from these traditions without becoming dogmatic.

> I am not trying to revamp some version of a cosmological or ontological 'argument' for the existence of God. I am merely indicating that, whatever we choose to call it, there is certainly more here than we have words for, or can expect ever to understand using reason alone. Such an expectation would itself be irrational. The proper response to this realisation is not argument, but awe. To be human, in my view, is to feel a deep gravitational pull towards something ineffable, that, if we can just for once get beyond words and reasons, is a matter of experience.[151]

Being Reasonable about God

I am not a philosopher, let alone a metaphysician or logician and yet, to try to solve the puzzle about God, or at least to develop an understanding that I can share, that goes beyond my experience, I have to rely on reason. I recognise, however, that any reasonable knowledge I develop, any words I use, will only be an approximation of this experience and that because it is logical, rational and scientific, there will be cracks, inconsistencies and even contradictions in my reasoning. And there will be cracks in the reasoning of others.

And this is where it gets difficult. I don't believe in the devil or hell. I don't believe in a God who intervenes in this world. However, I recognise and accept, and I think it is reasonable, for people to believe in an external, transcendental God who does participate in and direct the world. And, to go further, I think it is reasonable that all-knowing, all-powerful God could have become human. I think it is part of the human condition and the development of reason to think this.[152]

While it is reasonable to think that Jesus was the son of God, I don't believe it. I think that Jesus, like many prophets before and after him, was a very holy man and that he had plenty of good advice about how to live a good life. I believe that Jesus died on the cross, but I don't believe he rose from the dead.

And this is where religion and being religious gets a bad name. I am fearful when other people say, whatever their religious belief, that they know the truth about God and that they are as certain about this truth as they are that the sun will rise in the morning. I am fearful of dogmatists and fundamentalists. Worse still are those who declare that the beliefs I have are not only false, but the values I have and the way I live my life, are a source of contamination and that I pose a threat to them.

As soon as belief slips into dogmatism, it is easy to become righteous and tyrannical. And it is easy and often comfortable to live in a cocoon of unquestioned beliefs that are held to be true, that cannot be transcended, that cannot be penetrated by new ideas, experiences or ways of being.

If there is no definitive, eternal truth about God, the whole or the cosmos, and if I accept that your understanding of God is as acceptable or as good as mine then, the only way to avoid religious conflict, is to follow a version of the golden rule that says since I don't want you to impose your beliefs on me, I should not impose my beliefs on you.[153] I think it is necessary to accept that, since any knowledge of God is based more on emotion, experience and intuition than on reason, there are potentially as many understandings of God as there are individuals. Each of us has our own conception of God and each of us has a right to have this personal understanding. More importantly, this must be a universal right.[154]

But we do not live in a cosmopolitan religious world in which, when it comes to the notion of God, the whole or the cosmos, people are free to believe what they like. The symbolic and often violent domination that the Catholic Church exercised for so long in Ireland is evident in many societies around the world today. This dominance was part and parcel of the institutional era of being religious. It was perhaps little different from what happened, elsewhere for example, in Islam and Judaism. The problem is one of power. Religious domination and violence occur when people's firmly held beliefs and practices, usually those of the majority, impinge on the rights and freedoms of others, usually the minority. In many respects, it is no different from social, political and economic domination, and is often allied with them, it is just that it operates symbolically.

This is not to deny that religious beliefs and values can play an important role in a mature, democratic, civil society, particularly in terms of creating and maintaining shared values. People can be religious in any way they wish, they can find inspiration and fulfilment however they like, but when it comes to being part of wider society, they, and the religious institutions to which they belong, have to be able to rationally defend their beliefs in the court of human reason, especially when their rituals, beliefs and values impinge on others.

The big question, then, is how, given that most world religions are doctrinal and dogmatic, particularly Judaism, Islam and Christianity, is it possible for members to transcend their institutional beliefs and practices and to develop a shared understanding of what it is to live morally. Is it possible for humans, regardless of their personal beliefs and practices, to develop a shared understanding of what it is to be human?

In *Anatheism*, Richard Kearney explores the space between, on the one hand, 'militant atheism' and the quest to root God out of human thinking and being and, on the other hand, 'dogmatic theism' and the absolute certainty that not only does God exist, but that it is possible to know God and how 'He' thinks. If there is to be transcendence between these two extremes, it must begin, he argues, with an acceptance and admittance of 'not-knowing'. This begins with critical self-reflection which is at the heart of transcendence. It involves being able to question and challenge those who are certain that they do know the truth about God.[155]

I think, to avoid being dogmatic, there is a need for those who believe in God, to be open to the notion of what God might be and, consequently, the notion of what it is to be religious. Kearney believes in God. But he believes that the notion of a father figure in heaven is dead. Whatever God is, 'He' is beyond the cosmos as we know it. 'He' transcends the material, natural world. Kearney argues that this notion of God is found in Judaism, Christianity and Islam and, to a certain extent, in Hinduism and Buddhism. For Kearney, whatever God may be, it is a feeling. God is experienced in our bones, in our moods, affects, senses and emotions, before it becomes interrogated in language, theology and philosophy.[156] The question, then, is how to know something which can be sensed, that can be imagined, but is, to a certain extent, beyond reason and certainly beyond science.

We will never be able to know God in the same way that we know each other or the material world in which we live, but there are, and have always been, glimpses, insights, signs that can be read that give us a knowledge, or a sense, of what God might be like. It is through being open to these signs that we can transcend ourselves. For Kearney, the most important of these is the stranger, the 'other', the one who is different, not like us. The other can be an exotic, erotic, enchanting, charismatic figure who inspires us to change the way we live, or the other can be seen as a threat who instils a sense of fear, loathing and hatred. But the real challenge is to open up to those who, at first glance, put us off, who we see as threatening. To transcend ourselves we must reach out and invite them into our world, to provide them with hospitality.

We can find God and experience the awesomeness of the whole in the small moments of everyday life, in the way we see things differently, in the way we imagine, in the way we can laugh at life and with each other, in the way we make commitments and stay loyal and in the way we reach out and provide love, shelter and care to the stranger. We also can find God in letting go of our deeply entrenched notions of what God is, of being open to other notions, other traditions, beliefs and rituals. We can find God in the beauty of the mundane, in everyday life and the way in which this complex, fleshy world is revealed in the words of literature and poetry. We can find God in music, art and dance. We can find God in hugging and making love. Finally, we can be inspired by people who have transcended the way they were living in the world and who provide us with insights and examples of what it is to be good, especially in the way they reach out, welcome and provide hospitality to those who might be poor, marginalised or excluded. I think this continual attempt to reach out, understand and appreciate the 'other' – the one which we are not, those who don't belong to our way of being – is central to transcending the fear of the other, a fear that is easily turned into mistrust and hatred.

Being spiritual

Being spiritual and mystical is at the heart of being religious. It is going beyond the profane world of the everyday, of communicating, giving opinions, sharing information, attending to duties and responsibilities, working, learning, achieving, getting and spending. For most of us, most of the time, we are suspended in webs of meaning that are spun from a practical knowledge of the world.

Being spiritual is about transcendence, about going beyond received wisdoms, inherited, unquestioned truths about the world, about God and nature. It is about going beyond the institutionalised knowledges and what might be called passive learning. It is about questioning and challenging. But to be spiritual, there has to be a determination to change, to seek new truths about oneself.

If I am to get to the truth about myself, I have to be willing and able to change, to transform and shift my way of being and thinking, to the extent that I become other than myself. I can do this through love. I can also do it through a practice of self-discipline or asceticism. I can give up bad habits. I can fast and abstain. I can take up an exercise regime or maybe go on a pilgrimage. When I engage in disciplined care for myself, I might find the truth that will not only transform me, but it will also make me feel fulfilled and at peace with the world.[157]

As we saw earlier, Michel Foucault suggested that truth does not come about solely by thinking alone. There is a physical dimension. It requires mental and physical effort. Think of the early Christian monks going to live on Skellig Michael, or martyrs like Julian of Norwich and Theresa of Avila. The aim is to attain peace and tranquillity by controlling their desires, passions and emotions. They try and enter and stay in a space that is not of this world, but rather to be in the world of God or nature. We can call these mystics.[158]

The history of religion is full of groups, sects, cults that have attempted to transcend the world by becoming detached from it. They have broken away from mainstream churches and provided alternative ways of under-standing the meaning of life and of being religious. In the West, from after the end of WWII, there was a small explosion of what became known as 'new religious movements'.[159] Many of these were based on the importation of Eastern religious traditions, particularly Buddhism and Hinduism. There have been numerous new religious movements, such as the Moonies, who try to withdraw from the world which they see as sinful and evil. And then there are new age religions in which people live in communities such as Findhorn in Scotland, who eschew doctrine and are oriented towards living simple lives that are embedded in nature.

There are other, less radical, mystics, who realise that the way to flourish is to accept the necessity of being in the world, the need to work and make a living, but who seek ways of breaking their habits of being, of avoiding being sucked into the profane world of getting and spending by taking time out to be mystical or spiritual. There is an acceptance of being in the world, but the way to transcendence is to take time out to be still, to be in God, to be in nature.

I think this pertains to many people in Ireland today. It may come from doing yoga, meditation or, like Joan Gallagher and her group that we met earlier, chanting and singing. It may come from being in prayer groups, going on retreats and pilgrimages. It may come from kneeling and praying in a Church. And it may come from walking down a country lane. We could call this a form of inner-worldly spirituality, of engaging with the world, but taking time out to withdraw from it.

Another way to be spiritual is to be actively involved in helping those in need, in caring for the sick, poor and marginalised. In this way, one transcends oneself through the other. It brings people beyond the world of self-concern into a spiritual realm of self-sacrifice. Some are more disciplined in their approach. There is a whole host of Catholic religious orders, lay groups such as the Vincent de Paul as well many other lay charitable groups and organisations, who follow this path to transcendence. Many of these people feel they are doing God's work. I think my aunt Joan was a good example of this orientation, always looking to see how she could be in the service of others, all the time seeing herself as being a good Catholic and honouring and worshipping God.

But, as we saw earlier, it is not necessary to be a member of a religious group to attain this spiritual experience. They are many people who reach out and care for others who are not members of a religious group. The Samaritans are one example, but there are many others. And, of course, it is not necessary to be a member of any group. There is often a sense of spiritual well-being that comes from helping others in need which may be enhanced by them being strangers. This sense of well-being can also come about with helping animals and plants.

For others, being spiritual is achieved through self-discipline. This is very much self-centred and inner-worldly. It has little to do with caring for others or about being in God or nature. It is about working hard, being responsible, and controlling appetites, desires and passions. It makes you feel good about yourself. There is a sense of joy. A sense of being a good person.

This orientation is associated with Calvinism, Presbyterianism and other less institutionalised forms of Protestantism. It is based on the notion that if God is all-knowing then it is already known who will be saved and who will be damned. The aim, therefore, is convince oneself that one is going to be saved by living a life of hard work, frugality and abstinence. It is about stiving to be a good person by transcending self-indulgence. Someone might be successful by dedicating themselves to, for example, art, music, literature, sport, a craft, a trade or profession. Finding one's soul comes from dedication to one's work, rather than a craving for wealth, power, recognition or status. But there are many inner-worldly ascetics who seek to improve and flourish but have little or no interest in salvation in another life. If there is salvation, it is only in this world.

I think there is a link between transcendence and becoming unstuck from the glue of being and thinking into which we have become socialised and habituated. It revolves around a conscious attempt to change the patterns, strategies and tactics of our everyday lives. Following Foucault, I think the problem with knowing the world through literature, philosophy, psychology or sociology or any scholarly discipline, is that they all have their ways of framing, asking and answering questions. Being spiritual, on the other hand, involves some kind of challenge to existing ways of thinking which often involves some kind of physical engagement. It could be walking around a gallery, listening to music, walking across a mountain, going into a Church. It could be sitting looking at a candle. It could be just being still.

Maybe, most of all, being spiritual revolves around making love. It is not about the technology of having sex but more about trying to dissolve oneself in the flesh of the loved one. It is in the surrender of two bodies to each other that something else emerges that is neither one of them. It could lead to the creation of new life, but more often than not, it is two people flourishing in each other's fleshy company. I think this form of spirituality probably dates back to hunter-gathering times, when humans had more time to languish in each other's arms. It would seem that this way of being became diminished with the emergence of private property, reason and institutional religions.[160]

Being spiritual and mystical, then, is not necessarily about a Christian monk engaging in some penitential practice. Nor is it necessarily about sitting still and meditating. It may involve reaching out and caring for those who are poor, marginalised or oppressed. Whatever the path, it is about searching for new truths, of transcending inherited ways of being and thinking. For me, the way of transcending myself, of being mystical and spiritual, is trying to be more in nature.

Being in nature

I mentioned earlier how Ireland is full of holy mountains, lakes and wells. The writer and documentary maker, Manchán Magan, has documented the customs and beliefs of many of these. He writes, for example, about the power of Louch Gur in south Limerick near the border with County Cork. On his first visit there, an elderly local man, who Magan had come across by accident after his car broke down, invited him into his old cottage. He recognised Magan from a television documentary he had made. He took Magan to a spot near the gable wall of the kitchen and told him to stand still. Magan did as he was told and, instantly, he felt a most unusual sensation running up his spine. 'It was like a chill that ran from my coccyx straight up into my skull and made me feel nauseated, but there was also a mildly expansive, buzzing type of sensation in my forehead that was more pleasant.'[161] In all his travels around the world, Magan said he had never encountered anything like it. The local man attributed the sensation to the Goddess Áine.

Magan tells us that Ireland is full of goddesses and spirits. They are associated with rivers, trees, mountains, hills, caves, stones, ring forts and bogs. These pagan beliefs and practices were systematically ousted by a scientific interest in mapping, grabbing, owning and controlling the land and by Christianity and the Catholic Church which wanted to eliminate ancient forms of worship, to reduce the supernatural to being governed by one God, and to confine the divine to churches. Magan argues that 'our rational minds will want to dismiss them all as the imaginings of a pre-modern people, and yet everything that science is now telling us points to the fact that the world is a lot more indeterminate and wonder-filled than we ever imagined.[162] He argues that a return to pagan practices is not only good for our well-being – as with standing on one leg, there is scientific evidence to prove this – it also helps guide us to a more sustainable relationship with the land.[163]

Not all mapping is about legal ownership and control of the land. In his depictions of the Connemara landscape, Tim Robinson produced exquisite, detailed small-area maps depicting paths through local mountains, valleys, rivers and lakes. These were accompanied by legends, stories of people, of saints, druids, fairies and ghosts, and of mysterious, miraculous events. Many of the stories revolved around holy wells, mountains and rivers. The whole ethos of Robinson's writings and maps can be seen as an attempt to reconnect with landscape, to learn how to pay attention, to be mindful of the fauna, flora and history of a place, to learn the language of the people and the way they see and understand their habitat.[164]

There is a natural woodland around Lough Meelagh in which I like to go walking. In winter, the trees are covered with layers of deep green lichens. The complex of oaks, ashes, alders and birches as well as many shrubs, some which stand tall and strong, some of which have fallen to the ground with age or because of a storm, create a mesmerising, enchanting mosaic that is illuminated by the light of the low-lying sun. I sometimes get a feeling of what it must have been like to live and survive in these woods as millions of my ancestors did. It is a feeling of being part of some mysterious, magical whole of which I know little. I keep walking but I think that if I stayed there, for a day, let alone for a week or month, I would grow to see and understand the wood very differently.

It seems to me that our knowledge and understanding of nature changed radically when we stopped being hunter-gatherers and began to develop a knowledge of plants and animals that, in turn, led to technologies that enabled us to master and control the world. The land and other species were there to be exploited for our gain. It helped, of course, that not long after that Christian theologians and priests told us that humans had not just a God-given right to harness nature to our ends, but a moral command to do so.

I think that Darwin threw a spanner into the Christian way of thinking. He turned our knowledge and understanding of nature upside down. Whatever about the idea of creating the earth for the benefit and pleasure of humans, the idea that God did this in seven days was difficult to believe. But even after a hundred and fifty years, the idea that nature is there to be exploited by humans is still rampant and is propagated by many religious specialists.

Darwin shone a light on how little we know and understand nature and that realisation is growing all the time. In *Underland*, Robin McFarlane tells the story of Suzanne Simard, a Canadian forest ecologist. In the 1990s, she linked the rapid decline of Douglas Firs in the forest she was studying to the weeding out of paper birch trees. It had been thought that this weeding out was necessary to give the young Douglas saplings a better chance of surviving. But the opposite occurred. There was something going on underneath the surface and instead of depriving the Firs of important nutrients, the Birches through a process of carbon photosynthesis and fungi distribution were actually aiding the growth of the Firs. Her paper in *Nature* was groundbreaking and led to the concept of the 'wood wide web' which captured the beautiful structures and finely adapted languages of the forest network, that until then scientists had not been aware of.[165] This leads me to wonder if there could be a new symbiotic relationship between science, reason and being spiritual and mystical in nature. McFarlane comes close to this in his description of his being in the wood.

> Lying there among the trees, despite a learned wariness towards anthropomorphism, I find it hard not to imagine these arboreal relations in terms of tenderness, generosity and even – as Ginny Battson has written – of love; the respectful distance of their own shy crowns, the kissing branches that have pleached with one another; the unseen connections forged by root and hyphae between seemingly distant trees.[166]

I think it is the arrogance of reason and science, coupled with technology and the ability to master and control some parts of nature, that have prevented humans from developing a more intuitive, sensitive and appreciate way of being in nature. What is there for us in nature when we live in dense complex cities with a myriad of streets with buildings of concrete, stone, glass and steel? And so, am I deluding myself that I am being in nature when, once in a while I walk in these woods, or across the local mountains and along the beaches in Sligo?

There is a connection between seeing God in nature, and the American scientist James Lovelock's concept of Gaia. He saw the earth as being a sensitive, responsive ecosystem that comprises all of life and the environment. It is everything, from rocks, to oceans and the atmosphere, coming together to form one self-determining, self-regulating entity. There is nothing that is outside of Gaia.[167] He thought that it was useful to think of the earth as being alive, not like some goddess, but more like a tree that exists, 'never moving except to sway in the wind, yet endlessly conversing with the sun and the soil'.[168]

I think that as much as we want to touch and be touched, to hug and be hugged, there is a longing to belong to, to be immersed in nature. But over the last two and half thousand years, we have become detached from it. We have become like gods, looking at the activities of other species as if we had nothing to do with them. It would be possible for us to re-immerse ourselves in nature, to live like a hunter-gatherer, but it would be challenging and terrifying. The world would be full of such strange sights, sounds and smells. It would be so unpredictable and, of course, it would be so uncomfortable. We talk glibly about returning to nature but for the vast majority of humans today, they would be like fish out of water.

In *Being a Human*, Charles Foster argues that our increasing reliance on sight has led to the decay of the other senses that were central to our survival for hundreds of thousands of years. In hunter-gatherer societies this would mean trying to survive with just 20 per cent of the information available. But, worse than that, humans have lost their intuitive knowledge of the world.

> Our intuition is older, wiser and more reliable than our underused, atrophied senses. We intuit that the world is one way: our senses insist that it is another. There is a sickening gap between the two types of understanding. No wonder we don't feel at home in the world. We have no idea what it's like, and we *know* at some level that we don't know what it is like.[169]

Foster describes the trials, tribulations, agonies, fears, joys and rewards of trying to live with his son Tom in a wood in Derbyshire, England, as if they were upper Palaeolithic men of 40,000 years ago. They only use whatever technology would have been available at the time. They are constantly on the search for food. Most of the time they starve. 'The last thing I ate was a hedgehog. That was nine days ago.'[170] They become alive to the wood, to the movements of its inhabitants. He extends the sociological argument that we only understand ourselves through our relationships with others – the notion of the looking-glass self – and with other animals. We can only know ourselves as human beings through our relationship with the animals in our environment. He suggests that if we became more attuned with other animals and gave up our interest in mastering and controlling nature, we would transcend reason and science and rediscover a whole non-rational, intuitive way of being in the world. If we are more mindful of the creatures with whom we share the earth, we might be able to connect with another way of knowing ourselves.[171]

Foster lists a number of non-rational ways that we see and understand the world, that were common to our Palaeolithic ancestors, but which have, like many of our senses, fallen by the wayside. He thinks that we have a sense of being that transcends time and space. We get this in moments of clairvoyance, of having been somewhere before (déjà vu), in out of body and near-death experiences and in the sense of communication or shared presence-of-mind that we experience with non-humans.[172]

In many respects, this way of thinking is the opposite of slow, deliberate, rational, scientific thinking. But it is in line with ways of intuitive thinking which are part and parcel of everyday life.[173] Our intuitive knowledge of the world, which was only superseded by rational knowledge in the last two and a half thousand years, revolves around senses, emotions and body language. We read and react to each other's emotional states, we process the signals, without rationally working out the information. Our reaction to confronting a rattlesnake, is not worked out rationally. It is second nature.

Intuitive, second nature thinking, reacting spontaneously to the world, is part and parcel of being human and is included in many forms of religious rituals that are informal, open and fluid. We can see it in dance, chanting and 'talking in tongues'. The arrival of theology and the rationalisation of religious thought effectively marginalised this way of being religious. But it may well be that in the third era of religion, humans will engage more in rituals that revolve around intuitive ways of creating a sense of attunement and enchantment. And it is because religious thought and being religious is second nature to being human, it will not only transcend churches but will also transcend our scientific understanding of life.[174]

Being more attuned to the non-rational ways that we know each other and other species, and trying to connect with other animals, is part and parcel of being religious. As a consequence of the development and domination of rational, scientific thinking, there was a distancing of humans from each other, from other animals and from nature.[175] Being civilised meant not behaving like an animal. To engage in what was deemed to be animal behaviour, from eating with our hands, to farting and, indeed, to touching, came to be seen as impolite if not disgusting.[176] Endemic to this process was a way of seeing other animals not just as inferior but mindless, unintelligent and unemotional.

Palaeolithic humans would not have thought like this. But there is increasing recognition that other animals know, understand and appreciate the world not in inferior but rather different ways.[177] We now know that Egyptian fruit bats 'argue about food, about their sleeping quarters, and about sitting too close together.' We know that ants send complex messages to each other that are almost like sentences and that dolphins create 'words' by changing the volume and frequency of pulsed clicks.[178]

The more we can just be in the natural world, without any aim or purpose other than just being present in nature, and the more we try to transcend our senses and rely on intuition, emotion and empathy for the birds, animals and other species, the more we can communicate with them.[179] Spending time in the wild is good for us, we need to spend more time in nature. The problem, however, is that half the human population live in cities and that by the end of this century it could be more than three-quarters.[180]

It is hard to know what the impact of living in cities will be. It may well be that the freedom that individuals have, comes at a price. As well as being alienated from nature, people may be becoming disconnected and alienated from each other. Census data from America show that more than a quarter of the population live alone and a survey in 2010 found that 43 million Americans suffer from chronic loneliness.[181]

It might well be that the decline in the numbers of people in tight-knit families and small face-to-face groups has led to increased depression. The webs of meaning in which people are suspended have become thin and frail. The inability to identify, love and care for other human beings is linked to the inability to care for nature and other species. We delude ourselves into thinking we are free and in control. We have lost the sense of interdependency, of being part of a whole on which we depend.

In the Lane

I am privileged to live in a beautiful part of Ireland. The old schoolhouse in which I live overlooks a lake and I am easily absorbed by the mixture of green fields, grey water, grey and white cloud and sometimes blue sky. This is the stage for the comings and goings of all sorts of birds. The swans predominate but herons, cormorants, black-seagulls, shell ducks and moor hens play their part.

Most mornings, I go for a walk down the same lane. It is like many other lanes in rural Ireland. It twists and turns and eventually comes to a dead end in the form of a large steel gate that leads into a field. Beyond the field there is a bog that eventually leads down to the River Shannon.

There is nothing special about the lane and yet, for me, it is an enchanting place. I get a sense of timelessness, that I will cease to exist, but the lane and the landscape will go on without me. And, at the same time, there is a strong sense of circular time, of the seasons changing day by day, slowly but inexorably, of things coming into life and dying. I get a sense of belonging. I am part of a living, palpating organism. The more I pay attention to the small aspects of the lane, the more I get a sense of the whole. But try as I do, I only get a glimpse of what is going on in and around me. In a stretch of less than a hundred metres, there are over 2,000 different species.[182] My rational way of thinking means I cannot become attuned to them perhaps in the same way that they are to each other. I am accompanied by the calls and songs of the birds and their flight back and forth across the lane. I am often beaten down by the wind and the rain. But there are many days and times when I am lightened by the sun.

What makes the lane enchanting is the symbiosis, the interconnectedness and interdependency between the species. There is a sense of wonderment. The complexity of it all. I have the same sensation when I see an anthill or beehive. How do all the species in the lane come together to make it all work. I realise that whatever is in the lane, is in the eye of the beholder, of their interests and concerns. I suspect many would see the lane as very ordinary. It's just another Irish lane going nowhere. And yet, for me, it has become a sacred place. It is where I go every day to be mindful about nature.

John McGahern has captured the enchantment of Irish lanes. At the beginning of *Memoir*, he describes walking in early summer with his mother up the lane from their house to the school in Lisacarn where she taught.

> There was a drinking pool for horses along the way, gates to houses, and the banks were covered with all kinds of wild flowers and vetches and wild strawberries. My mother named these flowers for me as we walked, and sometimes we stopped and picked them for the jamjars. I must have been extraordinarily happy walking that lane to school. There are many such lanes all around where I live, and in certain rare moments over the years while walking in these lanes I have come into an extraordinary sense of security, a deep peace, in which I feel that I can live for ever.[183]

On another lane that I walk, I pass a small three-roomed cottage that has been derelict for years. The walls are of grey concrete. There is a corrugated iron roof. Each of the rooms has a small window shrouded in white lace curtains. The rooms are dark but on a bright day it is possible to make out some furniture, pictures and household items.

Tom, who lived there, was a bachelor farmer. He lived on his own until he was no longer able to take care of himself and he went to end his days in a nursing home. It is said that he was a quiet, gracious man who kept to himself. If people called to him or passed by on the lane, he was reluctant to invite them in and preferred to talk to them through one of the windows.

There is a big rusty shed beside the house and there are the outlines of some carrels for treating cattle hidden beneath ivy. There is a shed on the opposite side of the lane in which his small blue car used to sit. There is a green apple tree that sheds flowers onto the lane in Spring and its fruit in Autumn. There is another, grander two-storied house at the end of the lane. It too has been deserted for many years.

As I pass by, I wonder about Tom and how he lived his life. I imagine him awakening to the silence that surrounded him, thinking of the day ahead, the cattle to be cared for, the jobs to be done on the farm, a trip to the local town, the radio for company during the day, the television in the evening, and perhaps before bed, prayers to be said.

I imagine his was a hard life. I imagine he had little money to spend on pleasures or new technologies. His was not a life of getting and spending, coming and going. Did I hear tell that, like many others, he went to work in England for a while? Did he go to Dublin much? Was there anything in the city for him? There are many around here who find Dublin alienating; too busy, too fast, too anonymous, too intimidating.

Tom was probably more immersed in nature than I could ever be. I suspect that like many others around here, his life revolved around his cattle. He cared for them. They were his purpose in life. They gave him a place in the community and in nature.

Not so long ago, I would have seen Tom's cottage as a pitiful memory of time's past. There would have been little that I saw in his life as inspiring. What was there to admire about a man who lived on his own, in small, dark, rooms with nothing but frugal comforts. And yet, on refection, I see how he lived an ecologically sustainable life, that he was, in this world of consumer capitalism, a saint and that his cottage is a sacred place. I have no idea of what his conception of nature, God or the whole would have been. I suspect it was practical, that he accepted the explanation of life and the ways of living a good life that he had inherited.

It seems to me that there are many people like Tom who live quiet, unassuming virtuous lives. There is a joy to being in the world. They live a life of care, being polite and considerate, fulfilling their duties and responsibilities. They may be sustained by a Catholic identity and tradition and engaging in Catholic rituals but, I suspect, there is less concern about adhering to Church rules and regulations.

And, so, I come back to the idea of moral superiority and the notion that I have a better understanding of the meaning of life. The reality is that I live in a rural community in which I am the odd one out. I am a blow-in. I never spent any sustained time in the countryside. Growing up, I had no aunts or uncles who lived in rural areas. I was never on a farm until I was 24 years old. The people with whom I now live have found their own way of being in nature, of being part of this mysterious whole. It is up to me to find my own.

I think, like every plant, animal and insect, it is part of our nature to realise ourselves, to strive to fulfil our desires, particularly to survive and thrive, as much as possible.[184] This is our purpose. As Lovelock argues, everything in nature is interconnected and interdependent and yet each species tries to modify its environment to optimise its reproduction rate. In this way, when it comes to being in nature, like it or not, 'whatever we may do to the total system, we shall continue to be drawn, albeit unawares, into the

Gaian process of regulation.'[185] The last four hundred years have been about the enormous flourishing of human beings. The next four hundred may be about their demise. We used the environment and other species to realise ourselves in the best possible way. Maybe it will be the turn of ants next.

But there is room for optimism. It may well be, however, that in the same way that we learnt to communicate and cooperate with each other in striving to flourish, we need to think that, if this flourishing is to continue, we have to stop trying to master and control other species and, instead, learn how to live in harmony with them. If we are to survive, let alone flourish, we need the oceans and icecaps to flourish as well as the mountains, lakes, rivers, forests and fields.[186] But how far can we go? Can we really recognise and respect the right of all creatures to flourish? What about ants?

Jainism is one of the oldest religions in the world. Like Buddhism, it emerged from Hinduism. Jains practice a form of self-denial that makes the culture of Catholic self-denial look like heaven. It demands a life of removing oneself from the world, of having no possessions and not being violent to any creature, abstaining from sexual activity, always speaking the truth, not taking anything that is not given and not eating after dark.[187]

Jains believe that the spirit of God is contained in everything. In his book on religious lives in India, William Dalrymple spent time with a Jain nun. She told him:

> Our guru had taught us how to walk as Jains. While walking, as well as meditating on the earth and the scriptures, and thinking of the purpose of our lives, we were taught to concentrate on not touching or crushing any living creature. You have to be aware of every single step, and to look four steps ahead. If a single ant is in your path you should be ready to jump or step aside. For the same reason, we must avoid standing on green plants, dew, mud, clay or cobwebs – who knows what life forms may be there?[188]

I like the idea of humans being enmeshed in a complex, mysterious whole that we have never and will never understand but the emergence of reason and science has deluded us into thinking that we are the masters of the universe and that is only a matter of time before we find the meaning of everything and how it works. As much as we have inherited, unquestioned ways of thinking about God, we have inherited, unquestioned ways of thinking about nature.[189]

I don't think I could ever come close to the way a Jain sees and understands nature. And yet, I have this feeling that the main way to know and understand God is through nature. When I walk down the lane, I try to take in the glorious, sublime vista of the clouds and the light of the sky. It is easy to think of God being up there somewhere, beyond, outside, eternal and transcendent. But I try to transcend this way of thinking and, instead, see myself as part of nature and, in doing so, as part of God. I realise that, like all the flora and fauna of the lane, I will go as I have come, in the same way that every atom and cell comes and goes, and that are all part of one flow, one eternal consciousness, call it God or the cosmos, that is as it has always been and will always be.

I am trying to transcend an inherited romantic vision and understanding of nature. When I am in the lane, meditating, I think I am sharing in the same way of being as the curious robin, the dancing chaffinches, the busy bees, the placid donkeys, the beautiful plants not to mention the whole complex world below. I think we are all interconnected. Part of some great whole. And I think, or maybe hope, that I could become attuned to it all.

William James recognised that while the notion of being religious has been dominated by institutions, theologies and doctrines, it is fundamentally personal. It revolves around the interest of the individual in personal concerns and private personal destiny. This religious experience is primary to any intellectualisation about religion. In its most basic form, religion 'consists of the belief that there is an unseen order, and that our supreme good lies in harmoniously adjusting ourselves thereto.'[190]

The philosopher Timothy Morton has argued that when it comes to behaving ecologically, it is about taking small rather than drastic personal actions. As a start, he recommends spending time with pets and stroking them for no other reason than to connect with them.[191] I can see this as a form of love. In the same way that we reach out across the divide and try to love strangers, we can try to develop a relationship with other species that is not a means towards an end, but an attempt just to be in the world. Being loving and kind to each other and to other species may be at the heart of transcendence.[192]

But the uncertainty comes back. Maybe I don't know. Maybe I am projecting something onto the lane, something onto nature, that is not there. Maybe nature does not have a meaning. It is not beautiful, magical or enchanting. I am creating this meaning in the same way as I create an image of God. Maybe nature just is and we need to abandon the idea that just because we became self-consciousness, just because we developed language and meaning, that we are any better than the ants. And this leads to an even more perplexing problem, if I think of myself as being part of some enormous evolving interconnected web, that has been mutating and adapting, can I think of myself not just as a sophisticated ape that has evolved, but as no wiser or better than a sophisticated ant?[193]

There is a lot we can learn from ants. McGilchrist tells us that the carpenter ant is 'extraordinarily sophisticated – it forages and communicates food sources to comrades, carves wooden galleries to live in, and indulges in farming (the ants corral and protect aphids in order to get a sweet substance called honeydew from them, which they achieve by stroking the aphids with their antennae).' The problem is that the carpenter ant is itself used by the zombie ant fungus. While the ant forages on the forest floor, it becomes infected with the fungus. This takes over the nervous system of the ant and makes it behave entirely against its nature. The ant climbs a tree, goes to a height of 25 centimetres, travels out along a branch to a leaf, bites into the leaf and hangs upside down. Twenty-four hours later, it dies and falls to the ground. A day later the fungus bursts out of the corpse and infects more ants.[194] The moral of the story is that nature is not moral. It may be purposeful, but the purpose is not readily evident. Humans think that they are purposeful, sophisticated and moral. But they are destroying the habitat on which they depend. They have become infected with a cultural fungus which deludes then into believing they are God's chosen ones, set apart and different from other species.

My intention is, in some way, to approximate to the Jain nun and to become as detached from the consumer capitalism and the iron cage of rationality as possible, to try to be more other-worldly and mystical. I believe that the more time human beings can spend trying to be part of nature, to feel and understand it, the more we can live a good, ecologically sustainable life. I think it is through trying to let go of myself and be in the lane that I can achieve transcendence. I think that many of the thousands of species that live in the lane are aware of me and that my task is to be aware of them, to move away from my homocentric way of being. It is like being back in the apple tree. I had no real sense that by sitting in the tree there was some form of communication. But at the same time, there was a collision of atoms from which I derived a sense of awareness, belonging and solace.

We come, then, back to the notion that transcendence involves embodiment, a physical rather than mental being in the world. It is about feeling rather than thinking. It is about recognising that our knowledge of the world, of nature, of what it means to be alive, to be human, comes from moods and sensations that arise from engaging in an activity that, like Foucault suggested, transgresses the limits of our understanding and being in the world. This is what can happen when you wander into the middle of the desert, into an untamed jungle or onto a rocky island off the coast of Ireland. But it can also occur through loving, caring, walking a lane, listening to music, looking at art, dancing, singing, chanting and taking drugs.

Mammon and being religious

I sometimes go to the Dundrum Town Centre. The name conjures up an image of some imaginary small town in which local people come to do their shopping, where they meet and greet, stop and chat, and in which there is a sense of belonging to a community. But if ever there was an imagined community, the Town Centre may be a good example. On average, close to fifty thousand people go the Centre each day, that is, allowing for overlaps, over 18 million visits a year. The vast majority do not know each other. It is like any other vast shopping mall in the world. If you had something like the traditional god-like stance of David Attenborough looking down on this from above, it would appear like some giant anthill with thousands of ants winding their way in and out of the myriads of stores, cafes and restaurants, seemingly engaging in what one assumes is highly purposive, mindful, meaningful behaviour.

At the official opening of the centre in March 2005, a Catholic priest, a Church of Ireland minister and Methodist minister, gathered to pray. One of them intoned: 'God of Beauty, may we see in the magnificence of this centre a reflection of your beauty, variety, brightness and colour, may it fill us with wonder and may it raise our hearts and spirits to you.'[195]

When I go to Dundrum, I am amazed and bewildered by the corridors of stores, the lights, the big polished glassed windows, the doors leading into caverns of goodies. I can see how it could feel like heaven on earth, a wondrous paradise in which gorgeous, caring people invite me to fulfil my appetites and desires.

I am then like so many other human beings today, driven by my appetites, desires and passions. I'm like some over-stimulated rat chasing for some elixir that I believe exists but that when I find it, is never completely fulfilling, there is always something else, something newer, better, more satisfying. I can never get enough. I always want more. For me, it is not so much clothes, beauty products or machines, it is books, food and wine and exotic places.

But it is also the small things. I am now thinking of rewarding myself with a fried egg on toast. It is not just any egg. It is from a local producer who feeds his hens samphire. It is not just any bread. It is my own, made with yeast and a mixture of strong white and wholemeal flour. And it is not any oil, it is good Italian virgin olive oil. And it is not just any pan: it is my non-stick, aluminium single egg pan that works perfectly on my induction hob.

There are many times during the day, when my desires are dormant and don't well up inside me like some volcano wanting to explode. I am rarely overwhelmed when I am reading, writing, walking in the lane, and standing on one leg, trying to be a tree. Nor am I overcome when I sit still and look out over the lake or when I look into the eyes of the ones I love and feel their presence. Nor when I see the delight of Missy running wild through the fields, alert to every smell and sight, tail quivering with excitement and then, later, when she comes and sits, and we stare into each other's eyes. I imagine this coming together of mind and body, of being at peace with myself and the world, as an eternal moment of being as close as it is possible to understand and appreciate God.

And so, when I walk through the halls of temptation, I try to say to myself, I don't need. I have enough. I try to say to myself that I am not worthy, that in fulfilling my useless appetites and desires, I am destroying the habitat on which I depend, the nature of which I am a part. I am moving away from being in God. I have this feeling that the more still I am, the more I am connected with other people, other species, with nature and with God, I am like one of the daddy long legs, being quiet and calm, while the bats of passion, appetite and desire, fly past.

Being human, I am regularly if not continually blown off course by my emotions, passions, appetites and desires. I become hurt, angry, resentful, fearful, sad and despairing. Sometimes I think I am some kind of neurotic, over-stimulated rat seeking out new stimulations, sensations and pleasures. I realise that the best way out of this is to stop and to try to be at ease with myself. It is only when I am at ease with myself that I can be at easy in nature and in God. Whatever sense of free will I have may, in the infinite scheme of things, be illusory. My task is to use my self-consciousness and my ability to reason, to try and quell those emotions, passions and appetites that undermine my ability to be at ease with myself, to be part of nature, God, the whole.

Being Religious

It is estimated that up to 18,000 self-help books are published annually in the United States, with the total number available being over 85,000.[196] In a recent encyclical, *A Gift of Joy and Hope*, Pope Francis suggests that the simplest form of self-help is to smile more and that the best smile comes from thinking of Jesus as 'only He is the Saviour'.

He writes about hope, beauty, the promise of youth, compassion and the love of God. He identifies and describes fifteen diseases of the soul, that mainly come from self-absorption and involvement in the world. It is curious, however, that except for a short veneration of St Francis towards the end, there is little, or no connection made with *Laudato Si*, his earlier encyclical about the environment, and little about how being joyous and hopeful is linked to being more in nature. Instead, there is an anthropomorphic notion of God and the assertion of the primacy of human beings: 'He, the Lord, is the Great One, He who desired to create the world for humankind.'[197]

Francis is adamant that the way to overcome the malaise of modernity and self-absorption is to turn to Jesus. The problem is that for an ever-increasing number of people in Ireland, the colonisation of everyday life by the market and the media means that Jesus, God and the Catholic Church as a way of salvation and self-fulfilment, are increasingly irrelevant.

It is not so much that people are either dogmatic theists or militant atheists, it is more that God does not figure in the profane world of being in oneself. It may be that a return to God could come through a greater aware-ness, recognition and appreciation of our being in nature. It may well be that this comes about through being more reasonable about our relationship with other species, about rethinking that we have a god-given right to master and control nature. This might come about by returning to a greater reliance on our intuitive knowledge of what it is to be human and to be part of nature. There is a possibility of this happening as although there are many who deny that God exists, there are few who would deny that we are part of nature.

Again, this brings us back to where we began and the question of what it is to be religious. Is a Buddhist monk standing on one leg religious, while if I do so in my bedroom it is not? Is a priest walking around a garden read-ing his office being religious, while if I read a poem it is not? Is someone who does yoga as a means towards living a healthier life not being religious, while a Buddhist monk is? Is someone who tries to transcend themselves by reading self-help books, or by going on mindfulness courses not being religious, while someone who reads and follows Pope Francis's advice is?

It would seem, then, that when it comes to being religious, much depends on the motivation of the individual. As we saw at the outset of this journey, someone might do yoga as a means of being more productive, effective and successful in their work. For others, it may be less about control and more a way of finding peace and calmness in oneself, of taking time out from the profane world, and letting go, for a while, of the arbitrary ways of thinking and being which they have inherited and now embody.

When I invite family and friends into my home to eat and drink, am I trying to surrender my sense of self to the wider group? Am I striving to be attuned to them as a means of being attuned to God, or is it a form of collective self-indulgence in which God is irrelevant? When I meditate, when I stand doing my tree pose, when I walk the lane in the morning, I wonder is it about living longer and being more productive and successful and less about losing myself and becoming more attuned to the world, to other people and other species.

Who am I to say that people who sing and dance their hearts out at a concert, who are high on drugs, who lose themselves to the collective effervescence of the crowd and the musicians, are not being religious? That, in comparison to those gathered in a Church, they are self-indulgent, pro-fane and sacrilegious.[198] This relates to when and how an event becomes religious. If someone says a few words of Grace before a meal, does the meal become religious? However, it is not religious occasion if someone recites a poem.

I think the best way of becoming closer to nature and to God is to try to be at ease with myself, to overcome the distractions, stimulations and false gods of the material world. The more I am still and reflective, the more I try to empty my mind of the clutter of everyday life, the more I feel I am a better person. The way to transcendence is to be still. This is the way of the mystic. The mystic strives to be in God by renouncing the world.

When I walk down the lane, I try to see it differently every day. I am learning how to see myself in the lane, a bit like David Attenborough looking at an ant going along a path in the anthill, busily accomplishing some task that is part of a wider social whole whose structure and meaning is difficult to see. It is best to try not to decipher one total and complete explanation, some eternal truth about my walking in the lane. It is best to try and explain my being in the lane by concentrating on one local place enmeshed in a web of meaning; to try to see and understand the world differently by trying to walk differently in the lane each time. It is about stopping, focusing in on a particular sight, a tiny aspect of the enormous complex world that is the lane which is just a fleeting moment in time. I cannot understand the whole. I can only try and understand me being in the lane as an atom in time and space that like any spark only lasts a moment. It is these moments of enchantment, and when I am attuned with those I love, that I have any chance of finding God. It is only by grasping these moments that I come to see myself as a body in eternity. So, I may have been right when I said to Aunt Joan all those years ago, that unless I know and understand myself, I cannot know God.[199]

It is hard to stop, look and listen. There is a tendency to repeat the ritual, to become lost in mundane thoughts. Missy helps remind me that there is a wildness in the lane. After walking it for more than six years now, it is still mysterious and magical. I realise that, like God, it is something I will never fully see or understand. I am necessarily burdened with inherited ways of thinking and writing about the experience. My walking has become an attempt to transcend these ways of thinking and, indeed, to transcend language. But if it goes beyond language and, indeed, reason, is there anything to say? Maybe we should follow the advice of the philosopher Ludwig

Wittgenstein who suggested that when it comes to those things about which we cannot say anything, say nothing.

And so, I wonder if I have lived an ethical life. I think it has been like creating a collage sculpture. I have used the various elements that I have come across – people I have known and loved, events, experiences, trials and tribulations – to make a meaningful life that has, I think, some merit. I see it as another life among billions of others. But like every snowflake, it has its own individual beauty. I have been moulded by having known love, beauty, pain and suffering. I am fortunate. I have never experienced poverty, famine or war.

I have done many wrong things and still do. I do not live the ecologically sustainable life that I aspire to. I sin against nature. I drive my car, travel in planes, eat meat and chicken, wear cheap clothes made in Asia. I imagine that every time I do so, I am driving another nail into the womb of nature. They may be venial sins, but they mount up. The problem is that while I sometimes feel guilty, I know it is not enough. There is no sense of shame. I imagine a world in which if I committed a mortal sin such as polluting the lake on which I live and killing all the fish, that I would be taken away and incarcerated in a home for polluters. To avoid such a fate, I imagine going regularly to confession to a personal admonitor or counsellor who would help me live better.

CHAPTER 5

Conclusion

For tens of thousands of years being religious had little to do with belief, doctrine and dogma. It had more to do with ritual gatherings that morphed into practices of healers, druids, shamans and necromancers. This was the first era of religion. Over the last two and a half thousand years, these were slowly replaced, particularly in Judaism, Islam and Christianity by rabbis, imams and priests who constructed complex institutional structures with theologies, laws, rules and regulations. Rituals became less spontaneous, informal and ecstatic and more formal and doctrinal. These world religions colonised not just the notion of God, but our understanding and being in the world, and what it is to be religious.

It is important to take this long-term historical perspective, because being religious is closely tied into being social, into developing a collective sense of identity and belonging and about how to live an ethical life. Before the emergence of agriculture, humans mostly lived in small groups in which they developed shared ways of feeding and looking out for each other. Through nurturing, caring and grooming they began to emotionally relate to each other. The development of symbols and language contributed to the sense of bonding as well as the sharing of knowledge and technology. The impetus to share, care and belong, to marvel at nature, and to search for new ways of being in nature, have always been at the heart of being religious.

Over the last two hundred years in Ireland, the intuitive way that people knew and lived with nature, the land, each other and other species, was colonised by the Church which systematically suppressed pagan practices and coaxed and cajoled people into churches where its rituals, liturgies and theologies were embedded in the people. The Church developed a monopoly over the meaning of life and how to be ethical. It dominated the religious field, but its power came from obtaining a dominant position in other social fields including education, health and social welfare and to a lesser extent politics and the media. If we are to transcend our understanding of what it is to be religious and how to live morally, we need to understand how this colonisation took place.

Religious colonisation is different from political and economic colonisation. But it is similar in that it requires a myriad of dedicated personnel who through providing essential services are able to monitor, supervise and control many aspects of everyday life. The success of the Catholic colonisation was that it was able to recruit over a thousand priests, nuns and brothers who ran almost all the schools, hospitals and welfare homes, and who had a dominating influence in the civil service, universities and a myriad of social and cultural organisations. But its greatest success was in the colonisation of families. Homes became chapels, operating in Catholic time, full of Catholic prayer and language, and decorated with Catholic iconography. Not only could priests, nuns and brothers freely enter into these homes, they were often welcomed with open arms. Through house visitations as well as confessions and generally being at the centre of social life, the Church developed a well-oiled machine that was able to regulate and control behaviour.

What made the colonisation unique and most effective, is that most people, at least in the beginning, wanted to be colonised. They were happy to be good Catholics, to embrace a Catholic identity and fulfil the Church rituals, rules and regulations. It was a way of creating and maintaining their own power. The Church developed a monopoly over what it was to be a good mother, father, son or daughter. People accepted these definitions of themselves. As the power of the Church grew, it became increasingly difficult if not impossible to question or challenge it. When symbolic domination becomes so strong that the dominated take on the perspective of the dominators have of them, when they see themselves as sinners, it becomes symbolic violence.

I have tried to describe how this process took place in my own upbringing. My mother was a card-carrying, loyal, docile, obedient member of the Catholic Church. Everything she did and said would convince you that she was a saint. She wore a path up and down to the church. She did everything she could to raise her children as good Catholics and to live good Catholic lives. In many ways, she was like the millions of Catholic mothers in Ireland on which the Church depended to create vocations and maintain the allegiance of the laity.

But the more Ireland became global, the more it became penetrated by the market and the media, the less it was necessary to be a good Catholic to be seen as a good person. It was not necessary to embrace Catholic language, to identify as Catholic. The web of Catholic meaning began to break down. Families stopped saying the rosary and going to Mass, Holy Communion and Confession. People became less dependent on Church rituals as a means of keeping attuned with each other. They found other ways of being enchanted. They began to throw off the Catholic clothes that had leached into their bodies.

What has happened in Ireland over the last fifty years, is that being religious has become less institutional. In the nineteenth century, being religious moved into churches. Now it is moving back out. It is more informal and less hierarchical. It is less dependent on priests. People are devising their own rituals, their own ways of celebrating and mourning. Being religious is moving into alternative spaces with more personalised services and liturgies.

Taking a broader definition of religion and being religious, I have argued that people are religious when they engage in rituals that bring them together, that create and maintain a sense of bonding and belonging, that enable them to surrender their individual sense of self, to immerse themselves into a collective consciousness. I think that people are being religious when they recognise and accept the sense of awe, mystery, beauty and enchantment of life and nature. I think that people are religious when they say they don't know and when they are open to change, to continually searching for new experiences, new ways of being and understanding. Being religious involves going beyond reason, to being intuitive, but all the time recognising the need to be reasonable and to be cognisant of and vigilant against the will to dominate, master and control.

The notion of God into which I was socialised, and which is part and parcel of Abrahamic religions, is that He is above, beyond and separate from us. It is the idea, evoked by David Attenborough, of God looking down on us as if we are busy ants going about our lives. I don't think this is a good way of thinking about God. For me God is the inexplicable whole of which we are a part. But God is more than the sum of the parts, in the same way that I am more than the sum of the cells in my body.

I accept my understanding of what it is to be in nature, to be in God, to be a part of the cosmic whole, is personal, confused and ambiguous. I feel

I am enmeshed in some wonderous dynamic, fluid entity that is constantly re-emerging. I also realise that in writing these words, in writing this book, that I am suspended in a web of meaning that is also constantly changing. I accept that the creation of a centre, a total explanation, whether we call it 'God', Nature', the 'Cosmos', is an attempt to recognise, understand and appreciate the whole of which we are a part. This to me is not just central to being religious, it is central to being human.

The question then is how it is possible for me to develop a sense of bonding and belonging, a sense of harmony and attunement, with others who do not have the same belief. Is it possible for humans to develop a strong sense of belonging if they have different beliefs? I think this became a problem once humans started to become self-conscious. They could not be sure that they each saw and understood themselves in the same way but, to survive, they had to persuade themselves that they did. And this is why ritual is so important. When people come together, it is about them surrendering their individual beliefs in order to develop a collective consciousness. I think that this is probably best done in families and small groups that belong to wider communities of up to 150 people. It is something that is best achieved through face-to-face relations, through the expression of emotions and touch.

We need to get in touch with each other. I have little doubt that if a meteor was heading to earth and was going to bring an end to the planet, people would huddle together in small groups and hold onto each other for dear life. And yet this is what is happening. But it is not a meteor that will be the cause of our demise. It is not something external. It is coming from within us. We are destroying the planet. It may well be that the only way to stop this, is to become more attuned to each other, to recognise, respect and accept that we are living in an enchanted space and that the way to survive is to accept that we don't know and that we need to transcend our existing ways of being and knowing.

I often wake in the middle of the night and am unable to return to sleep. I lie still and thoughts wander in and out. They are about anything and everything; family and friends, concerns and anxieties, tasks to be done, books I am reading, sentences to be written. I realise these thoughts come from my being in this place on earth and this moment in time. I try to let go the thoughts and embrace being part of a wonderful infinite being, that I am happy to call God and that the more I am in God and nature, the more I can let go my passions, the happier I will be. And so, slowly breathing in, I imagine that I am a star that has emerged in time, that this life, this moment is all there is, that I should embrace and cherish it. I hold this breath and thought. I hold onto dear life. And then I slowly let go of my breath and see myself as collapsing into the infinite. And there is a sense of relief and joy because, in God, the whole or the cosmos, there is no beginning and there is no end. There is just this life on earth.

Notes

1   D. Skelton, 'Standing on one leg is a sign of good health – and practising is good for you' *The Conversation* (6 October 2021). There is plenty of evidence to suggest that being religious, or developing a spiritual mindset, is good for you. See David Robson, *The Expectation Effect: How Your Mindset Can Transform Your Life* (London: Cannongate, 2022). See also: Robin Dunbar, *How Religion Evolved and Why it Endures* (London: Pelican, 2022), 53–5.

2   See Tom Inglis, *Meanings of Life in Contemporary Ireland: Webs of Significance* (New York: Palgrave Macmillan, 2014), 17–39, 123–53.

3   Harrison suggests that in Christianity and probably in many other religions, doctrine is what people are taught to believe. They are indoctrinated. But doctrine, he claims, is different from what people believe, which is the source of self-understanding. He argues, that in the early years 'Christianity was understood more as a way of life than a body of doctrines.' Peter Harrison, *The Territories of Science and Religion* (Chicago: Chicago University Press, 2017), 49.

4   Quoted in Ronald Dworkin, *Religion Without God* (Cambridge [MA]: Harvard University Press, 2013), 3.

5   Much of this derives from Durkheim. Émile Durkheim, *The Elementary Forms of the Religious Life* (London: George Allen & Unwin (1915 [1976])).

6   See, Dworkin, *Religion without God*, 10–21.

7   Dunbar argues that religious specialists such as priests were linked to the concept of Moralising High Gods and doctrinal religions. These emerged with large scale societies, the development of private property and the need for a rule of law and prosocial behaviour. Dunbar, *How Religion Evolved*, 199–201.

8   Dunbar, *How Religion Evolved*, 258–61.

9   Dunbar, *How Religion Evolved*, 162–3.

10   Harrison goes further and argues the notion of 'religion' as a system of institutional doctrines and practices did not exist until the seventeenth century and that up to then, religion was generally seen as something personal and being religious as a virtue, a form of 'inner piety'. Harrison, *The Territories of Science and Religion*, 7–11.

11   Following the writings of Mark Abramowitz, Iain McGilchrist makes a distinction between architective religion that is characterised by knowledge that is codified, storied and accumulated and leads to domination, with connective religion which has great spiritual depth, but which is not easily codified. Examples of connective religions are Sufism, Zen Buddhism, the Kabbalah, Tantric Hinduism and

Christian mysticism. See, Iain McGilchrist, *The Matter with Things: Our Brains, Our Delusions and the Unmaking of the World* (London: Perspectiva, 2021), 833–37.

12   Dunbar refers to this as the 'mystical stance' and that not only is it a universal feature of religious behaviour, but it is also part and parcel of the human psyche, Dunbar, *How Religion Evolved*, 25–48,

13   See, Daniéle Hervieu-Léger, *Religion as a Chain of Memory* (*Cambridge: Polity Press*, 2000), 30–41. Roland Robertson, *The Sociological Interpretation of Religion* (Oxford: Basil Blackwell, 1970), 34–51.

14   'Ceremony is a primordial part of human nature, one that helps us connect, find meaning and discover who we are: we are the ritual species.' Dimitris Xygalatas, *Ritual: How Seemingly Senseless Acts Make Life Worth Living* (London; Profile, 2022), 268.

15   Xygalatas, *Ritual*, 110–3.

16   The concept of religious field comes from Bourdieu. See P. Bourdieu, 'Genesis and Structure of the Religious Field' in *Comparative Social Research: Religious Institutions*, Vol 13, 1991, 1–44. See also, Hervieu-Léger, *Religion as a Chain of Memory*, 108–11.

17   See Bourdieu, 'Genesis and Structure', 31–8. For an analysis of the power of the Catholic Church in other social fields, see Tom Inglis, *Moral Monopoly: The Rise and Fall of the Catholic Church in Modern Ireland* (Dublin: University College Dublin Press, 1998), 65–94.

18   Armstrong suggests that the best way of overcoming this speciesism is to follow the example of Jains and extend the golden rule of treating others the way one would like to be treated oneself, to other species. Karen Armstrong, *Sacred Nature: How we can recover our bond with the natural world* (London: Penguin, 2022), 166–7.

19   See Max Weber, 'Religious Rejections of the World and their Directions' in *From Max Weber: Essays in Sociology* (Oxford: Oxford University Press, 1946), 323–59. For a re-interpretation of this classic essay, see Hans Joas, *The Power of the Sacred: An Alternative to the Narrative of Disenchantment* (Oxford: Oxford University Press, 2021), 206–31.

20   In the Middle Ages, science and religion were seen as different but overlapping habits. Being scientific was an intellectual habit while being religious was a moral one. See Harrison, *The Territories of Science and Religion*, 11–19.

21   For a detailed discussion of religious freedom as a human right, see Dworkin, *Religion Without God*, 128–137.

22   Heelas and Woodward see this as part of the subjective turn in being religious. Paul Heelas and Linda Woodhead, *The Spiritual Revolution: why religion is giving way to spirituality* (Oxford: Blackwell, 2005) 2–5. See, also, Ulrich Beck, *A God of One's Own: Religion's Capacity for Peace and Potential for Violence* (Cambridge: Polity 2010) 81–92. For a more detailed discussion of the emergence of smorgasbord

Catholics, see T, Inglis, 'Catholic Identity in Contemporary Ireland: Belief and Belonging to Tradition', *Journal of Contemporary Religion*, 22.2, 2007, 205–220.

23 There have been numerous attempts in sociology to define the dimensions of being religious and to examine the extent to which they are prevalent in any given population. In a very early study of Irish university students, I identified the following dimensions: religious belief (faith), permeation (the extent to which religious belief permeated everyday life), legalism (adherence to Church teaching), ritualism (religious practice) and mysticism (religious experience), see T. Inglis, 'Dimensions of Irish Students' Religiosity', *The Economic and Social Review*, 11.4, 1980, 237–56.

24 In his pioneering and influential study, William James saw religion as the feelings, acts and experiences that people have of the 'divine', however they define it. He saw religion as personal. He ignored organised and institutionalised religion, particularly in terms of churches and their systematic theologies. He argued that 'the *founders*' of every Church owed their power originally to the fact that they had direct personal communion with the divine. William James, *The Varieties of Religious Experience*. (London: Penguin, 1902 [1982]), 31, 33, 30.

25 The appreciation of the world being an enchanted place is in opposition to Weber's notion that, with the rationalisation of every area of social life, including religion, the world is becoming increasingly disenchanted. See Weber, 'Science as a Vocation', in *From Max Weber*, 128–56. However, disenchantment suggests that there is no room for the sacred in everyday life, that the world is less magical and that individuals have no desire or interest in self-transcendence. See Joas, *Power of the Sacred*, 195–273. I don't think this is the case and that seeing the world as enchanting is part of being human and that there could be a renaissance of enchantment with the climate breakdown.

26 This relates to Durkheim's notion of collective consciousness. The group, family or community is externalised and symbolised. It is seen as above and beyond individual members. It becomes sacred and is worshipped. Rituals are central to the recreation of this collective consciousness. 'There can be no society which does not feel the need of upholding and reaffirming at regular intervals the collective sentiments and the collective ideas which make its unity and its personality.' Durkheim, *Elementary Forms*, 427.

27 As Armstrong notes: 'By rationalising nature and confining God to the heavens, we have so drastically reduced the divine that for many it has become either incredible or imperceptible. At the same time, in our industrialised societies, we have been systematically destroying the natural order.' *Sacred Nature*, 77.

28 Kearney argues transcendence marks a break from ingrained habits of thought and opens up novel possibilities of meaning. Without the suspension of received assumptions we cannot be open to the birth of the new. Richard Kearney, *Anatheism: Returning to God after God* (New York: Columbia University Press, 2011), 7.

29   The focus on feelings and experiences and how these are related to ritual is central
     to the analyses of James and Durkheim. See Joas, *Power of the Sacred*, 54–7.

30   For the variety and ambiguity in Irish Catholic beliefs, see Inglis, *Meanings of Life*,
     123–53.

31   This raises the key issue of the relation between religious belief and practice. This
     is related to social action generally. There is often a gap between what we say and
     what we do. See, Irwin Deutscher, *What we say/what we do* (Brighton: Scott,
     Foresman and Company, 1973). Davie coined the phrase 'believing without belong-
     ing' to characterise religion in contemporary Britain. See Grace Davie, *Religion
     in Britain: A Persistent Paradox* (Oxford: Wiley Blackwell, 2014). The question
     is to what extent can people believe in something if they don't put that belief into
     practice. Moreover, it might well be that in Ireland, there is a case to be made for
     belonging, that is engaging in rituals, without really believing. See Hugh Turpin,
     Unholy Catholic Ireland: Religious Hypocrisy, Secular Morality and Irish Irreligion
     (Stanford: Stanford University Press, 2022) 51–5.

32   See Sir David Attenborough On God- YouTube.

33   Goffman described and analysed this aspect of human behaviour in great detail.
     He recognised that social order was a consequence of moral norms but made little
     or no reference to the extent that this was religious. However, it could be argued
     that the level of coordination and cooperation in social interaction, particularly
     among strangers on city streets, has an element of trust that comes from a sense
     of attunement. See Erving Goffman, *Behavior in Public Places* (New York: The
     Free Press, 1963).

34   How and why the Catholic Church colonised the Irish for so long and so deeply
     is developed in Inglis, *Moral Monopoly*, 97–200.

35   When it came to the reproduction of power, the French sociologist Pierre Bourdieu,
     concentrated on the importance of socialisation. His concept of 'habitus' suggests
     that at some stage, as happened among Irish Catholics, the way in which people
     see and understand the world becomes so unquestioned, so taken-for-granted,
     that it is like the air they breathe. To criticise, let alone challenge the Church was
     beyond belief. See Pierre Bourdieu, *The Logic of Practice* (Cambridge: Polity Press,
     1990), 54–65.

36   The attempt to make links between the social and the psychological explana-
     tions for social evolution was central to the work of Norbert Elias. However,
     Elias never really explored the emotions of individuals in everyday life nor did he
     explore religion. Norbert Elias, *The Civilising Process: Sociogenetic and Psychogenetic
     Investigations* (Oxford: Blackwell. 2000).

37   Derek Scally, *The Best Catholics in the World: The Irish, the Church and the End
     of a Special Relationship* (Dublin: Sandycove, 2021). Scally interweaves personal
     experience with a systematic description and analysis of the way leaders of the
     church responded to the clerical child sex abuse scandals.

38 The notion of religious effervescence comes from Durkheim, *The Elementary Forms of the Religious Life*, 214–39.

39 The Census question changed in 2022 in that 'No Religion' was the first category offered instead of, as in previous censuses, 'Roman Catholic'. The 2016 Census found that 10 per cent of the population ticked 'no religion'. However, two years later, the European Social Survey put the figure at 32 per cent. It had a lead question: 'Do you consider yourself as belonging to any religion or denomination?' If a respondent answered 'yes', there was a selection of religions offered.

40 An international study of identity in 2003 found that in Ireland 35 per cent of participants ranked family or marital status as the most important form of self-description followed by nationality (16 per cent), occupation (14 per cent), gender (9 per cent) and religion (7 per cent). T. Inglis and S. Donnelly, 'Local and national belonging in a globalised world' *Irish Journal of Sociology* 19.2, 2011, 126–42.

41 For a description and analysis of cultural Catholics, see T. Inglis, 'Catholic Identity in Contemporary Ireland: Belief and Belonging to Tradition' *Journal of Contemporary Religion*, 22.2, 2007, 205–27 and Inglis, *Meanings of Life*, 140–4. It is this sense of identity, of wanting to be part of a shared tradition that creates a sense of belonging that distinguishes cultural Catholics from disenchanted or alienated Catholics. Many of the latter category want to disavow themselves of all that is Catholic in their being. For a description and analysis of this category of ex-Catholics, see Turpin, *Unholy Catholic Ireland*, 189–252.

42 The American historian Emmet Larkin conceptualised the attempt to eliminate pagan practices and beliefs and to bring religious practice away from outdoor sacred places and into churches as a 'devotional revolution'. See E. Larkin, 'The Devotional Revolution in Ireland, 1850–75' *American Historical Review*, 77. 3, 1972, 625–52.

43 Patsy McGarry's had an equally intense, if somewhat different, socialisation into the Irish Catholic life. Like me, he used to create an altar and say Mass with his younger brother Seán as the altar boy. See Patsy McGarry, *Well, Holy God: My Life as an Irish, Catholic, Agnostic Correspondent* (Dublin: Merrion Press, 2024), 22.

44 Durkheim argued that the division of the world into the domains of sacred and profane was the distinctive trait of religious thought. For him, what is sacred goes beyond gods and spirits. It could be 'a rock, a tree, a spring, a pebble, a piece of wood, a house, in a word anything can be sacred.' Durkheim, *The Elementary Forms of the Religious Life*, 37.

45 Henrich refers to these as 'credibility enhancing displays', See J. Henrich, 'The evolution of costly displays, cooperation and religion: credibility enhancing displays and their implications for cultural evolution,' *Evolution and Human Behaviour*, 30, 209, 244–60. Lanman argues that convincing displays of religious behaviour have a significant impact on religious socialisation. If children don't see their parents going to Mass or praying, they will be less likely to become ardent Catholics.

See, J. Lanman, 'The importance of Religious Displays for Belief Acquisition and Secularization' *Journal of Contemporary Religion*, 27. 1. 2012, 49–65. For a discussion and analysis of credibility enhancing displays in the Irish context, see Turpin, *Unholy Catholic Ireland*, esp. 48–55.

46   It was the Jesuit theologian Michael Paul Gallagher who characterised Irish Catholicism as being like an egg with a rock-hard shell that was based on high levels of practice but that, due to an absence of debate and discussion, did not have a strong yolk of belief to sustain it. Again, the notion of practising without believing.

47   For an overview of legal-orthodoxy in Irish Catholicism, See Inglis, *Moral Monopoly*, 30–6. Harrison points out that there were few catechisms until after the Reformation and then there was an explosion in the indoctrination of the laity. Harrison, *The Territories of Science and Religion*, 95.

48   McGilchrist argues that the notion of the many being contained within the whole is central not just to religious thought, but all of science and art. McGilchrist, *The Matter with Things*. 843–880.

49   The relation between religion and magic is a major debate in the sociology of religion. For a brief summary of the debate in relation to Irish Catholicism, see T. Inglis, 'Religion, Magic and Practical Reason: Meaning and Everyday Life in Contemporary Ireland', in C. Salazar and J. Bestard (eds) *Religion and Science as Forms of Life: Anthropological Insights into Reason and Unreason* (New York: Berghahn 2015), 188–206.

50   Weber argued that the rationalisation and intellectualisation of every sphere of social life necessarily led to the demagicalisation, demystification and disenchantment of life. Life could be explained and what could not be explained was taken as the way things are. See Max Weber, *Economy and Society* ed. G. Roth and C. Wittich (Berkeley: University of California Press, 1978), 506; Weber, 'Science as a Vocation', 139.

51   Research and Development Commission, *Solemn Novena to Our Lady of Perpetual Succour*. (St Patrick's College Maynooth, 1979).

52   Colm Tóibín (ed.) *Seeing is Believing* (Dublin: Pilgrim Press; 1988); and M. MacCurtain, 'Moving Statues and Irish Women' *Studies*, 76: 302, 1987, 139–47.

53   This is a very inadequate paraphrase of McGilchrist's argument in *The Matter with Things* and in his earlier 2009, *The Master and his Emissary: The Divided Brain and the Making of the Western World* (New Haven: Yale University Press, 2009).

54   Michael Carroll, *Irish Pilgrimage: Holy Wells and Popular Catholic Devotion* (Baltimore: The John Hopkins University, 1999), 144–5.

55   M. Nic Ghiolla Phádraig, 'Religion in Ireland: Preliminary Analysis' *Social Studies*, 5.2, 1976, 113–64.

56   Nic Ghiolla Phádraig, 'Religion in Ireland', 120.

57   Inglis, *Moral Monopoly*, 53–7.

58 Tony Flannery, 2020, *From the Outside: Rethinking Church Doctrine* (Dublin: Red Stripe, 2020), 10.

59 McGarry, *Well, Holy God*, 145. The power of the Church was well-recognised by the Irish Times. Conor Cleary described the caution that was taken when he began to investigate the Bishop Casey scandal. He was extremely cautious. He talked to a leading churchman who was also a canon lawyer and he told Cleary that 'if you're wrong or if you can't prove it, the church will destroy *The Irish Times*.' *The Irish Times*, 8 October 2005.

60 The confession was a great example of creating docile, obedient subjects through a continual system of observing, examining and judging them. If instituted at a young age, external forms of constraint became internalised. See Michel Foucault, *Confessions of the Flesh: The History of Sexuality Volume 4* (London: Penguin, 2020), 79–110; Elias, *The Civilising Process*, 365–87.

61 Foucault, *Confessions of the Flesh*, 101–10.

62 Of course, probably unwittingly, my mother was raising a fundamental question that was first raised by Socrates. What is the self? What is the subject? See Michel Foucault, *The Hermeneutics of the Subject: Lectures at the Collège de France 1981–1982* (London: Picador, 2005), 38.

63 There is evidence to suggest that gossiping, ridicule, shame and shunning were used among the first human groups as a means of bringing braggarts and bullies back into line and it is these strategies that distinguish them from other primates. See Christopher Boehm, *Hierarchy in the Forest: The Evolution of Egalitarian Behavior.* (Cambridge [MA]: Harvard University Press, 1999) 73–7.

64 Nancy Scheper-Hughes, *Saints, Scholars, and Schizophrenics: Mental Illness in Rural Ireland* (Berkeley: University of California Press, 2001), 253.

65 David Graeber and David Wengrow, *The Dawn of Everything: A New History of Humanity* (London: Penguin, 2021), 86.

66 For a more detailed discussion of the history of Irish sexuality see Diarmaid Ferriter, *Occasions of Sin: Sex & Society in Modern Ireland* (London: Profile, 2009); T. Inglis, 'Foucault, Bourdieu, and the Field of Irish Sexuality' *Irish Journal of Sociology*, 6: 1997, 5–28; Tom Inglis, *Lessons in Irish Sexuality* (Dublin: University College Dublin Press, 1998); T. Inglis, 'Origins and Legacies of Irish Prudery: Sexuality and Social Control in Modern Ireland' *Éire-Ireland*, 40:3&4, 2005, 9–37.

67 This is often reduced to there was no sex in Ireland until television. As Ferriter points out, 'it became the most hackneyed phrase to date about the history of sex in twentieth century Ireland.' Ferriter, *Occasions of Sin*, 374.

68 Research and Development Commission, *Irish Priests & Religious 1970–75.* (Dublin, 1977), 77.

69 In his short story, 'The Recruiting Officer', John McGahern captures the reign of terror exercised by a local priest in a visit to a school classroom and how it contrasted with the language and demeanour of a recruiting Christian brother

shortly afterwards. John McGahern, 1992, 'The Recruiting Officer' in *Collected Stories* (London: Faber & Faber, 1992) 100–11.

70   Inglis, *Moral Monopoly*, 178–200.

71   Inglis, *Moral Monopoly*, 212.

72   B. Hilliard, 'The Catholic Church and Married Women's Sexuality: Habitus Change in Late Twentieth Century Ireland' *Irish Journal of Sociology*, 12.2, 2003, 28–49.

73   Bourdieu developed the notions of symbolic domination and violence as a means of overcoming a more materialistic, physical conception and to see domination as rooted in culture, in inherited ways of being, talking and seeing. See Pierre Bourdieu, Outline *of a Theory of Practice* (Cambridge: Cambridge University Press, 1977) 190–7; Pierre Bourdieu, *Masculine Domination* (Stanford: Stanford University Press, 2001).

74   Peggy McCarthy's brother, Seán, wrote and sang a song 'In Shame Love, in Shame' that became popular in folk music circles in the 1960s. Tony Guerin (son of John Guerin the hackney driver in the story), wrote a play *Solo Run*. In 2018, RTÉ made a radio documentary with the same title Documentary On One - In Shame, Love, In Shame (rte.ie).

75   Tom Inglis, *Truth, Power and Lies: Irish Society and the Case of the Kerry Babies* (Dublin: University College Dublin Press, 2003), 125–6.

76   For an overview and analysis of the case, see T. Inglis, 'The Neary Case' in M. Corcoran and P. Share (eds) *Belongings: Shaping Identity in modern Ireland* (Dublin: Institute of Public Administration, 2008), 199–214.

77   Ferriter, *Occasions of Sin*, 455–6.

78   There were exceptions like, for example, Dr Paddy Randles who led a campaign against corporal punishment in schools in the late 1960s but was criticised for his stance by Church spokespeople. See Peter Mulholland, *Love's Betrayal The Decline of Catholicism and the Rise of New Religions in Ireland* (Oxford: Peter Lang, 2019) 106–11, 116–20. Dr Randles's campaign was the subject of Sinéad O'Shea's documentary film (2022) *Pray for Our Sinners*. Of course, dissidents within the Church were also ostracised. Fr Kevin Hegarty was removed from his position as editor of the Church's in-house magazine and sent to a remote parish in the West of Ireland after he published a series of articles that were critical of the Church. See Louse Fuller, *Irish Catholicism since 1950: The Undoing of a Culture* (Dublin: Gill and MacMillan, 2002), 263–4.

79   Report of the Commission of Investigation into the Catholic Archdiocese of Dublin (Murphy Report) (Dublin: Government Publications, 2009), 177–87.

80   For a detailed description of the strategies and tactics of Fr Fortune, see Alison O'Connor, *A Message from Heaven: The Life and Crimes of Father Sean Fortune* (Dingle: Brandon Press, 2000).

81 Marie Keenan, *Child Sexual Abuse & The Catholic Church: Gender, Power, and Organizational Culture* (Oxford: Oxford University Press, 2012).

82 Sunday Mass Readings for 30 October 2022. www <https://catholicreadings.org>.

83 This distinction between conscious action fulfilling a particular interest and almost automatic action, reflexive action that produces an intended effect, is central to Pierre Bourdieu's sociology. See, Pierre Bourdieu and Loïc Wacquant, *An Invitation to Reflexive Sociology* (Cambridge: Polity Press, 1992), 24–6.

84 <https://youtube.com/watch?v=Std83Ia9AEcE>.

85 Sunday Mass Readings for 30 October 2022. www <https://catholicreadings.org>.

86 Kerry bishop apologises after priest's controversial sermon in Listowel (irishexaminer.com)

87 'Priest who attacked homosexuality during mass in Listowel, Kerry, previously supported convicted sex offender' - Independent.ie Fr Sheehy has long been a troublesome priest. In 2009, he joined a queue of local people from Listowel who had gathered to publicly shake the hand of Danny Foley who, having been convicted of an aggravated sexual assault on a local woman, was about to be sentenced. Fr Sheehy had already supplied the court with a character reference. Foley was sentenced to seven years. Fr Sheehy was reported as saying that all that was wrong in the case was that Foley and his victim had engaged in a sexual act outside of marriage and such behaviour was immoral. For a more detailed description and analysis of this case, see T. Inglis and C. MacKeogh, 'The Double Bind: women, honour and sex in contemporary Ireland' *Media, Culture & Society*, 34.1, 2012, 68–82.

88 Browne challenged the power of the Catholic Church by trying to provide health care for mothers. He lost and was forced to resign. See Noël Browne, *Against the Tide* (Dublin: Gill & Macmillan, 1996)

89 There are some notable exceptions; Brian D'Arcy, *It Has to Be Said* (Dublin: Sliabh Ban; 2019); Tony Flannery, *A Question of Conscience* (Dublin: Londubh, 2013).

90 The nineteenth century can be seen as a relentless movement to bring the Catholic Church under Roman control not just in terms of the regulation and control of clergy but in relation to teachings and liturgy. This became known as ultramontanism and culminated in the declaration of Papal Infallibility in 1870. Inglis, *Moral Monopoly* 116–7.

91 Emma Donoghue, *Haven* (London: Picador, 2022).

92 For an overview of this moral panic and why so few Irish people took to new ways of being religious, see Mulholland, *Love's Betrayal*, 25–51; 248–52. See, also, V. Malešević, 'Situating New Religious Movements in Contemporary Ireland' in B. McNamara and H. O'Brien (eds) *The Study of Religions in Ireland: Past, Present and Future* (London: Bloomsbury, 2022), 106–118.

93 Max Weber, 'Religious Rejections', 343–50.

94   See, T. Inglis, 'Sexual Transgression and Scapegoats: A Case Study from Modern Ireland' *Sexualities*, 5.1, 2002, 5–24.

95   Michel Foucault, *The History of Sexuality: An Introduction* (London: Penguin, 1979); *The Use of Pleasure: The History of Sexuality Volume 2* (London: Penguin; 1985) *The Care of the Self: The History of Sexuality Volume Three* (London: Penguin, 1988). A fourth volume *Confessions of the Flesh* was published posthumously (London: Penguin, 2021). See, also, Inglis, 'Foucault, Bourdieu and the Field of Irish Sexuality, 8–15.

96   Michel Foucault, *The Archaeology of Knowledge* (London: Tavistock, 1972), 120; Michel Foucault, *The Order of Things: An Archaeology of the Human Sciences* (New York: Vintage, 1973), 308–312.

97   James Miller, *The Passion of Michel Foucault* (London: Flamingo, 1994), 262–74.

98   Foucault, *The Hermeneutics of the Subject*, 15.

99   This comes from Max Weber. 'The term "charisma" will be applied to a certain quality of an individual personality by virtue of which he is considered extraordinary and treated as endowed with supernatural, superhuman, or at least specifically exceptional powers or qualities. These are not accessible to the ordinary person but are regarded as of divine origin or as exemplary, and on the basis of them the individual concerned is treated as a "leader". Weber, *Economy and Society*, 241.

100   The sacralisation of the political in which rulers come to be seen as divine seems to have been a feature of many human societies. Their symbolic domination is such that they are deemed to have extraordinary, supernatural powers. They become like gods. When rulers become absolute, they can easily go on to become totalitarian. See Jonas, *The Power of the Sacred*, 262–273.

101   Weber, *Economy and Society*, 1139–41.

102   The synchronicities and tensions between reason and religion were teased out by Habermas and Ratzinger (Pope Benedict XVI) in a debate in Bavaria in January 2004. Habermas Jürgen and Joseph Ratzinger *The Dialectics of Secularization: On Reason and Religion*. San Francisco: Ingatius, 2005. These issues are dealt with more thoroughly in Joas, *The Power of the Sacred*, 133–53.

103   Gladys Ganiel, *Transforming Post-Catholic Ireland: Religious Practice in Late Modernity* (Oxford: Oxford University Press, 2016).

104   Inglis, *Meanings of Life*, 145–6.

105   Census of Population 2022, <https://data.cso.ie/table/FY030>.

106   This distinction between what the sacred and the profane world of everyday life is from Durkheim, *The Elementary Forms*, 38–9.

107   McCarraher argues, contrary to Weber, that with rationalisation and capitalism, the world has not become disenchanted but, rather, '*mis*enchanted'. Enlightenment, modernity, capitalism and the belief in technology have given rise to a consumer culture that 'is a counterfeit beatific vision, a realm of coruscating misenchantment, a corporate atlas for a parodic sacramental way of being in the world.' Eugene

McCarraher, *The Enchantments of Mammon: How Capitalism Became the Religion of Modernity* (Cambridge [MA]: Harvard University Press, 2019), 227.

108 Durkheim, *Elementary Forms*, 205–39.

109 Joas, *The Power of the Sacred*, 241.

110 Dunbar, *How Religion Evolved*, 131–7; Xygakatras, *Ritual*, 110–7. Durkheim suggests that religious rituals are the origins of games and art and not related to specific ends or beliefs but rather at reaffirming a collective consciousness, *Elementary Forms*, 350–414.

111 McGilchrist, *The Matter with Things*, 846.

112 For a rich description of how this operates in a small village in Ireland, see Adrian Peace, *A World of Fine Difference: The Social Architecture of a Modern Irish Village* (Dublin: University College Dublin Press, 2001), 19–28.

113 Elias saw shifting balances between 'we' and 'I' throughout the civilising process, but a steady swing towards the 'I' in contemporary society. See, Norbert Elias, *The Society of Individuals*. (Oxford: Blackwell, 1991). For a discussion of how this shift in balance is related to Individualisation, see Cas Wouters, *Informalization: Manners & Emotions since 1890*. (London: Sage, 2007), 191–6.

114 See Beck, *A God of One's Own*, 164–200. See, also, Joas, *The Power of the Sacred*, 72–3.

115 Xygaltas, *Ritual*, 252–9.

116 Quoted in Xygaltas, *Ritual*, 255–6.

117 Inglis, *Meanings of Life*, 107–14.

118 Nic Ghiolla Phádraig, 'Religion in Ireland', 127.

119 Inglis, *Meanings of Life*, 114–5.

120 Benedict Anderson, *Imagined Communities* (London: Verso, 1983).

121 Dunbar, *How Religion Evolved*, 99–102.

122 Dunbar, *How Religion Evolved*, 88–94.

123 Dunbar, *How Religion Evolved*, 96.

124 Tom Inglis, *Love* (London: Routledge, 2103), 26–36.

125 See Hervieu-Léger, *Religion as a Chain of Memory*, 87.

126 Hervieu-Léger argues that the type of solidarity that takes place in lay voluntary groups is similar to bonding that occurs in elective fraternities that revolve around shared commitments, experiences and values. These elective fraternities, separated from families, have been a part of religious life since ancient Judea. See, Hervieu-Léger, *Religion as a Chain of Memory*, 149–53.

127 Richard Kearney, *Touch: Recovering Our Most Vital Sense* (New York: Columbia University Press, 2021), 3.

128 Kearney, *Touch*, 125.

129 Kearney, *Touch*, 2.

130 The strict codes around touch can be seen as part of a more long-term civilising process that developed in the West from the 16th century. There was an increasing

demand for people to behave in predictable, regulated ways. This focused on not engaging in animal like behaviour. The more society became civilised, the more people became disgusted by bodily functions, by sweat, smells, dirt and hair. As part of this process, inappropriate touch has come to be seen not just as impolite, but as offensive. Touching has become a source of shame and repugnance to the same extent as spitting, farting or nose picking. See, Elias, *The Civilising Process*, 109–42.

131   Tom Inglis, *To Love a Dog*. (Dublin: Penguin, 2020) Kearney said that one of the ways he was able to overcome his depression was by walking with his dog, *Touch*, 100.

132   See Thomas Laqueur, *Solitary Sex: A Cultural History of Masturbation*. (Princeton [NJ]: Zone Books. 2003).

133   Weber points out that the tension between religion and sex did not exist in earlier forms of religion and only became an issue within Christianity with the chastity of priests. See Weber, 'Religious Rejections', 343–4.

134   Gregory Curtis, *The Cave Painters: Probing the Mysteries of the World's First Artists* (New York: Anchor, 2007).

135   B. Ehrenreich, 'Humans were not centre stage': how ancient cave art puts us in our place.' *The Guardian*. 12 December 2019.

136   McGilchrist writes: 'Creatures are not the passive playthings of necessity, but determine their environment as much as the environment determines them. The idea of a niche, separate from an animal whose niche it is, is nonsensical. The animal shapes the niche to its purposes, the niche in turn shapes the animal to its own.' McGilchrist, *The Matter with Things*, 1172.

137   Weber, 'Religious Rejections' 328.

138   Weber, 'Religious Rejections' 328.

139   I regularly have experiences that seem to reveal the wonder of nature, of infinite being, of God that come out of the blue and yet are, as Spinoza says, so strong, so revealing that they are like a bulb that lightens up a darkened room. Spinoza, *Ethics*, (E2P43), 58.

140   McGilchrist, *The Matter with Things*, 1233.

141   See John Cottingham, *In Search of the Soul: A Philosophical Essay* (Princeton [NJ]: Princeton University Press, 2020), 117.

142   For a detailed discussion of the implausibility of the universe happening by chance, see Phillip Goff, *Why? The Purpose of the Universe* (Oxford: Oxford University Press, 2023), 16–46. See, also, McGilchrist, *The Matter with Things*, 1114–5.

143   McGilchrist argues that cells are not just aware but smart, that they make decisions, plan responses and contain memory. See McGilchrist, *The Matter with Things*, 464–5; 1073–4.

144 This is derived from Spinoza who had the notion of a worm in the blood not being able to conceive of itself as part of a whole. See Clare Carlisle, *Spinoza's Religion: A New Reading of the Ethics* (Princeton: Princeton University Press, 2021), 75.

145 For a detailed description of consciousness, how it is related to matter and the role of the brain, see McGilchrist, *The Matter with Things*, 1037–1120.

146 Stephen Greenblatt, *The Swerve: How the Renaissance Began* (London; Vintage, 2012), 188.

147 For a discussion of the different theories of consciousness and how they relate to the God question, see Thomas Nagel, *Mind & Cosmo: Why the Materialist Neo-Darwinian Conception of Nature is Almost Certainly False* (Oxford: Oxford University Press, 2012), 35–69.

148 Goff, *Why?* 150.

149 Michel Foucault, *The Hermeneutics of the Subject: Lectures at the Collège de France 1981–1982.* (London: Picador, 2005). 15.

150 For a more detailed discussion of all this, see Dworkin, *Religion Without God*.

151 McGilchrist, *The Matter with Things*, 1195.

152 These is a crude and simplistic digestion of very complex philosophical questions. For a more thorough review and understanding of these issues and a strong defence of a Christian concept of God, see Patrick Masterson, *In Reasonable Hope: Philosophical Reflections on Ultimate Meaning* (Washington: Catholic University Press of America, 2021).

153 The challenge for humanity is to balance that right to join churches and sects, to assert shared beliefs, with individual freedom. 'By emphasizing the sacredness of the person, I have problematized forms of universalism that do not respect the dignity of every individual. This applies, for example, to theocratic authoritarianisms as to laicist dictatorships.' Joas, *The Power of the Sacred*, 273.

154 See Beck, *A God' of One's Own*. Looking back over the last two thousand years, it is easy to see a relationship between the emergence of the notion of a personal God and the salvation of the individual and the rise of individual religious freedom and then the political ideology of liberal individualism. For a more detailed discussion of this, see D. Hervieu-Léger, 'Religious Individualism, Modern Individualism and Self-Fulfilment: A few Reflections on the Origins of Contemporary Religious Individualism' in E. Barker (ed.) *The Centrality of Religion in Social Life: Essays in Honour of James A. Beckford* (London: Ashgate, 2008), 29–40.

155 Kearney, *Anatheism*, 16.

156 Kearny, *Anatheism*, 5.

157 Foucault, *The Hermeneutics of the Self*, 15–16.

158 The following typology about ways to attains transcendence is derived from Weber's typology of religious orientations. Weber, *Economy and Society*, 541–6. On the importance of mysticism in being religious, see Dunbar, *How Religion Evolved*, 25–48.

159 For a detailed description and analysis of New Religious Movements and how they morphed into New Age Movements and the history of these movements in Ireland, see Mulholland, *Love's Betrayal*, 5–66.

160 Foucault, *The Hermeneutics of the Subject*, 15. Foucault lists four characteristics for spiritual knowledge, the first of which is that the subject cannot properly know by remaining where he is. The second is that it requires a shift in position. The third is that it requires stepping outside of oneself, a form of self-viewing and, finally, in seeing the truth of one's being 'one finds a mode of being, which is one of happiness and of every perfection of which he is capable,' 308. The extent to which he saw making love as a spiritual exercise is unclear. However, the titles and content of the second (*The Use of Pleasures*) and third volumes (*The Care of the Self*) of *The History of Sexuality*, suggest that there was a close connection.

161 Manchán Magan, *Listen to the Land Speak* (Dublin: Gill Books, 2022), 151.

162 Magan, *Listen to the Land Speak*, 88.

163 Magan, *Listen to the Land Speak*, 129.

164 Tim Robinson, Tim, *Connemara: listening to the wind* (London: Penguin 2006); *Connemara: the last pool of darkness* (London: 2008); *Connemara: A Little Gaelic Kingdom.* (London: Penguin. 2011).

165 Robert McFarlane, *Underland: A Deep Time Journey* (London: Penguin, 2019), 88–91. The argument is that to understand and explain the upper-story of any wood, we have to understand what is going on below the ground, and then below that again. Ecologists have seen and been aware of this understory but have never come close to understanding its complexity.

166 McFarlane, *Underworld*, 99.

167 B. Latour, 'Why Gaia is not a God of Totality' *Theory, Culture & Society*, 34.2, 2017, 65.

168 James Lovelock, *Gaia: The Practical Science of Planetary Medicine.* (London: Hamlyn, 2000), 12.

169 Charles Foster, *Being a Human: Adventures in 40.000 Years of Consciousness.* (London: Profile, 2021), 65 (italics in original).

170 Foster, *Being a Human*, 71.

171 Foster, *Being a Human*, 295–329. In an earlier book, Foster describes his attempts to live like a beast, to inhabit the world and see, understand and appreciate it from the point of view of a badger, otter, fox, stag and swift. See, Charles Foster, *Being a Beast: An Intimate and Radical Look at Nature* (London: Profile, 2016).

172 Foster, *Being a Human*, 307.

173 R. McCauley, 'Maturationally Natural Cognition Impedes Professional Science and Facilitates Popular Religion' in C. Salazar and J. Bestard (eds), *Religion and Science as Forms of Life: Anthropological Insights into Reason and Unreason* (New York: Berghahn, 2015), 25–48.

174 McCauley argues that the ways in which scientists gather evidence to test theories is imbued with, what he calls, maturational ways of thinking, see McCauley, 'Maturationally Natural Cognition', 31–34.

175 McGilchrist links this to the dominance of the left hemisphere of the brain which is directed towards knowing as a means of isolating, dividing, mastering and controlling over the right hemisphere that sees knowing more as a means of sensitivity, awareness, bonding, belonging, understanding and appreciation. McGilchrist, *The Master and his Emissary*.

176 This is a central tenet of Elias, see Elias, *The Civilising Process*.

177 Richard Louv, *Our Wild Calling: How connecting with animals can transform our lives—and save theirs* (Chapel Hill [NC]: Algonquin Books, 2019), 45–52.

178 Louv, *Our Wild Calling*, 64.

179 Louv, *Our Wild Calling*, 80–1.

180 J. Chesire and M. Batty, 'The Era of the Megalopolis: How the World's Cities are Merging', *The Conversation*, 22 November 2022.

181 Louv, *Our Wild Calling*, 15.

182 Foster, *Being a Human*, 164.

183 John McGahern, *Memoir* (London: Faber & Faber, 2005), 4.

184 This comes from Spinoza who argues that we strive for anything that aids and increases the power of our bodies and minds. Benedict Spinoza, *The Ethics*. (London: Penguin, 1996), E3P11, 76.

185 See James Lovelock, *Gaia* (Oxford: Oxford University Press, 1979), 120. There are close connections and distinctions between Spinoza's concept of God and Lovelock's concept of Gaia, see B. Lord, 'We are nature' in Aeon 28 April 2020 Even the Anthropocene is nature at work, transforming itself | Aeon Essays.

186 For an elucidation of this argument, see Lord, 'We are nature'.

187 John Bowker, *World Religions: The great faiths explained and explored* (London: Penguin Random House, 2021), 73–81.

188 William Dalrymple, *Nine Lives: In Search of the Sacred in Modern India.* (London: Bloomsbury, 2010), 22.

189 Trying to find ways of transcending our ideas about nature and the way we see and understand it, is central to the work of Timothy Morton. See Timothy Morton, *The Ecological Thought* (Cambridge [Mass]: Harvard University Press, 2010).

190 James, *Variety of Religious Experience*, 491, 53.

191 Timothy Morton, *All Art is Ecological* (London: Penguin, 2018), 42.

192 Carlisle argues that loving-kindness is at the heart of Spinoza's notion of what it is to be religious. It is a struggle to be virtuous not as a means towards an end, but as an end in itself. See Carlisle, *Spinoza's Religion*, 164–83.

193 Morton argues that we should not think of nature, or animals, or creatures or plants but rather as belonging to one enormous complex, unimaginable mesh which has no centre or edge and in which everything is adapting to everything else. See, Morton, *The Ecological Thought*, 38–50.

194   McGilchrist, *The Matter with Things*, 1183.

195   T. Cunningham, 'Jesus in Dundrum: Between God and Mammon' in M. Corcoran
      and P. Share (eds) Belongings: *Shaping Identity in Modern Ireland* (Dublin: IPA,
      2008), 231.

196   'The pope versus Peterson: whose self-help advice is better?' *The Irish Times*,
      2 October 2022. The History of Self-Help Books – Tagari.com.

197   Pope Francis, *A Gift of Joy and Hope* (London: Hodder & Stoughton, 2020),
      x, 154–5, 87.

198   Dunbar argues that the mystical stance that produces raw feelings that can be
      overpowering has a very long history and is still identifiable in the contemporary
      world. 'I suggest that, with or without psychoactive drugs, this mystical component,
      with its strong emotional overtones, underpins all religious behaviour, no matter
      how sophisticated the religion. It is the motor of religiosity and consequently
      colours everything that emerges from this experience in the form of religion.'
      How Religion Evolved, 48.

199   See Spinoza, *Ethics*, P30, 174. 'Insofar as our mind knows itself and the body under
      a species of eternity, it necessarily has a knowledge of God.'

Select Bibliography

Armstrong, Karen *Sacred Nature: How we can recover our bond with the natural world* (London: Penguin, 2022)

Barker, Ellen (ed.) *The Centrality of Religion in Social Life: Essays in Honour of James A. Beckford* (London: Ashgate, 2008)

Beck, Ulrich, *A God of One's Own: Religion's Capacity for Peace and Potential for Violence* (Cambridge: Polity 2010)

Carlisle, Clare, *Spinoza's Religion: A New Reading of the Ethics* (Princeton: Princeton University Press, 2021)

Carroll, Michael, *Irish Pilgrimage: Holy Wells and Popular Catholic Devotion* (Baltimore: The John Hopkins University, 1999)

Cottingham, John, *In Search of the Soul: A Philosophical Essay* (Princeton [NJ]: Princeton University Press, 2020)

Dunbar, Robin, *How Religion Evolved and Why it Endures* (London: Pelican, 2022)

Durkheim, Émile, *The Elementary Forms of the Religious Life* (London: George Allen & Unwin 1976)

Dworkin, Ronald, *Religion Without God* (Cambridge [MA]: Harvard University Press, 2013)

Foster, Charles, *Being a Human: Adventures in 40.000 Years of Consciousness.* (London: Profile, 2021)

Ferriter, Diarmaid, *Occasions of Sin: Sex & Society in Modern Ireland* (London: Profile, 2009)

Fuller, Louse, *Irish Catholicism since 1950: The Undoing of a Culture* (Dublin: Gill and MacMillan, 2002)

Ganiel, Gladys, *Transforming Post-Catholic Ireland: Religious Practice in Late Modernity* (Oxford: Oxford University Press, 2016)

Goff, Phillip, *Why? The Purpose of the Universe* (Oxford: Oxford University Press, 2023)

Peter Harrison, *The Territories of Science and Religion* (Chicago: Chicago University Press, 2017)

Paul Heelas and Linda Woodhead, *The Spiritual Revolution: why religion is giving way to spirituality* (Oxford: Blackwell, 2005)

Hervieu-Léger, Daniéle, *Religion as a Chain of Memory* (Cambridge: Polity Press, 2000)

Louv, Richard, *Our Wild Calling: How connecting with animals can transform our lives—and save theirs* (Chapel Hill [NC]: Algonquin Books, 2019)

Inglis, Tom, *Moral Monopoly: The Rise and Fall of the Catholic Church in Modern Ireland* (Dublin: University College Dublin Press, 1998)

Inglis, Tom, *Meanings of Life in Contemporary Ireland: Webs of Significance* (New York: Palgrave Macmillan, 2014)

James, William, *The Varieties of Religious Experience* (London: Penguin, 1982)

Joas, Hans, 2021, *The Power of the Sacred: An Alternative to the Narrative of Disenchantment* (Oxford: Oxford University Press, 2021)

Kearney, Richard, *Anatheism: Returning to God after God* (New York: Columbia University Press, 2011)

Kearney, Richard *Touch: Recovering Our Most Vital Sense* (New York: Columbia University Press, 2021)

Magan, Manchán, *Listen to the Land Speak* (Dublin: Gill Books, 2022)

Masterson, Patrick, *In Reasonable Hope: Philosophical Reflections on Ultimate Meaning* (Washington: Catholic University Press of America, 2021)

Timothy Morton, *The Ecological Thought* (Cambridge [Mass]: Harvard University Press, 2010)

McGarry, Patsy, *Well, Holy God: My Life as an Irish, Catholic, Agnostic Correspondent.* (Dublin: Merrion Press, 2024).

McFarlane, Robert, *Underland: A Deep Time Journey* (London: Penguin, 2019), 88–91

McGilchrist, Iain, *The Matter with Things: Our Brains, Our Delusions and the Unmaking of the World* (London: Perspectiva, 2021)

Mulholland, Peter, *Love's Betrayal: The Decline of Catholicism and the Rise of New Religions in Ireland* (Oxford: Peter Lang, 2019)

Nagel, Thomas, *Mind & Cosmo: Why the Materialist Neo-Darwinian Conception of Nature is Almost Certainly False* (Oxford: Oxford University Press, 2012)

Scally, Derek, *The Best Catholics in the World: The Irish, the Church and the End of a Special Relationship* (Dublin: Sandycove, 2021)

Turpin, Hugh, *Unholy Catholic Ireland: Religious Hypocrisy, Secular Morality and Irish Irreligion* (Stanford: Stanford University Press, 2022)

Xygalatas, Dimitris, *Ritual: How Seemingly Senseless Acts Make Life Worth Living* (London; Profile, 2022)

Index

Abrahamic religions, 5
abortion, 63, 76, 78
asceticism, 136
acid, 88
Aileen, MacKeogh,
　baptism of first child, 65
　death, 121–3, 125
　first meeting, 86
　Fr Lennon, 57
　marriage, 37, 64
　magical beliefs, 37–8
　son Luke, 80
　schooling, 94
alienation, 21
altar (boys), 25–9, 46, 58, 77
anarchism, 63
animism, 123, 125
ants, 14, 30, 109, 128, 142, 146, 148
apple-tree, being in, 119
Armstrong, Karen, 162 (n18), 163 (n27)
Arron, Inglis, 47
Ash Wednesday, 28
atheists, 129, 151
attunement
　as couples, 111
　among strangers, 113, 158, 164 (n33)
　part of being religious, 12, 21, 24, 98,
　　101–3, 108, 112, 157
　through ritual, 105
Attenborough, David, 15, 30, 128, 153, 157
axial age, 5

belonging
　as a species, 109
　levels of, 109–11

parish, 111
tribal, 110
beliefs. *See* also Catholic and religious
　beliefs
belittling, 51–2
Bennett, Don, 63
Bernard, Brother, 59
Bible, 10, 30
big bang, 126–7
bonding, non-verbal, 112
Bourdieu, Pierre, 162 (n16), 164 (n35),
　　168 (n73), 169 (85)
Breda, daughter of Peggy McCarthy, 67–8
Brennan, Canon Patrick, 67–8
Browne, Bishop Ray, 78
Browne, Nöel, 79
Buddhism, 2, 10, 86, 99, 132, 134, 146
Burning Man Festival, 105

Calvinism, 19, 136
Camino de Santiago, 84
Carol MacKeogh, 112, 115
Carlisle, Clare, 173 (n144), 175 (192)
Catholic being
　beliefs, 10, 14, 21, 39–40, 82, 164 (n30)
　ceremonies, 26, 28–9, 36, 77
　cultural, 82
　iconography, 66
　and identity, 20
　and Irishness, 21
　like an eggshell, 31
　in Northern Ireland, 15
　orthodox, 82
　tradition, 20, 77–8
　socialisation, 17, 22, 29

Catholic Marriage Bureau, 41
celebration, 6
Census of Population, 165 (n39)
charisma, 64, 75–6, 89–93, 133, 170 (n99)
Charismatic Renewal, 36
Christian Brothers, 60
Church
    agencies, 63–4
    deference to, 69
    loyalty to, 73
    power, 7, 21–4, 34, 43–6, 53, 65–6, 68,
        72, 73, 76, 79–82, 91–4
    and state, 61, 66–69
civilised, being, 81, 93, 116, 120, 142, 171
    (n130)
climate breakdown, 19, 108, 113, 125, 163
    (n25)
colonisation
    of everyday life, 152, 156
    religious, 7, 156
    post-religious, 97, 116–7
collective spirit, 102
commandments
    ten, 47–8, 58
    Church, 47–8, 58
community,
    moral, 108
    imagined, 149
confession, 26, 29, 40, 47–9, 154, 167 (60)
Connell, Fr Desmond, 62
consciousness,
    collective, 53, 76–7, 97–8, 101–2, 104,
        107, 109, 157–8, 163 (n26),
        171 (n110)
    cosmic, 3, 117, 126–8, 147
    parapsychic, 128–9
    self-consciousness, 12–3, 114, 118, 126,
        128, 148, 151
consumerism, 53
cosmopolitanism, 96, 104, 106, 131
Croagh Patrick, 13, 39, 84
Crowe, Fr Bertie, 63

daddy long legs, 109
Daly, Cardinal Cathal, 46–7
Davie, Grace, 164 (n31)
De La Salle, Brothers, 59–60, 86
Dancing, 141
delusion, collective, 70
devil (Satan), 14, 34, 38–40, 50, 78, 130
Deutscher, Irwin, 164 (n31)
diocesan clergy, 60
discourses, 88
doctrine, 2
    acceptance, 8, 14, 82, 155, 161
        (n7, n19)
    as central to Church power, 39–47, 98
    church sacraments, 6
    as opposed to experience, 11, 14, 32, 83,
        102, 106, 147
    and sex, 69, 77
    as truth, 96
dogmatism, 131–2
Donoghue, Emma, 83
Dorrie (aunt), 50
Dougan, Rev Prof., 72
drugs, 7, 13, 84, 87, 101, 149, 152, 176
    (n198)
Dunbar, Robin, 110–111, 161 (n7),
        162 (n12), 176 (n198)
Dundrum Town Centre, 149
Dunn, Fr Joe, 36

ecological sustainability, 145, 154
ecstasy, 26–7, 58, 84, 87, 103
effervescence (collective)
    as central to being religious, 21, 23, 31,
        97, 101, 103, 105
    Catholic, 99
Einstein, Albert, 4
Elias, Norbert, 164 (n36), 171 (n130)
emergence in life, 109, 128
enchantment,
    as central to being religious, 4, 81,
        91–2, 118–9, 142

Catholic, 20–2, 24–39, 59, 72, 97–9
dancehalls, 119
in garden, 119
in nature, 119, 144, 153, 153
shopping malls, 118–9
eras of religion,
first era, 5, 96, 155
second era, 5, 84, 96, 98, 126
third era, 9–10, 96, 98, 101–23, 141
ethical being, 16, 23, 154, 155
Eucharistic, Congress 1932, 75

faith-healing, 37
father, my, 25, 29–30, 45, 48, 50–1, 59, 65,
114, 119
family,
and Church, 40, 79
identity and sense of self, 20, 30, 41,
44, 50, 101, 111
and mothers and vocations, 61
rituals, 6, 25, 31, 77, 111, 152
as sacred and religious, 6, 12, 14, 23,
102–3, 113
and sport, 107
and threat of sex, 87
Faye Inglis, 115
fear,
of being religious, 104
of Church, 58–9, 73
within Church, 73, 120
of evil, 38
living without, 76
of mysticism, 13
of the other, 133
as part of life, 21, 24, 79, 115
of power, 91
of sex, 55, 64, 69
of touch, 133
Ferns, diocese, 74
Flaherty, Michael, 59
Flannery, Fr Tony, 45
Flynn, Eileen, 69–70

Foucault, Michel, 49, 88, 134, 136, 149
Fortune, Fr Seán, 74
Foster, Charles, 120, 140–1, 174 (n171)
Francis, Pope, 76
Francis, Saint, 151
Fundamentalism, 131

GAA, 45, 108
Gaia, 139–40
Gallagher, Christina, 37
Gallagher, Joan, 97, 135
Gallagher, Fr Michael Paul, 166 (n46)
Gallagher, Fr Raphael, 94
Ganiel, Gladys, 96
Gift-economy, 105
Good Samaritan, 113
God
ambiguity about, 125–6
anatheism, 132
atheism, 63
being reasonable about, 130–3
Catholic, 82, 97, 151–2, 173 (n152)
consciousness and, 173, (n147)
experiencing, 27–9, 38, 86, 120, 132,
146–7, 152, 157, 172 (n139)
as father figure, 32, 136, 163 (n27)
knowing, 34, 39, 78, 81, 84, 122, 125,
129, 148
Mammon, 149–51
one (monotheism), 84, 157
nature of, 3, 8, 27, 48, 98, 120
in nature, 99, 125, 140, 148
personal, 14, 173, (n154)
Jesus as, 32–3
talking about, 4
transcending existing notion,
163 (n28)
as the whole, 126–9, 147, 158–9
Goff, Phillip, 128–9, 172 (n142)
Goffman, Erving, 164 (n33)
Good Shepard (Church of), 25, 28–9, 58
Gossip, 73

Griffin, Gerry, 87
Grooming, 110

Habermas, Jürgen, 170 (n102)
Harding-Clark, Justice Maureen, 71
Harrison, Peter, 161 (n3, n10), 162 (n20),
    166 (n47)
Harvey, Lee, 105
healthy, being, 2
heaven, 14, 17, 26, 32, 80, 93, 99, 125–6,
    132, 150
hell, 14, 17, 40, 49, 78–9, 99, 120, 126
Hervieu-Léger, Danielle, 171 (n126),
    173 (n154)
Hesse, Herman, 85
High School, The, 60
Hobson, Tom, 84–5
Holy Communion
    first, 27, 47, 77
    sacrament 27, 29, 47–9, 157
Holy, Spirit (Ghost), 30, 33–4, 42–3
homocentrism, 148, 151
horoscopes, 38
House of Prayer, Achill, 37
hugging, 114
humour, 42, 52, 53
hunter gatherers, 101, 110, 136, 138, 140
hymns, 28, 35, 107
hysterectomies, 71–2

individualism, 104
Irish society, changes, 61–2
Isla Inglis, 115

Jainism, 146
James, William, 147
Jesuits, 38, 48, 51, 167 (n46)
Jesus, 10–11, 29, 32–4, 43, 90, 130–1,
    151
Joan Inglis, 38–43, 58, 87, 93, 135, 153
John Inglis, 87
John, Paul Pope, 75, 103, 110

Jonas, Hans, 170 (n100), 173 (n153)
Jones, Rev Jim, 90

Kavanagh, Bishop James, 63
Karma Sutra, 117
Kearney, Richard, 115, 132–3, 163 (n28), 172
    (n131)
Kelly, John, T.D., 80
Kenny, Mary, 79
Kerry, Co., 67–9
Knowledge *see also* science
    approximate, 31, 112, 127
    and Foucault, 88
    intimate, 112
    intuitive, 123, 126, 140–1, 152
    and power, 34, 45–6
    practical, 134
    reasonable, 130
    scientific 4, 9, 137
    of nature, 138, 149
    theological, 33

Larkin, Emmet, 165 (n42)
Lascaux, caves, 118
Laity, 32, 34, 36, 48, 53, 57, 77–8, 81–2,
    87, 95
lane, waling in, 3, 143–9
Legion of Mary, 40
Lennon, Fr Jim, 57, 65, 76
life after death, 4, 8, 10, 122
liturgy, 77
love
    of God, 29, 133, 151
    as heavenly, 125
    in *Narcissus and Goldmund*, 85
    making love, 112
    of mother, 26
    as primary emotion, 21, 86, 92, 125, 134
    of pets, 147, 150
    as sacred, 113
    and transcendence, 84
Lovelock, James, 139, 145–6, 175 (n185)

Lough Derg, 84
Lough Gur, 137
Lucretius, 128
Luke, Inglis, 80, 125

McCarthy, Peggy, 67–9
McCauley, R., 175 (n174)
McFarlane, Robin, 139, 174 (n165)
McGahern, John, 144
McGarry, Patsy, 46–7, 165 (n43)
MacGréil, Fr Micheál, 39
McGilchrist, Iain, 102, 130, 148, 161 (n11),
    166 (n48), 172 (n136, 142),
    173 (n145), 175 (n175)
McNamee, Fr James, 74
McQuaid, Archbishop John Charles,
    43–4
Magdalene, laundry, 42, 55, 68, 72
magical thinking, 11, 35, 37, 39, 120–3, 125
magpies, 121
Manchester United, 106
Manchán, Magan, 137
marriage, outside Church, 77
market and media, 53, 99, 112, 151, 157
Masterson, Paddy, 63, 173 (n152)
materialism, 128
Maura, MacKeogh, 80
Maurice, Inglis, 41–2, 65
meaning(s) (of life)
    Catholic colonisation of, 30, 32, 52,
        155, 157
    family, 104
    origins, 4, 118, 126
    as part of religion, 16, 20, 97, 134
    searching for, 6, 66, 83–9, 145, 148
    and science, 92, 114, 146
    webs of, 3, 52, 104, 134, 142, 153
meditation and mindfulness, 2, 84, 95, 99,
    138, 152
Meelagh, Lough, 138
Missy (dog) 116, 150, 153
Moral Monopoly, 79, 94

Moral
    being, 148
    panic, 87
    superiority, 145
Morrison, Van, 84
Morton, Timothy, 147, 175 (n193)
mother (my), 24–31, 35–7, 41–2, 48, 50, 59,
    65, 120, 121, 156
mothers, role of in vocations, 61–2
mourning, 6
music,
    being musical, 7, 58, 119
    and being religious, 58, 77, 84, 96–7,
        102, 136, 153
    self-transcendence 13, 84
Mykonos, 52
Mysticism, 13, 35–6, 84, 134

Narcissus and Goldmund, 85
nature,
    being in, 138–40, 147
    second, 141
Nagel, Thomas, 173 (n147)
new age religion, 97–8
Nunan, Jim, 28

Olwen, Inglis, 94
Our Lady, 25–7, 29, 31, 34–37, 40
Our Lady of Lourdes Hospital, 71

Palaeolithic, 140–2
paganism, 98, 117, 137
panpsychism, 128–9
Pascal, Blaise, 31
passions, 151
pathological and normal, 67
patriarchy, 74
penitential (practices) 7, 13, 28, 30, 39, 83,
    137
People's Temple, 90
pets 147, 166
power, *see also* Church,

charismatic, 89–90
learning about, 91
over the body, 88
profane, the, 29, 39, 58, 107, 112, 133–5,
    151–2, 165 (n44)
Protestants (ism), 15, 24, 39, 43–5, 60
Priests
    as celebrities, 64
    celibacy, 56, 77
    in church ceremonies, 26–7
    in community, 32, 45, 68–9, 80, 94–5
    as enforcers, 78–9, 81–3
    as explainers, 33–4, 72
    fear of, 58
    paedophile, 73–5
    playing role of as children, 28
    numbers, 60
    reverence of, 64, 81–2
    as servants, 76–7
    visitations, 80–1
    vocations, 60–1
purposiveness, 128–9, 148

randomness, 128
rational
    being, 9–10, 15, 24, 132, 137
    not being, 101–2, 141
rationalisation
    of life, 114, 120–1, 163 (n25), 167 (n50),
        171 (n107)
    of religious thought, 5, 9, 35, 89, 141
Reformation
    The Reformation, 39, 166 (n47)
    contemporary, 96–9, 166 (n47)
Religious being
    and art, 86
    charitable works, 135
    and civil society, 132
    and cultural imperialism, 19
    dimensions of, 11–13
    as experience, 4, 11
    and institutional religion, 3, 8

new age, 97–8, 134
new religious movements, 134
personnel, numbers, 60–1
rights, 131
and sex, 87
Research and Development Unit, 63
retreats religious, 38, 48, 51
Rice, Rodney, 80
rituals,
    Catholic, 6, 10, 21–3, 24–6, 28, 95,
        145, 157
    creating sense of sacred, 4, 6, 8, 9, 12,
        16, 31, 77, 141, 155
    and collective consciousness, 163 (n26)
    daily, 2, 97, 153, 155
    and effervescence, 102–5
    among family and friends, 6, 31, 111–113
    mourning, 6
    performative, 31, 49, 164 (n31)
    personal, 1–3, 17, 23
    as origins of games and art, 171 (n110)
    religious, 5, 7, 11, 13–14, 20, 97, 105,
        162 (14), 164 (n29), 98, 102
    rosary, 3, 6, 11, 25, 29, 108, 157
    sporting, 106–8
    and transcendence, 83, 92–3, 98
Robinson, Tim, 138
RTÉ, 74, 80, 168 (n74)
rural life, 103, 145
Ryan, Bishop Larry, 74
Ryan, Justice, Nöel, 70

sacred,
    being, 6, 38, 74, 81, 98, 143
    and profane, 29, 39, 58, 112, 132, 144
        (n44), 153
    rituals, 31, 77
    spaces, 28, 39, 73, 83, 151, 138
    texts, 35, 77
sacrilegious, 102
Saints,
    above, 34–9

Anthony, 35
Brigid, 25
Christopher, 35
Columba, 35
Jude, 35
Patrick, 33
Joseph, 26
Francis, 35, 151
Salvation
    attaining, 5, 10, 14, 40, 82, 87, 104, 151,
        173 (n154)
    inner-worldly, 99, 107, 136
Samaritans, 135
Scally, Derek, 164 (n37)
Scheper-Huges, Nancy, 51
Screamers (sect), 87
Self
    consciousness, 12, 13, 118, 128, 148, 151
    denial, 50–3, 62, 99, 146
    help, 151
    realisation, 152
sensationalism, 115
sex (sexuality),
    abuse, 46, 72, 76
    being sexual, 10, 14, 69, 117, 146
    in the classroom, 59
    sexual repression, 53–8
    sexual subjects, 49, 87
    shame, 56, 69
    silence, about, 69
science
    and big bang, 126
    beyond scientific thinking, 16, 23, 35,
        84, 132, 141
    dependency on, 39, 92, 96, 108, 113,
        120–3
    origins, 110, 161 (n3), 162 (n10)
    and understanding nature, 139
shame, 49, 91, 154
shaman, 122
Sheehy, Fr Seán, 78–9
Skellig Michael, 83–4

Simard, Suzanne, 139
Social order (maintaining) 16, 51, 65, 87,
    120, 264 (n33)
social, surveys, 39
soul-searching, 2, 85, 87, 136
species,
    mastering and controlling other, 8
    attunement with other, 12, 109, 113
Spinoza, Benedict, 172 (n139), 174 (n184,
    n185), 176 (n199)
spirituality, 2, 12, 97, 133
sport
    as religion, 7, 104, 106–8
statues, moving, 37, 70
stoicism, 99
stranger, the, 133, 135
superstitious thinking, 121
surveillance, 73
symbols, 4, 13, 66, 98, 103, 114, 120, 128,
    140, 155
symbiotic relationships, 61, 108, 139, 143
symbolic
    capital, 108
    domination, 24, 44, 66–70, 90, 156,
        168 (n73), 170 (n100)
    life, 114
    violence, 67–69, 132, 156, 168 (n73)
symphysiotomies, 72

theists, 151
theology, 23, 32, 36, 63, 82, 101–2, 132, 141
transcendence
    asceticism, 99
    my attempts, 84–5, 148
    being charitable, 135
    being still, 153
    being spiritual, 134–7
    as breaking fee, 16, 86, 89, 99, 134, 136,
        163 (n28)
    as experience, 149
    and friendship, 85
    in Michel Foucault, 88, 134, 136, 149

in not knowing, 8, 132
mystical, 83, 135
in religious history, 83–4
and self-consciousness, 13
in sport, 107
and transgression, 87
transgenderism, 78
truth,
    Church monopoly, 67, 71, 81
    knowing the, 16, 96, 131–2
    and power, 71
    as reasonable and scientific, 39
    searching for, 13, 49, 55, 81, 83, 129,
        134, 153
    sexual, 57
    and transcendence, 88–9, 134
    as virtue, 129
Turner, Denys, 62

Turpin, Hugh, 164 (n31), 165 (n41)

Uncle Tom (Grand), 38, 42–3, 75–7

vocations, 61–2, 75

Ward, Fr Conor, 63
Weber, Max, 116, 120–1, 163 (n25), 166
        (n50), 170 (n99, 107), 172 (n133),
        173 (n158)
we-I balance, 104
whistleblower, 70
whole, part of, 127, 143, 147
Wittgenstein, Ludwig, 154
women, 62, 67, 71–2
wonder, as central to being religious, 4–5
'wood wild world', 139

Yoga, 1–2

Reimagining Ireland

Series Editor: Dr Eamon Maher, Technological University Dublin

The concepts of Ireland and 'Irishness' are in constant flux in the wake of an ever- increasing reappraisal of the notion of cultural and national specificity in a world assailed from all angles by the forces of globalisation and uniformity. Reimagining Ireland interrogates Ireland's past and present and suggests possibilities for the future by looking at Ireland's literature, culture and history and subjecting them to the most up-to-date critical appraisals associated with sociology, literary theory, historiography, political science and theology.

Some of the pertinent issues include, but are not confined to, Irish writing in English and Irish, Nationalism, Unionism, the Northern 'Troubles', the Peace Process, economic development in Ireland, the impact and decline of the Celtic Tiger, Irish spirituality, the rise and fall of organised religion, the visual arts, popular cultures, sport, Irish music and dance, emigration and the Irish diaspora, immigration and multiculturalism, marginalisation, globalisation, modernity/postmodernity and postcolonialism. The series publishes monographs, comparative studies, interdisciplinary projects, conference proceedings and edited books.

Proposals should be sent either to Dr Eamon Maher at eamon.maher@ittdublin.ie or to ireland@peterlang.com.

Vol. 1   Eugene O'Brien: 'Kicking Bishop Brennan up the Arse': Negotiating Texts and Contexts in Contemporary Irish Studies
ISBN 978-3-03911-539-6. 219 pages. 2009.

Vol. 2   James P. Byrne, Padraig Kirwan and Michael O'Sullivan (eds): Affecting Irishness: Negotiating Cultural Identity Within and Beyond the Nation
ISBN 978-3-03911-830-4. 334 pages. 2009.

Vol. 3   Irene Lucchitti: The Islandman: The Hidden Life of Tomás O'Crohan
ISBN 978-3-03911-837-3. 232 pages. 2009.

Vol. 4   Paddy Lyons and Alison O'Malley-Younger (eds): No Country for Old Men: Fresh Perspectives on Irish Literature
ISBN 978-3-03911-841-0. 289 pages. 2009.

Vol. 5   Eamon Maher (ed.): Cultural Perspectives on Globalisation and
          Ireland
          ISBN 978-3-03911-851-9. 256 pages. 2009.

Vol. 6   Lynn Brunet: 'A Course of Severe and Arduous Trials': Bacon, Beckett
          and Spurious Freemasonry in Early Twentieth-Century Ireland
          ISBN 978-3-03911-854-0. 218 pages. 2009.

Vol. 7   Claire Lynch: Irish Autobiography: Stories of Self in the Narrative of
          a Nation
          ISBN 978-3-03911-856-4. 234 pages. 2009.

Vol. 8   Victoria O'Brien: A History of Irish Ballet from 1927 to 1963
          ISBN 978-3-03911-873-1. 208 pages. 2011.

Vol. 9   Irene Gilsenan Nordin and Elin Holmsten (eds): Liminal Borderlands in
          Irish Literature and Culture
          ISBN 978-3-03911-859-5. 208 pages. 2009.

Vol. 10   Claire Nally: Envisioning Ireland: W. B. Yeats's Occult Nationalism
          ISBN 978-3-03911-882-3. 320 pages. 2010.

Vol. 11   Raita Merivirta: The Gun and Irish Politics: Examining National History
          in Neil Jordan's Michael Collins
          ISBN 978-3-03911-888-5. 202 pages. 2009.

Vol. 12   John Strachan and Alison O'Malley-Younger (eds): Ireland: Revolution
          and Evolution
          ISBN 978-3-03911-881-6. 248 pages. 2010.

Vol. 13   Barbara Hughes: Between Literature and History: The Diaries and
          Memoirs of Mary Leadbeater and Dorothea Herbert
          ISBN 978-3-03911-889-2. 255 pages. 2010.

Vol. 14   Edwina Keown and Carol Taaffe (eds): Irish Modernism: Origins,
          Contexts, Publics
          ISBN 978-3-03911-894-6. 256 pages. 2010.

Vol. 15   John Walsh: Contests and Contexts: The Irish Language and Ireland's
          Socio-Economic Development
          ISBN 978-3-03911-914-1. 492 pages. 2011.

Vol. 16   Zélie Asava: The Black Irish Onscreen: Representing Black and Mixed-Race Identities on Irish Film and Television
ISBN 978-3-0343-0839-7. 213 pages. 2013.

Vol. 17   Susan Cahill and Eóin Flannery (eds): This Side of Brightness: Essays on the Fiction of Colum McCann
ISBN 978-3-03911-935-6. 189 pages. 2012.

Vol. 18   Brian Arkins: The Thought of W. B. Yeats
ISBN 978-3-03911-939-4. 204 pages. 2010.

Vol. 19   Maureen O'Connor: The Female and the Species: The Animal in Irish Women's Writing
ISBN 978-3-03911-959-2. 203 pages. 2010.

Vol. 20   Rhona Trench: Bloody Living: The Loss of Selfhood in the Plays of Marina Carr
ISBN 978-3-03911-964-6. 327 pages. 2010.

Vol. 21   Jeannine Woods: Visions of Empire and Other Imaginings: Cinema, Ireland and India, 1910–1962
ISBN 978-3-03911-974-5. 230 pages. 2011.

Vol. 22   Neil O'Boyle: New Vocabularies, Old Ideas: Culture, Irishness and the Advertising Industry
ISBN 978-3-03911-978-3. 233 pages. 2011.

Vol. 23   Dermot McCarthy: John McGahern and the Art of Memory
ISBN 978-3-0343-0100-8. 344 pages. 2010.

Vol. 24   Francesca Benatti, Sean Ryder and Justin Tonra (eds): Thomas Moore: Texts, Contexts, Hypertexts
ISBN 978-3-0343-0900-4. 220 pages. 2013.

Vol. 25   Sarah O'Connor: No Man's Land: Irish Women and the Cultural Present
ISBN 978-3-0343-0111-4. 230 pages. 2011.

Vol. 26   Caroline Magennis: Sons of Ulster: Masculinities in the Contemporary Northern Irish Novel
ISBN 978-3-0343-0110-7. 192 pages. 2010.

Vol. 27 Dawn Duncan: Irish Myth, Lore and Legend on Film
ISBN 978-3-0343-0140-4. 181 pages. 2013.

Vol. 28 Eamon Maher and Catherine Maignant (eds): Franco-Irish
Connections in Space and Time: Peregrinations and Ruminations
ISBN 978-3-0343-0870-0. 295 pages. 2012.

Vol. 29 Holly Maples: Culture War: Conflict, Commemoration and the
Contemporary Abbey Theatre
ISBN 978-3-0343-0137-4. 294 pages. 2011.

Vol. 30 Maureen O'Connor (ed.): Back to the Future of Irish
Studies: Festschrift for Tadhg Foley
ISBN 978-3-0343-0141-1. 359 pages. 2010.

Vol. 31 Eva Urban: Community Politics and the Peace Process in
Contemporary Northern Irish Drama
ISBN 978-3-0343-0143-5. 303 pages. 2011.

Vol. 32 Mairéad Conneely: Between Two Shores/*Idir Dhá Chladach*: Writing
the Aran Islands, 1890–1980
ISBN 978-3-0343-0144-2. 299 pages. 2011.

Vol. 33 Gerald Morgan and Gavin Hughes (eds): Southern Ireland and the
Liberation of France: New Perspectives
ISBN 978-3-0343-0190-9. 250 pages. 2011.

Vol. 34 Anne MacCarthy: Definitions of Irishness in the 'Library of
Ireland' Literary Anthologies
ISBN 978-3-0343-0194-7. 271 pages. 2012.

Vol. 35 Irene Lucchitti: Peig Sayers: In Her Own Write
ISBN 978-3-0343-0253-1. Forthcoming.

Vol. 36 Eamon Maher and Eugene O'Brien (eds): Breaking the
Mould: Literary Representations of Irish Catholicism
ISBN 978-3-0343-0232-6. 249 pages. 2011.

Vol. 37 Mícheál Ó hAodha and John O'Callaghan (eds): Narratives of the
Occluded Irish Diaspora: Subversive Voices
ISBN 978-3-0343-0248-7. 227 pages. 2012.

Vol. 38   Willy Maley and Alison O'Malley-Younger (eds): Celtic
            Connections: Irish–Scottish Relations and the Politics of Culture
            ISBN 978-3-0343-0214-2. 247 pages. 2013.

Vol. 39   Sabine Egger and John McDonagh (eds): Polish–Irish Encounters in
            the Old and New Europe
            ISBN 978-3-0343-0253-1. 322 pages. 2011.

Vol. 40   Elke D'hoker, Raphaël Ingelbien and Hedwig Schwall (eds): Irish
            Women Writers: New Critical Perspectives
            ISBN 978-3-0343-0249-4. 318 pages. 2011.

Vol. 41   Peter James Harris: From Stage to Page: Critical Reception of Irish
            Plays in the London Theatre, 1925–1996
            ISBN 978-3-0343-0266-1. 311 pages. 2011.

Vol. 42   Hedda Friberg-Harnesk, Gerald Porter and Joakim Wrethed
            (eds): Beyond Ireland: Encounters Across Cultures
            ISBN 978-3-0343-0270-8. 342 pages. 2011.

Vol. 43   Irene Gilsenan Nordin and Carmen Zamorano Llena (eds): Urban
            and Rural Landscapes in Modern Ireland: Language, Literature and
            Culture
            ISBN 978-3-0343-0279-1. 238 pages. 2012.

Vol. 44   Kathleen Costello-Sullivan: Mother/Country: Politics of the Personal
            in the Fiction of Colm Tóibín
            ISBN 978-3-0343-0753-6. 247 pages. 2012.

Vol. 45   Lesley Lelourec and Gráinne O'Keeffe-Vigneron (eds): Ireland and
            Victims: Confronting the Past, Forging the Future
            ISBN 978-3-0343-0792-5. 331 pages. 2012.

Vol. 46   Gerald Dawe, Darryl Jones and Nora Pelizzari (eds): Beautiful
            Strangers: Ireland and the World of the 1950s
            ISBN 978-3-0343-0801-4. 207 pages. 2013.

Vol. 47   Yvonne O'Keeffe and Claudia Reese (eds): New Voices, Inherited
            Lines: Literary and Cultural Representations of the Irish Family
            ISBN 978-3-0343-0799-4. 238 pages. 2013.

Vol. 48   Justin Carville (ed.): Visualizing Dublin: Visual Culture, Modernity and the Representation of Urban Space
ISBN 978-3-0343-0802-1. 326 pages. 2014.

Vol. 49   Gerald Power and Ondřej Pilný (eds): Ireland and the Czech Lands: Contacts and Comparisons in History and Culture
ISBN 978-3-0343-1701-6. 243 pages. 2014.

Vol. 50   Eoghan Smith: John Banville: Art and Authenticity
ISBN 978-3-0343-0852-6. 199 pages. 2014.

Vol. 51   María Elena Jaime de Pablos and Mary Pierse (eds): George Moore and the Quirks of Human Nature
ISBN 978-3-0343-1752-8. 283 pages. 2014.

Vol. 52   Aidan O'Malley and Eve Patten (eds): Ireland, West to East: Irish Cultural Connections with Central and Eastern Europe
ISBN 978-3-0343-0913-4. 307 pages. 2014.

Vol. 53   Ruben Moi, Brynhildur Boyce and Charles I. Armstrong (eds): The Crossings of Art in Ireland
ISBN 978-3-0343-0983-7. 319 pages. 2014.

Vol. 54   Sylvie Mikowski (ed.): Ireland and Popular Culture
ISBN 978-3-0343-1717-7. 257 pages. 2014.

Vol. 55   Benjamin Keatinge and Mary Pierse (eds): France and Ireland in the Public Imagination
ISBN 978-3-0343-1747-4. 279 pages. 2014.

Vol. 56   Raymond Mullen, Adam Bargroff and Jennifer Mullen (eds): John McGahern: Critical Essays
ISBN 978-3-0343-1755-9. 253 pages. 2014.

Vol. 57   Máirtín Mac Con Iomaire and Eamon Maher (eds): 'Tickling the Palate': Gastronomy in Irish Literature and Culture
ISBN 978-3-0343-1769-6. 253 pages. 2014.

Vol. 58   Heidi Hansson and James H. Murphy (eds): Fictions of the Irish Land War
ISBN 978-3-0343-0999-8. 237 pages. 2014.

Vol. 59   Fiona McCann: A Poetics of Dissensus: Confronting Violence in
           Contemporary Prose Writing from the North of Ireland
           ISBN 978-3-0343-0979-0. 238 pages. 2014.

Vol. 60   Marguérite Corporaal, Christopher Cusack, Lindsay Janssen and
           Ruud van den Beuken (eds): Global Legacies of the Great Irish
           Famine: Transnational and Interdisciplinary Perspectives
           ISBN 978-3-0343-0903-5. 357 pages. 2014.

Vol. 61   Katarzyna Ojrzyn'ska: 'Dancing As If Language No Longer
           Existed': Dance in Contemporary Irish Drama
           ISBN 978-3-0343-1813-6. 318 pages. 2015.

Vol. 62   Whitney Standlee: 'Power to Observe': Irish Women Novelists in
           Britain, 1890–1916
           ISBN 978-3-0343-1837-2. 288 pages. 2015.

Vol. 63   Elke D'hoker and Stephanie Eggermont (eds): The Irish Short
           Story: Traditions and Trends
           ISBN 978-3-0343-1753-5. 330 pages. 2015.

Vol. 64   Radvan Markus: Echoes of the Rebellion: The Year 1798 in Twentieth-
           Century Irish Fiction and Drama
           ISBN 978-3-0343-1832-7. 248 pages. 2015.

Vol. 65   B. Mairéad Pratschke: Visions of Ireland: Gael Linn's *Amharc Éireann*
           Film Series, 1956–1964
           ISBN 978-3-0343-1872-3. 301 pages. 2015.

Vol. 66   Una Hunt and Mary Pierse (eds): France and Ireland: Notes and
           Narratives
           ISBN 978-3-0343-1914-0. 272 pages. 2015.

Vol. 67   John Lynch and Katherina Dodou (eds): The Leaving of
           Ireland: Migration and Belonging in Irish Literature and Film
           ISBN 978-3-0343-1896-9. 313 pages. 2015.

Vol. 68   Anne Goarzin (ed.): New Critical Perspectives on Franco-Irish
           Relations
           ISBN 978-3-0343-1781-8. 271 pages. 2015.

Vol. 69   Michel Brunet, Fabienne Gaspari and Mary Pierse (eds): George
           Moore's Paris and His Ongoing French Connections
           ISBN 978-3-0343-1973-7. 279 pages. 2015.

Vol. 70   Carine Berbéri and Martine Pelletier (eds): Ireland: Authority
           and Crisis
           ISBN 978-3-0343-1939-3. 296 pages. 2015.

Vol. 71   David Doolin: Transnational Revolutionaries: The Fenian Invasion of
           Canada, 1866
           ISBN 978-3-0343-1922-5. 348 pages. 2016.

Vol. 72   Terry Phillips: Irish Literature and the First World War: Culture,
           Identity and Memory
           ISBN 978-3-0343-1969-0. 297 pages. 2015.

Vol. 73   Carmen Zamorano Llena and Billy Gray (eds): Authority and
           Wisdom in the New Ireland: Studies in Literature and Culture
           ISBN 978-3-0343-1833-4. 263 pages. 2016.

Vol. 74   Flore Coulouma (ed.): New Perspectives on Irish TV Series: Identity
           and Nostalgia on the Small Screen
           ISBN 978-3-0343-1977-5. 222 pages. 2016.

Vol. 75   Fergal Lenehan: Stereotypes, Ideology and Foreign
           Correspondents: German Media Representations of Ireland,
           1946–2010
           ISBN 978-3-0343-2222-5. 306 pages. 2016.

Vol. 76   Jarlath Killeen and Valeria Cavalli (eds): 'Inspiring a Mysterious
           Terror': 200 Years of Joseph Sheridan Le Fanu
           ISBN 978-3-0343-2223-2. 260 pages. 2016.

Vol. 77   Anne Karhio: 'Slight Return': Paul Muldoon's Poetics of Place
           ISBN 978-3-0343-1986-7. 272 pages. 2017.

Vol. 78   Margaret Eaton: Frank Confessions: Performance in the Life-Writings
           of Frank McCourt
           ISBN 978-1-906165-61-1. 294 pages. 2017.

Vol. 79   Marguérite Corporaal, Christopher Cusack and Ruud van den Beuken
           (eds): Irish Studies and the Dynamics of Memory: Transitions and
           Transformations
           ISBN 978-3-0343-2236-2. 360 pages. 2017.

Vol. 80   Conor Caldwell and Eamon Byers (eds): New Crops, Old
           Fields: Reimagining Irish Folklore
           ISBN 978-3-0343-1912-6. 200 pages. 2017.

Vol. 81   Sinéad Wall: Irish Diasporic Narratives in Argentina: A
           Reconsideration of Home, Identity and Belonging
           ISBN 978-1-906165-66-6. 282 pages. 2017.

Vol. 82   Ute Anna Mittermaier: Images of Spain in Irish Literature, 1922–1975
           ISBN 978-3-0343-1993-5. 386 pages. 2017.

Vol. 83   Lauren Clark: Consuming Irish Children: Advertising and the Art of
           Independence, 1860–1921
           ISBN 978-3-0343-1989-8. 288 pages. 2017.

Vol. 84   Lisa FitzGerald: Re-Place: Irish Theatre Environments
           ISBN 978-1-78707-359-3. 222 pages. 2017.

Vol. 85   Joseph Greenwood: 'Hear My Song': Irish Theatre and Popular Song
           in the 1950s and 1960s
           ISBN 978-3-0343-1915-7. 320 pages. 2017.

Vol. 86   Nils Beese: Writing Slums: Dublin, Dirt and Literature
           ISBN 978-1-78707-959-5. 250 pages. 2018.

Vol. 87   Barry Houlihan (ed.): Navigating Ireland's Theatre Archive: Theory,
           Practice, Performance
           ISBN 978-1-78707-372-2. 306 pages. 2019.

Vol. 88   María Elena Jaime de Pablos (ed.): Giving Shape to the Moment: The
           Art of Mary O'Donnell: Poet, Novelist and Short Story Writer
           ISBN 978-1-78874-403-4. 228 pages. 2018.

Vol. 89   Marguérite Corporaal and Peter Gray (eds): The Great Irish Famine
           and Social Class: Conflicts, Responsibilities, Representations
           ISBN 978-1-78874-166-8. 330 pages. 2019.

Vol. 90   Patrick Speight: Irish-Argentine Identity in an Age of Political
           Challenge and Change, 1875–1983
           ISBN 978-1-78874-417-1. 360 pages. 2020.

Vol. 91   Fionna Barber, Heidi Hansson, and Sara Dybris McQuaid
           (eds): Ireland and the North
           ISBN 978-1-78874-289-4. 338 pages. 2019.

Vol. 92   Ruth Sheehy: The Life and Work of Richard King: Religion,
           Nationalism and Modernism
           ISBN 978-1-78707-246-6. 482 pages. 2019.

Vol. 93   Brian Lucey, Eamon Maher and Eugene O'Brien (eds): Recalling the
           Celtic Tiger
           ISBN 978-1-78997-286-3. 386 pages. 2019.

Vol. 94   Melania Terrazas Gallego (ed.): Trauma and Identity in Contemporary
           Irish Culture
           ISBN 978-1-78997-557-4. 302 pages. 2020.

Vol. 95   Patricia Medcalf: Advertising the Black Stuff in Ireland 1959–1999:
           Increments of Change
           ISBN 978-1-78997-345-7. 218 pages. 2020.

Vol. 96   Anne Goarzin and Maria Parsons (eds): New Cartographies, Nomadic
           Methologies: Contemporary Arts, Culture and Politics in Ireland ISBN
           978-1-78874-651-9. 204 pages. 2020.

Vol. 97   Hiroko Ikeda and Kazuo Yokouchi (eds): Irish Literature in the British
           Context and Beyond: New Perspectives from Kyoto
           ISBN 978-1-78997-566-6. 250 pages. 2020.

Vol. 98   Catherine Nealy Judd: Travel Narratives of the Irish Famine: Politics,
           Tourism, and Scandal, 1845–1853
           ISBN 978-1-80079-084-1. 468 pages. 2020.

Vol. 99   Lesley Lelourec and Gráinne O'Keeffe-Vigneron (eds): Northern Ireland after the Good Friday Agreement: Building a Shared Future from a Troubled Past?
ISBN 978-1-78997-746-2. 262 pages. 2021.

Vol. 100   Eamon Maher and Eugene O'Brien (eds): Reimagining Irish Studies for the Twenty-First Century
ISBN 978-1-80079-191-6. 384 pages. 2021.

Vol. 101   Nathalie Sebbane: Memorialising the Magdalene Laundries: From Story to History
ISBN 978-1-78707-589-4. 334 pages. 2021.

Vol. 102   Roz Goldie: A Dangerous Pursuit: The Anti-Sectarian Work of Counteract
ISBN 978-1-80079-187-9. 268 pages. 2021.

Vol. 103   Ann Wilson: The Picture Postcard: A New Window into Edwardian Ireland
ISBN 978-1-78874-079-1. 282 pages. 2021.

Vol. 104   Anna Charczun: Irish Lesbian Writing Across Time: A New Framework for Rethinking Love Between Women
ISBN 978-1-78997-864-3. 320 pages. 2022.

Vol. 105   Olivier Coquelin, Brigitte Bastiat and Frank Healy (eds): Northern Ireland: Challenges of Peace and Reconciliation Since the Good Friday Agreement
ISBN 978-1-78997-817-9. 298 pages. 2022.

Vol. 106   Jo Murphy-Lawless and Laury Oaks (eds): The Salley Gardens: Women, Sex, and Motherhood in Ireland
ISBN 978-1-80079-417-7. 338 pages. 2022.

Vol. 107   Mercedes del Campo: Voices from the Margins: Gender and the Everyday in Women's Pre- and Post-Agreement Troubles Short Fiction
ISBN 978-1-78874-330-3. 324 pages. 2022.

Vol. 108   Sean McGraw and Jonathan Tiernan: The Politics of Irish Primary Education: Reform in an Era of Secularisation
ISBN 978-1-80079-709-3. 532 pages. 2022.

Vol. 109   Gerald Dawe: Northern Windows/Southern Stars: Selected Early
           Essays 1983–1994
           ISBN 978-1-80079-652-2. 180 pages. 2022.

Vol. 110   John Fanning: The Mandarin, the Musician and the Mage:
           T. K. Whitaker, Seán Ó Riada, Thomas Kinsella and the Lessons of
           Ireland's Mid-Twentieth-Century Revival
           ISBN 978-1-80079-599-0. 296 pages. 2022.

Vol. 111   Gerald Dawe: Dreaming of Home: Seven Irish Writers
           ISBN 978-1-80079-655-3. 108 pages. 2022.

Vol. 112   John Walsh: One Hundred Years of Irish Language Policy, 1922–2022
           ISBN 978-1-78997-892-6. 394 pages. 2022.

Vol. 113   Bertrand Cardin: Neil Jordan, Author and Screenwriter: The
           Imagination of Transgression
           ISBN 978-1-80079-923-3. 286 pages. 2023.

Vol. 114   David Clark: Dark Green: Irish Crime Fiction 1665–2000
           ISBN 978-1-80079-826-7. 450 pages. 2022.

Vol. 115   Aida Rosende-Pérez and Rubén Jarazo-Álvarez (eds): The Cultural
           Politics of In/Difference: Irish Texts and Contexts
           ISBN 978-1-80079-727-7. 274 pages. 2022.

Vol. 116   Tara McConnell: "Honest Claret": The Social Meaning of Georgian
           Ireland's Favourite Wine
           ISBN 978-1-80079-790-1. 346 pages. 2022.

Vol. 117   M. Teresa Caneda-Cabrera (ed.): Telling Truths: Evelyn Conlon and
           the Task of Writing
           ISBN 978-1-80079-481-8. 228 pages. 2023.

Vol. 118   Alexandra Maclennan (ed.): The Irish Catholic Diaspora: Five
           Centuries of Global Presence
           ISBN 978-1-80079-516-7. 264 pages. 2023.

Vol. 119   Brian J. Murphy: Beyond Sustenance: An Exploration of Food and
           Drink Culture in Ireland
           ISBN 978-1-80079-956-1. 328 pages. 2023.

Vol. 120   Fintan Cullen (ed.): Ireland and the British Empire: Essays on Art and Visuality
           ISBN 978-1-78874-299-3. 264 pages. 2023.

Vol. 121   Natalie Wynn and Zuleika Rodgers (eds): Reimagining the Jews of Ireland: Historiography, Identity and Representation
           ISBN 978-1-80079-083-4. 308 pages. 2023.

Vol. 122   Paul Butler: A Deep Well of Want: Visualising the World of John McGahern
           ISBN 978-1-80079-810-6. 244 pages. 2023.

Vol. 123   Carlos Menéndez Otero: The Great Pretenders: Genre, Form, and Style in the Film Musicals of John Carney
           ISBN 978-1-80374-135-2. 258 pages. 2023.

Vol. 124   Gerald Dawe: Politic Words: Writing Women | Writing History
           ISBN 978-1-80374-259-5. 208 pages. 2023.

Vol. 125   Marjan Shokouhi: From Landscapes to Cityscapes: Towards a Poetics of Dwelling in Modern Irish Verse
           ISBN 978-1-80079-870-0. 260 pages. 2023.

Vol. 126   Pat O'Connor: A 'proper' woman? One woman's story of success and failure in academia
           ISBN 978-1-80374-305-9. 248 pages. 2023.

Vol. 127   Natalie Wynn: Community, Identity, Conflict: The Jewish Experience in Ireland, 1881–1914
           ISBN 978-1-78707-483-5. 338 pages. 2024.

Vol. 128   Marie-Violaine Louvet: The Irish Against the War: Post-Colonial Identity & Political Activism in Contemporary Ireland
           ISBN 978-1-80079-998-1. 296 pages. 2024.

Vol. 129   Anne Rainey: Hiberno-English, Ulster Scots and Belfast Banter: Ciaran Carson's Translations of Dante and Rimbaud
           ISBN 978-1-80374-070-6. 338 pages. 2024.

Vol. 130   Nicole Volmering, Claire M. Dunne, John Walsh and Noel Ó Murchadha (eds): Irish in Outlook: A Hundred Years of Irish Education
           ISBN 978-1-80374-090-4. *Forthcoming*. 2024.

Vol. 131 Grace Neville, Sarah Nolan and Eugene O'Brien (eds): 'Getting the Words Right': A *Festschrift* in Honour of Eamon Maher
ISBN 978-1-80374-144-4. 382 pages. 2024.

Vol. 132 Hiroko Ikeda: Sweeney's Revival: Translating and transcending the liminal
ISBN 978-1-80374-429-2. 192 pages. 2024.

Vol. 133 Maria Gaviña-Costero, Dina Pedro, Dónall Mac Cathmhaoill (eds): 'Lost, Unhappy and at Home'. The Impact of Violence on Irish Culture. Volume I: Literature
ISBN 978-1-80374-321-9. 296 pages. 2024

Vol. 134 Maria Gaviña-Costero, Dina Pedro, Donall Mac Cathmhaoill (eds): 'Lost, Unhappy and at Home'. The Impact of Violence on Irish Culture. Volume II: Socio-Cultural Aspects
ISBN 978-1-80374-318-9. 312 pages. 2024

Vol. 135 Spencer, Graham: The SDLP, Politics and Peace. The Mark Durkan Interviews.
ISBN 978-1-80079-940-0. 288 pages. 2025.

Vol. 136 Seán William Gannon , Natalie Wynn (eds): The Limerick Boycott in Context.
ISBN 978-1-80079-899-1. 318 pages. 2025.

Vol. 137 Connai Parr, Stephen Hopkins (eds): Paving the Path to Peace Civil Society and the Northern Ireland Peace Process.
ISBN 978-1-80374-332-5. 330 pages. 2025.

Vol. 138 Madalina Armie, Verónica Membrive, Germán Peral (eds): A Nation, not A Parish. The Homewhere-s and Elsewhere-s of 1930s Irish Culture
ISBN 978-1-80374-848-1. 294 pages. 2025.

Vol. 139 Tom Inglis: Unbecoming Catholic. Being Religious in Contemporary Ireland.
ISBN 978-1-80374-817-7. 210 pages. 2025.

www.ingramcontent.com/pod-product-compliance
Ingram Content Group UK Ltd.
Pitfield, Milton Keynes, MK11 3LW, UK
UKHW021313140825
7399UKWH00029B/696

9 781803 748177